MODERN BAKING

cakes, cookies AND *everything* IN BETWEEN

Fourth Estate
An imprint of HarperCollins*Publishers*

First published in Australia and New Zealand in 2018
by HarperCollins*Publishers* Australia Pty Limited
ABN 36 009 913 517   harpercollins.com.au

HarperCollins*Publishers*
Level 13, 201 Elizabeth Street, Sydney NSW 2000
Unit D1, 63 Apollo Drive, Rosedale, Auckland 0632, New Zealand
A 53, Sector 57, Noida, UP, India
1 London Bridge Street, London SE1 9GF, United Kingdom
Bay Adelaide Centre, East Tower, 22 Adelaide Street West, 41st floor, Toronto, Ontario M5H 4E3, Canada
195 Broadway, New York NY 10007, USA

A catalogue record for this book is available from the National Library of Australia
ISBN: 978 1 4607 5671 3

On the cover: cupcake papers, photographed by Anson Smart

Reproduction by News PreMedia Centre
Printed and bound in China by RR Donnelley on 140gsm Lucky Bird Uncoated Woodfree
6 5 4 3 2 1   18 19 20 21

donna hay

—

MODERN BAKING
cakes, cookies AND everything IN BETWEEN

—

FOURTH ESTATE

CHAPTERS

---

chocolate
pages 8 – 55

QUICK FIX
pages 56 – 65

FRESH AND LIGHT
pages 66 – 81

caramel, toffee and coffee
pages 82 – 129

QUICK FIX
pages 130 – 139

FRESH AND LIGHT
pages 140 – 155

sugar and spice
pages 156 – 197

QUICK FIX
pages 198 – 207

FRESH AND LIGHT
pages 208 – 223

fruit and berries

pages 224 – 277

QUICK FIX
pages 278 – 287

FRESH AND LIGHT
pages 288 – 303

milk and cream

pages 304 – 351

QUICK FIX
pages 352 – 361

FRESH AND LIGHT
pages 362 – 377

glossary and index

pages 378 – 397

*Ingredients marked with an asterisk have a glossary entry

introduction

Anyone who knows me will tell you baking is my therapy – it's my own form of mindfulness meditation! Plus, it's the way I nurture the people I love. When I can't sleep, I often tiptoe into the kitchen and, in the calm quiet of the early morning, will begin to measure and mix – maybe a batch of oat cookies for my boys, a cake for a girlfriend's birthday or some raw caramel slice for my team at the office. Surely it's good for the soul! After all, is there anything better than curling up with coffee and a freshly baked brownie, warm from the oven? Or the way the comforting smell of muffins fills the house on a cold, rainy day? I hope you enjoy these recipes as much as I do. With all my years of tweaks and updates, they're my favourite sweet things to make in my own kitchen right now. Whether you're in the mood for pure indulgence, a balanced treat or a sneaky shortcut dessert – I've got you covered.

CHAPTER

—

chocolate

—

ONE

I often think of chocolate as having a mysterious kind of power which, when woven through birthday cakes, rich truffles or fudgy brownies, brings joy to whoever I'm baking for. A nod to its pure decadence, these recipes pair that dark, exotic magic with everything from cream to nuts to marshmallow.

chocolate and maple banana cake

chocolate and maple banana cake

250g unsalted butter, chopped
2¼ cups (335g) self-raising (self-rising) flour, sifted
½ cup (50g) cocoa powder, sifted
1 teaspoon bicarbonate of (baking) soda, sifted
1 cup (220g) caster (superfine) sugar
¾ cup (135g) light brown sugar
⅓ cup (80ml) maple syrup
4 eggs
1 cup (260g) mashed banana (about 3 bananas)
1½ cups (375ml) milk
½ cup (150g) store-bought thick caramel or dulce de leche*
quick dark chocolate ganache
1 cup (240g) sour cream*
200g dark chocolate, melted

Preheat oven to 180°C (350°F). Line a 24cm round springform tin with non-stick baking paper. Place the butter in a large non-stick frying pan over high heat. Cook, stirring, for 5 minutes or until melted and nutty brown in colour. Transfer to a large bowl. Add the flour, cocoa, bicarbonate of soda, both the sugars, the maple syrup, eggs, banana and milk and whisk until smooth. Bake for 1 hour 10 minutes or until cooked when tested with a skewer. Allow to cool in the tin for 10 minutes before turning out onto a wire rack to cool completely.

To make the quick dark chocolate ganache, place the sour cream and chocolate in a large bowl and whisk until smooth and combined.

Place the cake on a cake stand or plate and spread with the ganache. Spoon the caramel over the top and swirl gently to serve. **SERVES 10–12**

dark chocolate pretzel cake

115g unsalted butter, chopped
450g dark chocolate, chopped
4 eggs, separated
¼ cup (55g) caster (superfine) sugar
2 teaspoons sea salt flakes
1 cup (50g) store-bought mini pretzels*

Preheat oven to 160°C (325°F). Line a 22cm round springform tin with non-stick baking paper. Place the butter and chocolate in a large heatproof bowl over a saucepan of simmering water (the bowl shouldn't touch the water). Stir until melted and smooth.

Place the eggwhites in the bowl of an electric mixer. Whisk on high speed until soft peaks form. Gradually add the sugar and whisk until thick. Scrape down the sides of the bowl and whisk for a further 2–3 minutes or until the mixture is thick and glossy.

Add the egg yolks and salt to the chocolate mixture and whisk to combine. In 3 batches, add the eggwhite mixture to the chocolate mixture and gently fold to combine. Pour into the tin and arrange the pretzels on top. Bake for 25–30 minutes or until the edges are cooked when tested with a skewer and the centre is just set. Allow to cool to room temperature in the tin. Refrigerate for 3 hours or until chilled[+].

Remove the cake from the tin and place on a cake stand or plate. Slice to serve. **SERVES 8–10**
+ *If you'll be refrigerating this cake for longer than the specified 3 hours, remove it from the fridge 1 hour before serving to allow it to come to room temperature.*

dark chocolate pretzel cake

salted dark chocolate layer cake with milk chocolate ganache

salted dark chocolate layer cake with milk chocolate ganache

2½ cups (375g) self-raising (self-rising) flour, sifted
½ cup (50g) cocoa powder, sifted
1½ cups (330g) caster (superfine) sugar
4 eggs
1½ cups (375ml) milk
250g unsalted butter, melted
200g dark chocolate, melted
2 teaspoons vanilla extract
2 teaspoons black sea salt flakes*
quick milk chocolate ganache
1 cup (240g) sour cream*
400g milk chocolate, melted

Preheat oven to 180°C (350°F). Line 2 x 20cm round cake tins with non-stick baking paper. Place the flour, cocoa, sugar, eggs, milk, butter, chocolate and vanilla in a large bowl and whisk until smooth. Divide the mixture between the tins and bake for 40–45 minutes or until cooked when tested with a skewer. Allow to cool in the tins for 10 minutes before turning out onto wire racks to cool completely.

To make the quick milk chocolate ganache, place the sour cream and chocolate in a large bowl. Mix to combine and refrigerate for 10 minutes or until firm.

Place 1 of the cakes on a cake stand or plate. Spread with half the ganache. Top with the remaining cake and ganache. Sprinkle with the salt to serve. SERVES 8-10

chocolate custard poke cake

2½ cups (375g) self-raising (self-rising) flour, sifted
½ cup (50g) cocoa powder, sifted
1 cup (220g) caster (superfine) sugar
½ cup (90g) light brown sugar
4 eggs
1¾ cups (430ml) buttermilk
250g unsalted butter, melted
2 teaspoons vanilla extract
200g 70% dark chocolate, melted
chocolate custard icing
200g dark chocolate, finely chopped
1½ cups (325g) store-bought good-quality thick custard
1 cup (250ml) buttermilk
chocolate curls
400g dark chocolate, melted

Preheat oven to 180°C (350°F). Line a 20cm x 30cm cake tin with non-stick baking paper, leaving 4cm paper above the long edges. Place the flour, cocoa, both the sugars, the eggs, buttermilk, butter, vanilla and chocolate in a large bowl and whisk until smooth. Pour into the tin and bake for 40–45 minutes or until cooked when tested with a skewer. Allow to cool in the tin.

While the cake is cooling, make the chocolate custard icing. Place the chocolate and custard in a medium saucepan over low heat. Cook, stirring, for 2–3 minutes or until melted and smooth. Remove from the heat, add the buttermilk and whisk to combine.

Using the handle of a wooden spoon, poke deep holes, about 4cm apart, into the cake. While the icing is still warm, slowly pour it over the cake and tap the tin gently to release any air bubbles. Refrigerate until cold.

To make the chocolate curls, pour the chocolate onto the underside of a large baking tray. Spread it evenly to 5mm thick and refrigerate until set. Using a sharp knife, scrape the chocolate away from you to create shavings.

Use the paper lining to help you lift the cake from the tin. Place onto a serving plate and top with the chocolate curls to serve. SERVES 10-12

chocolate custard poke cake

chocolate swirl loaf cake

1¾ cups (255g) self-raising (self-rising) flour, sifted
125g unsalted butter, melted
1 cup (220g) caster (superfine) sugar
1 teaspoon vanilla extract
3 eggs
⅔ cup (160ml) buttermilk
100g 70% dark chocolate, melted
¼ cup (60ml) buttermilk, extra
2 teaspoons cocoa powder

Preheat oven to 160°C (325°F). Line a 21cm x 10cm loaf tin with non-stick baking paper. Place the flour, butter, sugar, vanilla, eggs and buttermilk in a medium bowl and whisk until smooth. Place one-third of the mixture in a separate medium bowl and add the chocolate, extra buttermilk and the cocoa and whisk to combine.

   Pour the chocolate mixture into one end of the tin. Pour the remaining cake mixture into the other end. Using a palette knife, stir gently to create a swirl effect. Bake for 1 hour – 1 hour 10 minutes or until cooked when tested with a skewer. Allow to cool in the tin for 5 minutes before turning out onto a wire rack to cool completely. Slice to serve. SERVES 6
Tip: Gently tap the tin after you have swirled the cake mixture to help it sit evenly.

2 cups (300g) self-raising (self-rising) flour, sifted
1 cup (220g) caster (superfine) sugar
250g white chocolate, melted
185g unsalted butter, melted
1¼ cups (310ml) milk
3 eggs
1 teaspoon vanilla extract
2 cups (160g) crushed store-bought amaretti biscuits*,
   plus 2 tablespoons, finely crushed, extra

Preheat oven to 180°C (350°F). Grease a 3-litre-capacity Bundt tin. Place the flour, sugar, chocolate, butter, milk, eggs and vanilla in a large bowl and whisk until smooth. Pour half the cake mixture into the tin, sprinkle with the amaretti and top with the remaining mixture. Bake for 40–45 minutes or until cooked when tested with a skewer. Invert the tin onto a wire rack and allow to stand for 10 minutes before removing the tin. Allow the cake to cool completely.

   Place the cake on a cake stand or plate and dust with the extra amaretti to serve. SERVES 8-10

white chocolate and amaretti bundt cake

chocolate, malt and pecan cookies

chocolate, malt and pecan cookies

200g unsalted butter, melted and cooled
1 cup (175g) light brown sugar
¾ cup (165g) white (granulated) sugar
1 egg
1 egg yolk, extra
2 teaspoons vanilla extract
¼ teaspoon baking powder
½ teaspoon bicarbonate of (baking) soda
1 teaspoon water
2 cups (300g) plain (all-purpose) flour
¾ cup (75g) malted milk powder
¼ teaspoon table salt
200g dark chocolate, chopped
1 cup (120g) pecans, chopped

Preheat oven to 160°C (325°F). Line 2 large baking trays with non-stick baking paper. Place the butter and both the sugars in the bowl of an electric mixer and beat on medium speed for 6–8 minutes or until sandy in texture. Add the egg, extra yolk and vanilla, increase the speed to high and beat for 2 minutes or until pale and creamy. Place the baking powder, bicarbonate of soda and water in a small bowl and mix to combine. Add the baking powder mixture, the flour, milk powder and salt to the butter mixture and beat on low speed until combined. Add the chocolate and pecans and fold to combine.

Working in batches, shape ¼-cup (60ml) portions of the dough into balls and place on the trays, allowing room to spread⁺. Bake for 20 minutes or until golden and firm to the touch. Allow to cool on the trays for 10 minutes before transferring onto wire racks to cool completely. Repeat with the remaining dough to make a total of 15 cookies. MAKES 15
+ *This recipe makes 15 large cookies. To make regular-sized cookies, simply shape 2-tablespoon portions of the dough into balls and place onto the trays, allowing room to spread. Bake for 14–16 minutes.*
Tip: You can store these cookies in an airtight container for up to 4 days.

candied clementine and chocolate pudding

¾ cup (255g) store-bought orange marmalade
2 tablespoons caster (superfine) sugar
5 store-bought candied clementines (200g)⁺, thinly sliced
10 soft fresh dates (200g), pitted
1 teaspoon bicarbonate of (baking) soda
½ cup (125ml) boiling water
60g unsalted butter, chopped and softened
¾ cup (135g) light brown sugar
1 teaspoon vanilla extract
4 eggs
¾ cup (110g) self-raising (self-rising) flour, sifted
¼ cup (25g) cocoa powder, sifted
½ cup (60g) almond meal (ground almonds)
100g dark chocolate, melted

Place the marmalade and caster sugar in a small saucepan over high heat. Bring to the boil and cook, stirring, for 2–3 minutes or until reduced slightly. Strain into a small bowl, discarding any solids, and refrigerate until cold.

Line a 1.75-litre-capacity metal pudding bowl with non-stick baking paper. Arrange the clementine slices, slightly overlapping, in the base of the bowl and spoon over the marmalade mixture. Set aside.

Place the dates, bicarbonate of soda and water in a small bowl and allow to soften for 10 minutes. Place in a small food processor and process until smooth.

Place the butter, brown sugar and vanilla in the bowl of an electric mixer and beat on high speed for 4–5 minutes or until pale and creamy. Add the eggs, 1 at a time, beating well after each addition. Add the flour, cocoa, almond meal, chocolate and the date mixture and beat on low speed until just combined. Spoon into the pudding bowl and top with a round of non-stick baking paper. Cover with aluminium foil and tie with kitchen string to secure.

Place the bowl in a large saucepan over low heat and fill with boiling water until it reaches three-quarters of the way up the sides of the bowl. Cover the saucepan with a tight-fitting lid and cook for 2 hours, adding more boiling water if necessary. Carefully remove the bowl from the saucepan and allow to stand for 15 minutes.

Turn out onto a cake stand or plate to serve. SERVES 6–8
+ *You can buy candied clementines in packs or jars at gourmet food stores and delicatessens.*

candied clementine and chocolate pudding

fig and dark chocolate teardrop truffles

fig and dark chocolate teardrop truffles

200g store-bought plain chocolate biscuits
1½ cups (300g) dried figs, chopped
2 tablespoons amaretto or almond liqueur
1 teaspoon finely grated orange rind
200g dark chocolate, melted
edible gold leaf, for decorating[+]
chocolate coating
300g 70% dark chocolate, melted
3 teaspoons vegetable oil

Place the biscuits, fig, amaretto and orange rind in a
food processor and process until finely chopped. Add
the chocolate and pulse until just combined. Place the
mixture in a large bowl, cover with plastic wrap and
refrigerate for 30 minutes or until firm.

Roll 1-tablespoon portions of the mixture into balls
and pinch the ends to create a teardrop shape.

To make the chocolate coating, place the 70% dark
chocolate and the oil in a tall glass and mix to combine.

Insert a toothpick into the base of each truffle and
dip into the chocolate coating, shaking off any excess.
Stand the truffles in a piece of Styrofoam or thick
cardboard and refrigerate until set.

Decorate the tips of the truffles with the gold leaf
to serve. MAKES 20
+ Edible gold leaf is available from gourmet food shops,
cake-decorating stores and online. It's best to follow
the instructions on the packet, as products can vary.
Tip: Keep truffles refrigerated in an airtight container
for up to 1 week.

fudgy brownie muffins

225g unsalted butter, chopped
200g dark chocolate, chopped
350g 70% dark chocolate, chopped
4 eggs
1 cup (220g) white (granulated) sugar
1 cup (175g) light brown sugar
2 teaspoons vanilla extract
1 cup (150g) plain (all-purpose) flour, sifted
¼ teaspoon baking powder

Preheat oven to 180°C (350°F). Line 12 x ½-cup-capacity
(125ml) muffin tins with paper cases. Place the butter,
dark chocolate and 200g of the 70% dark chocolate in
a medium saucepan over low heat and stir until melted
and smooth. Remove from the heat and set aside.

Place the eggs, both the sugars and the vanilla in a
large bowl and whisk to combine. Add the chocolate
mixture and whisk to combine. Add the flour, baking
powder and the remaining 150g of 70% dark chocolate
and mix until well combined.

Divide the mixture between the tins and bake for
30–35 minutes or until slightly fudgy when tested
with a skewer. Serve warm or allow to cool completely
in the tins. MAKES 12
Tips: If you're not serving the muffins straight away,
let them cool in the tins so they continue to set but
stay soft and fudgy in the centre. Keep muffins in an
airtight container for up to 1 week.

fudgy brownie muffins

salted chocolate brownie cookies

salted chocolate brownie cookies

225g unsalted butter, chopped
200g dark chocolate, chopped
200g 70% dark chocolate, chopped
4 eggs
1 cup (220g) white (granulated) sugar
1 cup (175g) light brown sugar
2 teaspoons vanilla extract
2 cups (300g) plain (all-purpose) flour, sifted
sea salt flakes, to serve

Preheat oven to 180°C (350°F). Line 2 large baking
trays with non-stick baking paper. Place the butter
and both the chocolates in a medium saucepan over
low heat and stir until melted and smooth.
   Place the eggs, both the sugars and the vanilla in
a large bowl and whisk to combine. Add the chocolate
mixture and whisk until smooth. Add the flour and
mix until combined. Refrigerate for 10 minutes to firm.
   Working in batches, spoon 2-tablespoon portions
of the mixture onto the trays, allowing room to spread.
Bake for 8 minutes or until firm to the touch. Allow
to cool on the trays for 5 minutes before transferring
onto a wire rack to cool completely. Repeat with the
remaining mixture to make a total of 30 cookies.
Sprinkle with salt to serve. MAKES 30

whisky-frosted brownie cake

225g unsalted butter, chopped
200g dark chocolate, chopped
200g 70% dark chocolate, chopped
4 eggs
1 cup (220g) white (granulated) sugar
1 cup (175g) light brown sugar
2 teaspoons vanilla extract
1 cup (150g) plain (all-purpose) flour, sifted
whisky frosting
250g unsalted butter, chopped and softened
1½ cups (240g) icing (confectioner's) sugar mixture, sifted
1 teaspoon cocoa powder
1 tablespoon smoked whisky[+]

Preheat oven to 180°C (350°F). Line a 22cm round
springform tin with non-stick baking paper. Place the
butter and both the chocolates in a medium saucepan
over low heat and stir until melted and smooth.
   Place the eggs, both the sugars and the vanilla in
a large bowl and whisk to combine. Add the chocolate
mixture and whisk until smooth. Add the flour and
mix until well combined. Pour into the tin and bake
for 40–45 minutes or until slightly fudgy when tested
with a skewer. Allow to cool in the tin completely.
   To make the whisky frosting, place the butter, sugar,
cocoa and whisky in the bowl of an electric mixer and beat
on medium speed for 3–4 minutes or until pale and fluffy.
   Remove the cake from the tin, place on a cake stand or
plate and spread with the frosting. Slice to serve. SERVES 10
*+ We used a smoked whisky to complement the flavour of
the rich dark chocolate. If unavailable, use regular whisky.*

whisky-frosted brownie cake

peanut butter brownies

peanut butter brownies

2 cups (560g) smooth peanut butter
225g unsalted butter, chopped
200g dark chocolate, chopped
200g 70% dark chocolate, chopped
4 eggs
1 cup (220g) white (granulated) sugar
1 cup (175g) light brown sugar
2 teaspoons vanilla extract
1 cup (150g) plain (all-purpose) flour, sifted

Preheat oven to 180°C (350°F). Line a 20cm x 30cm slice tin with non-stick baking paper. Place the peanut butter in a small saucepan over low heat. Cook for 2–3 minutes or until melted and smooth and set aside.

Place the butter and both the chocolates in a medium saucepan over low heat and stir until melted and smooth.

Place the eggs, both the sugars and the vanilla in a large bowl and whisk to combine. Add the chocolate mixture and whisk until smooth. Add the flour and mix until well combined. Pour half the mixture into the tin. Freeze for 5 minutes to firm slightly.

Pour the melted peanut butter into the tin and spread evenly. Top with the remaining brownie mixture and bake for 35–40 minutes or until slightly fudgy when tested with a skewer. Allow to cool in the tin completely.

Remove the brownie from the tin and slice into pieces to serve. MAKES 20

Tip: Keep these brownies refrigerated in an airtight container for up to 1 week.

cocoa panna cottas

⅓ cup (80ml) warm water
3 teaspoons gelatine powder*
2 cups (500ml) single (pouring) cream*
1½ cups (330g) caster (superfine) sugar
2 teaspoons vanilla bean paste or vanilla extract
1 cup (100g) cocoa powder
1 cup (250ml) milk

Place the water in a small bowl, sprinkle over the gelatine and mix to combine. Set aside for 5 minutes or until the gelatine is absorbed.

Place the cream, sugar, vanilla and cocoa in a medium saucepan over medium heat. Bring to the boil, stirring frequently, and add the gelatine. Stir to combine and remove from the heat. Strain the mixture into a bowl, discarding any solids. Add the milk, stir to combine and divide the mixture between 6 x 10cm round (¾-cup-capacity) fluted tart tins. Refrigerate for 3–4 hours or until set[+].

Turn out onto serving plates to serve. MAKES 6
+ It's easiest to make these panna cottas a day in advance, then simply refrigerate them overnight.
Tip: To turn the panna cottas out, invert the tins onto serving plates and give them a gentle shake.

cocoa panna cottas

glazed chocolate bundt cake

glazed chocolate bundt cake

250g unsalted butter, chopped
200g 70% dark chocolate, finely chopped
1⅓ cups (330ml) milk
1 cup (220g) caster (superfine) sugar
1 cup (175g) light brown sugar
1 teaspoon vanilla extract
2 eggs
1¾ cups (260g) self-raising (self-rising) flour, sifted
⅓ cup (35g) cocoa powder, sifted
chocolate glaze
200g 70% dark chocolate, finely chopped
100g unsalted butter, chopped
¼ cup (90g) liquid glucose[+]
1 teaspoon vegetable oil

Preheat oven to 160°C (325°F). Grease a 2.75-litre-capacity Bundt tin. Place the butter and chocolate in a medium saucepan over low heat and stir until melted and smooth.

Place the milk, both the sugars and the vanilla in a large bowl and whisk to combine. Add the chocolate mixture and the eggs to the milk mixture and whisk to combine. Add the flour and cocoa and whisk until well combined. Pour into the tin and bake for 1 hour – 1 hour 10 minutes or until cooked when tested with a skewer. Invert the tin onto a wire rack and allow to stand for 15 minutes before removing the tin. Allow the cake to cool completely.

To make the chocolate glaze, place the chocolate, butter and glucose in a medium saucepan over low heat and stir until melted and smooth. Add the oil and stir to combine.

Place the cake on a wire rack over a tray and spoon on the glaze. Allow the glaze to set before transferring the cake to a cake stand or plate to serve. SERVES 6–8
+ *Liquid glucose is available from the baking aisle of most supermarkets.*

chocolate s'more cookie sandwiches

100g dark chocolate, chopped
40g unsalted butter, softened
¾ cup (135g) light brown sugar
1 egg
1 teaspoon vanilla extract
⅔ cup (100g) plain (all-purpose) flour, sifted
¼ cup (25g) cocoa powder, sifted
2 teaspoons baking powder, sifted
100g store-bought plain sweet malt biscuits, crushed
24 white marshmallows
50g dark chocolate, extra, melted

Place the chopped chocolate in a small heatproof bowl over a saucepan of simmering water (the bowl shouldn't touch the water). Stir until melted and smooth. Allow to cool slightly. Place the butter and sugar in the bowl of an electric mixer and beat for 1–2 minutes or until well combined. Add the egg, vanilla and the cooled chocolate and beat to combine. Add the flour, cocoa and baking powder and beat until combined. Refrigerate the dough for 30 minutes or until firm.

Preheat oven to 180°C (350°F). Line 2 baking trays with non-stick baking paper. Place the crushed biscuits in a bowl. Shape 1½-teaspoon portions of the dough into 24 balls and roll in the biscuit crumbs to coat. Place on the trays, allowing room to spread. Bake for 8 minutes or until the surfaces crack, the edges are crispy and the centres are still a little soft. Allow to cool completely on the trays.

Top half the cookies with 2 marshmallows each. Spread the remaining cookies with the extra melted chocolate and sandwich together. Using a kitchen blowtorch, lightly toast the outside of the marshmallow to caramelise. MAKES 12

chocolate s'more cookie sandwiches

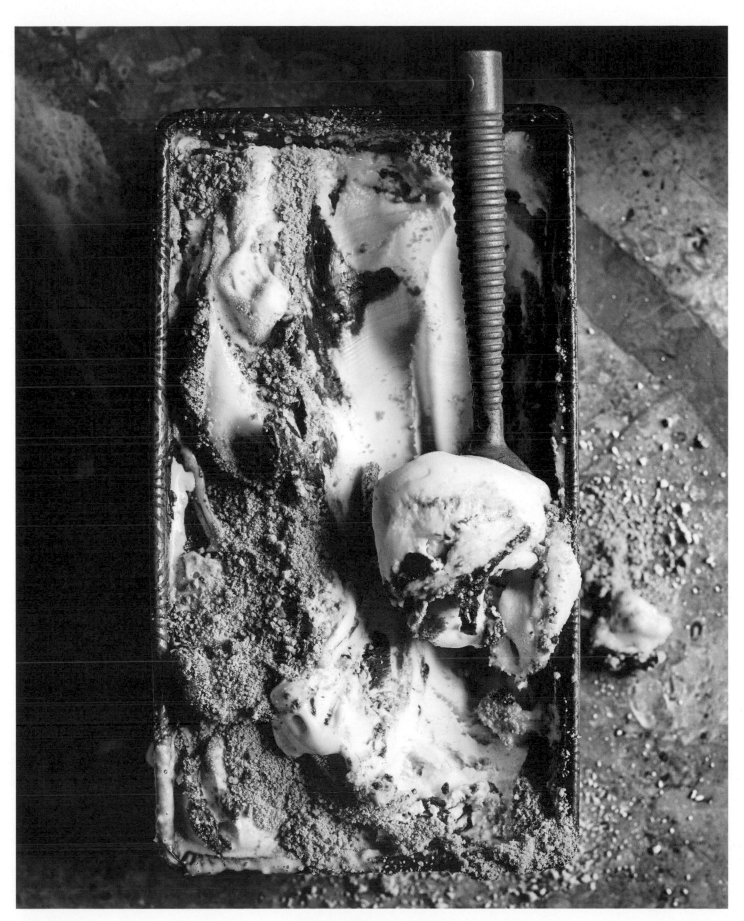

chocolate s'more ice-cream

chocolate s'more ice-cream

100g dark chocolate, finely chopped
¼ cup (60ml) single (pouring) cream*
2 cups (180g) white marshmallows
1 tablespoon milk
2 litres store-bought vanilla ice-cream
100g store-bought plain sweet malt biscuits, finely crushed

Place a 1.3-litre-capacity loaf tin or metal container in the freezer until ready to use. Place the chocolate in a small heatproof bowl. Place the cream in a small saucepan over high heat and bring almost to the boil. Pour the cream over the chocolate and stir until melted and smooth. Refrigerate for 20 minutes to cool.

While the ganache is cooling, place the marshmallows and milk in a medium saucepan over low heat and stir until melted. Scoop the ice-cream into the bowl of an electric mixer and beat on low speed for 1 minute or until softened. Working quickly, add the marshmallow mixture, chocolate ganache and biscuit crumbs to the ice-cream and gently fold to combine. Spoon into the tin and freeze for 3–4 hours or until set. **MAKES 1.3 LITRES**
Tip: The ice-cream will keep in an airtight container in the freezer for up to 2 days.

chocolate s'more meringue pie

250g store-bought plain sweet malt biscuits
125g unsalted butter, melted
600g dark chocolate, chopped
1½ cups (375ml) single (pouring) cream*
marshmallow meringue topping
2 cups (440g) caster (superfine) sugar
½ teaspoon cream of tartar
½ cup (125ml) water
150ml eggwhite (about 4 eggs), at room temperature[+]

Place the biscuits in a food processor and process until fine. Add the butter and process until combined. Using the back of a spoon, press the biscuit mixture into the base of an 18cm round (1-litre-capacity) pie dish. Refrigerate until needed.

Place the chocolate and cream in a medium saucepan over low heat, stirring until melted and smooth. Pour into the pie dish and refrigerate for 45 minutes or until firm.

To make the marshmallow meringue topping, place 1½ cups (330g) of the sugar, the cream of tartar and water in a small saucepan over high heat. Bring to the boil, reduce the heat to low and cook, without stirring, for 3–4 minutes or until slightly reduced and syrupy. Place the eggwhites in the bowl of an electric mixer and whisk on high speed until soft peaks form. Add the remaining sugar, 1 tablespoon at a time, whisking for 30 seconds before adding more. Scrape down the sides of the bowl. With the mixer still on high speed, gradually pour the sugar syrup into the eggwhite in a thin, steady stream and whisk for a further 3–4 minutes or until thick and glossy.

Spoon the meringue on top of the pie. Using a hand-held kitchen blowtorch or placing the pie under the grill (broiler) for 30 seconds, lightly toast the meringue to caramelise the top. Slice to serve. **SERVES 6-8**
+ Making meringue is a science – be sure to measure the eggwhites carefully, remembering egg sizes do vary.
Tip: This pie is best eaten on the day it's made.

chocolate s'more meringue pie

chocolate and raspberry marshmallow slice

chocolate and raspberry marshmallow slice

1½ cups (225g) plain (all-purpose) flour
¾ cup (60g) desiccated coconut
¾ cup (135g) light brown sugar
200g unsalted butter, melted
200g dark chocolate, melted
1 tablespoon vegetable oil
raspberry jam
500g raspberries
1¼ cups (275g) caster (superfine) sugar
1 tablespoon lemon juice
marshmallow
⅔ cup (160ml) warm water
2 tablespoons gelatine powder*
1½ cups (330g) caster (superfine) sugar
⅔ cup (230g) liquid glucose+
½ cup (125ml) warm water, extra

Preheat oven to 180°C (350°F). Line a 23cm x 35cm baking tray with non-stick baking paper. Place the flour, coconut, sugar and butter in a large bowl and mix to combine. Using the back of a spoon, press the mixture into the base of the tray and bake for 18 minutes or until golden brown.

To make the raspberry jam, place the raspberries, sugar and lemon juice in a large non-stick frying pan over high heat and stir until the sugar is dissolved. Cook, stirring occasionally, for 15 minutes or until thickened. Allow to cool before spreading over the base.

To make the marshmallow, place the warm water in the bowl of an electric mixer, sprinkle over the gelatine and stir to combine. Set aside for 5 minutes or until the gelatine is absorbed. Place the sugar, glucose and extra water in a small saucepan over medium heat and cook, stirring, until the sugar is dissolved. Increase the heat to high and bring to the boil. Cook, without stirring, for 5–7 minutes or until the temperature reaches 115°C (239°F) on a sugar (candy) thermometer. With the mixer on high speed, gradually pour the hot sugar syrup into the gelatine mixture in a thin, steady stream. Beat for 3 minutes or until thickened.

Working quickly, pour the marshmallow mixture evenly over the jam. Refrigerate for 10 minutes or until firm.

Place the chocolate and oil in a small bowl and mix to combine. Pour over the marshmallow and refrigerate until set. Cut into slices to serve. **MAKES 15**

+ *Liquid glucose is available from the baking aisle of most supermarkets.*

rum and raisin truffles

½ cup (75g) raisins, chopped
⅓ cup (80ml) dark rum
¾ cup (180ml) single (pouring) cream*
600g dark chocolate, finely chopped
1 cup (100g) cocoa powder

Place the raisins and rum in a small bowl and set aside to soak. Place the cream in a small saucepan over high heat and bring to the boil. Place the chocolate in a medium heatproof bowl and top with the hot cream. Place the bowl over a saucepan of simmering water (the bowl shouldn't touch the water) and, using a metal spoon, stir until melted and smooth. Add the raisin mixture and stir to combine. Allow to stand at room temperature for 10 minutes, before refrigerating for 2–3 hours or until just firm.

Roll 1-teaspoon portions of the truffle mixture into balls+ and place on a large tray. Dust with cocoa to serve. **MAKES 50**

+ *If the truffle mixture becomes too firm to roll, allow it to stand at room temperature for 15 minutes or until softened.*
Tip: You can keep these truffles refrigerated for up to 2 weeks, meaning they're easy to prepare in advance.

rum and raisin truffles

salted peanut butter and choc-chip skillet cookies

salted peanut butter and choc-chip skillet cookies

1½ cups (225g) plain (all-purpose) flour
1 teaspoon bicarbonate of (baking) soda
¾ cup (135g) light brown sugar
½ cup (110g) white (granulated) sugar
1 egg
1 teaspoon vanilla extract
⅔ cup (190g) smooth peanut butter
175g unsalted butter, melted
200g dark chocolate, chopped
½ cup (70g) unsalted peanuts
sea salt flakes, for sprinkling
store-bought vanilla ice-cream, to serve

Preheat oven to 180°C (350°F). Place the flour, bicarbonate of soda, both the sugars, the egg, vanilla, peanut butter, butter, chocolate and peanuts in a large bowl and mix to combine. Divide between 8 x 10cm round (1-cup-capacity) heavy-based ovenproof frying pans (skillets) and press to cover the bases evenly, with the mixture coming halfway up the sides of the pans. Place on a large oven tray and bake for 15–18 minutes or until golden brown but still a little soft in the centre. Allow to cool slightly.

Sprinkle with salt and top with ice-cream to serve. SERVES 8

chocolate, banana and coconut muffins

2½ cups (375g) self-raising (self-rising) flour
½ cup (40g) desiccated coconut
1 cup (175g) light brown sugar
¼ cup (25g) cocoa powder
2 eggs, lightly beaten
2 teaspoons vanilla extract
½ cup (125ml) coconut milk
½ cup (125ml) vegetable oil
2 cups (520g) mashed banana (about 6 bananas)
200g dark chocolate, chopped
icing (confectioner's) sugar, for dusting

Preheat oven to 180°C (350°F). Line 12 x ½-cup-capacity (125ml) muffin tins with paper cases. Place the flour, coconut, sugar and cocoa in a large bowl and mix to combine. Add the egg, vanilla, coconut milk, oil, banana and chocolate and, using a butter knife, mix until just combined.

Spoon the mixture into the tins and bake for 25 minutes or until cooked when tested with a skewer. Allow to cool in the tins for 2 minutes before transferring onto wire racks to cool completely. Dust with icing sugar to serve. MAKES 12

chocolate, banana and coconut muffins

lamington ice-cream bars

lamington ice-cream bars

2 litres store-bought coconut ice-cream+
400g 70% dark chocolate, chopped
⅓ cup (80ml) vegetable oil
4 cups (300g) shredded coconut

Line a 20cm x 30cm slice tin with non-stick baking paper and freeze until ready to use. Scoop the ice-cream into the bowl of an electric mixer and beat on low speed until softened. Spoon into the tin and spread evenly with a palette knife. Freeze for 4–5 hours or until frozen.

Line a tray with non-stick baking paper. Remove the ice-cream from the tin and slice into 12 bars. Place the bars on the tray and freeze for a further 1 hour.

Place the chocolate and oil in a heatproof bowl over a saucepan of simmering water (the bowl shouldn't touch the water) and stir until melted. Allow to cool completely.

Spread the coconut in a thin layer on a tray. Working quickly, remove 2–3 ice-cream bars at a time from the tray in the freezer. Use 2 forks to dip each bar into the chocolate, then press gently into the coconut to coat. Return to the tray in the freezer immediately and repeat with the remaining bars, chocolate and coconut. Freeze for 1–2 hours or until very firm, before serving. MAKES 12
+ *You can buy coconut ice-cream at specialty grocers, gourmet food stores and major supermarkets.*

chocolate stout doughnuts with chipotle stout praline

½ cup (125ml) stout beer
1 teaspoon vanilla bean paste or vanilla extract
2¼ cups (335g) plain (all-purpose) flour, plus extra for dusting
¼ cup (25g) cocoa powder
⅓ cup (75g) caster (superfine) sugar
2 teaspoons dry yeast
4 egg yolks
¼ cup (60ml) double (thick) cream*
80g unsalted butter, chopped and softened
¼ cup (90g) honey
120g dark chocolate, finely chopped
chipotle stout praline
1 cup (220g) coffee sugar or Demerara sugar*
2 tablespoons stout beer
3 dried chipotle chillies*, finely chopped

Place the stout and vanilla in a small saucepan over medium heat until just warm. Place the flour, cocoa, sugar and yeast in the bowl of an electric mixer fitted with a dough hook and beat on medium speed until combined. Add the stout mixture and the egg yolks and beat until just combined. Add the cream and 50g of the butter and beat for 6–8 minutes or until a smooth dough forms. Place the dough in a lightly greased bowl, cover with a clean damp tea towel and set aside in a warm place for 1 hour or until doubled in size.

Line a large baking tray with non-stick baking paper. Roll out the dough on a lightly floured surface to 1.5cm thick. Using an 8.5cm round cookie cutter+, cut 6 rounds from the dough. Arrange on the tray, allowing room to spread. Using a 4cm round cutter, cut and remove the centre of each round. Set aside at room temperature for 30 minutes or until risen.

To make the praline, preheat oven to 180°C (350°F). Line a large baking tray with non-stick baking paper. Place the sugar, stout and chilli in a bowl and mix until just combined. Spread onto the tray and bake for 20 minutes or until dark golden. Allow to set and break into small crumbs.

Bake the doughnuts for 8–10 minutes or until puffed and golden. Allow to cool completely.

Place the remaining 30g of butter, the honey and chocolate in a small saucepan over low heat and cook for 2–3 minutes or until melted and smooth. Dip the top halves of the doughnuts into the chocolate glaze and sprinkle half of each doughnut with the crumbled praline to serve. MAKES 6
+ *It helps to dust the cutters in flour before cutting the rounds.*

chocolate stout doughnuts with chipotle stout praline

chocolate and pecan cake

chocolate and pecan cake

350g dark chocolate, chopped
150g unsalted butter, chopped
6 eggs, separated and at room temperature
1 vanilla bean, split and seeds scraped
1 cup (175g) light brown sugar
2 tablespoons brandy
1⅔ cups (200g) pecan meal (ground pecans)+
cocoa powder, for dusting

Preheat oven to 160°C (325°F). Line a 22cm round springform tin with non-stick baking paper. Place the chocolate and butter in a large heatproof bowl over a saucepan of simmering water (the bowl shouldn't touch the water) and stir until melted and smooth. Remove from the heat and allow to cool slightly. Add the egg yolks, vanilla seeds, half the sugar, the brandy and pecan meal and mix well to combine.

Place the eggwhites in the bowl of an electric mixer and whisk on high speed until stiff peaks form. Gradually add the remaining sugar and whisk until thick.

In 2 batches, add the eggwhite mixture to the chocolate mixture and gently fold to combine. Pour into the tin and bake for 1 hour 10 minutes – 1 hour 20 minutes or until the top is crisp and just a few crumbs are attached when tested with a skewer. Allow to cool in the tin completely.

Gently run a small knife around the inside edge of the tin. Remove the cake from the tin and place on a cake stand or plate. Dust with cocoa to serve. SERVES 8–10
+ *Buy pecan meal at your local health food store or specialty grocer. If you can't find it, it's very easy to make your own. Simply process the required quantity of nuts in a food processor until a fine meal forms. Store any leftover nut meal in an airtight container, as you would flour.*

chocolate mousse cake

300g store-bought cream-filled chocolate biscuits
100g unsalted butter, melted
400g dark chocolate, finely chopped
½ cup (125ml) single (pouring) cream*
4 eggs, separated
¼ cup (45g) light brown sugar
1½ cups (375ml) double (thick) cream*, whipped
chocolate glaze
½ cup (125ml) single (pouring) cream*
2 tablespoons liquid glucose+
100g 70% dark chocolate, finely chopped
1 teaspoon vegetable oil

Line a deep-sided 20cm round springform tin with non-stick baking paper. Place the biscuits in a food processor and process into fine crumbs. Add the butter and process to combine. Using the back of a spoon, press the mixture into the base of the tin and refrigerate until ready to use.

Place the chocolate and single cream in a large heatproof bowl over a saucepan of simmering water (the bowl shouldn't touch the water) and stir until melted and smooth. Remove from the heat and allow to cool slightly. Add the egg yolks and whisk to combine.

Place the eggwhites in the bowl of an electric mixer and whisk on high speed until soft peaks form. Gradually add the sugar and whisk until thick and glossy.

Add the whipped cream to the chocolate mixture and gently fold to combine. In 2 batches, add the eggwhite and fold to combine. Spoon the mousse onto the biscuit base and smooth the top. Refrigerate for 4–5 hours or until set.

To make the chocolate glaze, place the cream and glucose in a small saucepan over medium heat and bring to the boil. Remove from the heat, add the chocolate and allow to stand for 5 minutes or until the chocolate is melted. Add the oil and whisk until smooth. Allow to cool slightly.

Pour the glaze over the cake, gently tilting and tapping until even. Refrigerate for a further 1 hour or until set.

Carefully remove the cake from the tin and place on a cake stand or plate to serve. SERVES 10–12
+ *Liquid glucose is available from the baking aisle of most supermarkets.*

chocolate mousse cake

crunchy chocolate caramel layer cake

crunchy chocolate caramel layer cake

1¾ cups (260g) plain (all-purpose) flour, sifted,
    plus extra for dusting
¼ cup (25g) cocoa powder, sifted
½ cup (80g) icing (confectioner's) sugar, sifted
40g unsalted butter, melted
¼ cup (60ml) water
1 egg
2 egg yolks, extra
chocolate caramel filling
¾ cup (165g) caster (superfine) sugar
⅓ cup (80ml) water
½ cup (125ml) single (pouring) cream*
75g unsalted butter, softened
300g dark chocolate, chopped

Preheat oven to 180°C (350°F). Line 2 large baking trays
with non-stick baking paper. Place the flour, cocoa and
sugar in a food processor and pulse to combine. Add the
butter, water, egg and extra yolks and process until a smooth
dough forms. Turn out the dough and bring it together on a
lightly floured surface. Divide into 8 equal pieces. Roll each
piece into a very thin rectangle and trim to 10cm x 35cm.
Prick each layer all over with a fork and place on the trays.
Bake for 8–10 minutes or until just crisp. Transfer to wire
racks and allow to cool at room temperature until crisp.

To make the chocolate caramel filling, place the sugar
and water in a medium saucepan⁺ over medium heat and
stir to dissolve the sugar. Bring to the boil and cook for
8–10 minutes or until deep golden in colour. Remove from
the heat and, working quickly, add the cream in a thin
steady stream. Add the butter, return to the heat and cook,
stirring, until well combined. Place the chocolate in a
heatproof bowl, pour the caramel mixture over and stir
until melted and smooth. Refrigerate until just cold,
whisking occasionally. Once cooled, whisk for 1–2 minutes
or until creamy and smooth.

To assemble, place 1 of the pastry layers on a cake stand
or plate. Spread evenly with ⅓ cup (80ml) of the chocolate
caramel filling. Repeat with the remaining pastry and
filling, finishing with a pastry layer. Refrigerate the cake
for 1–2 hours or until set. Slice to serve. **SERVES 10–12**
*+ Use a deep saucepan to prevent the hot mixture from
overflowing – once the cream and butter are added the
caramel will begin to bubble.*

chocolate canelés

2¼ cups (560ml) milk
1 vanilla bean, split and seeds scraped
50g unsalted butter, chopped
200g dark chocolate, chopped
2 eggs
2 egg yolks, extra
1½ cups (240g) icing (confectioner's) sugar, sifted twice
⅔ cup (100g) plain (all-purpose) flour, sifted twice
cooking oil spray, for greasing
⅔ cup (160ml) butterscotch schnapps

Place the milk, vanilla seeds, butter and chocolate in
a medium saucepan over medium heat and bring to the
boil. Remove from the heat, stir to combine and allow
to cool completely.

Place the eggs, extra yolks and the sugar in a large bowl
and gently stir to combine⁺. Add the flour and fold to
combine. Add the chocolate mixture and stir to combine.
Strain the mixture through a sieve, discarding any solids,
and allow to stand at room temperature for 2 hours.

Preheat oven to 220°C (425°F). Use the cooking oil
spray to grease 16 x ⅓-cup-capacity (80ml) canelé moulds
well⁺⁺. Place the moulds upside-down on a wire rack over
a baking tray and refrigerate for 10 minutes or until cold.

Skim the foam from the surface of the canelé mixture,
add the schnapps and gently stir to combine. Place the
moulds on the baking tray and fill each three-quarters
full with the mixture. Bake for 10 minutes, reduce the
oven temperature to 180°C (350°F) and bake for a further
50–55 minutes or until golden but still soft in the centre.
Remove the canelés from the moulds immediately and
place on a wire rack to cool completely. **MAKES 16**
*+ Be sure to stir, not whisk, the canelé mixture to prevent
the texture from becoming too light and fluffy.*
*++ Canelés are traditionally baked in copper tins that
have been coated in beeswax (check manufacturer's
instructions). These days, silicone canelé moulds are
also readily available.*

chocolate canelés

coffee, hazelnut and cocoa crisps

coffee, hazelnut and cocoa crisps

⅓ cup (45g) hazelnuts, roasted and skins removed
½ teaspoon coffee beans
⅔ cup (150g) white (granulated) sugar
60g unsalted butter, chopped
1 tablespoon milk
1 tablespoon liquid glucose[+]
1 vanilla bean, split and seeds scraped
1½ tablespoons cocoa powder

Preheat oven to 180°C (350°F). Place the hazelnuts and coffee beans in a small food processor and process until fine. Place the sugar, butter, milk, glucose and vanilla seeds in a small saucepan over medium heat. Stir until the butter is melted and bring to the boil. Cook for 2–3 minutes or until the temperature reaches 100°C (212°F) on a sugar (candy) thermometer. Remove from the heat and add the hazelnut mixture and the cocoa. Stir until well combined and allow to cool slightly[++].

Line 3 large baking trays with non-stick baking paper. Spoon 1-teaspoon portions of the mixture onto the trays, allowing room to spread. Bake for 6–8 minutes or until flat and golden. Allow to cool on the trays for 5 minutes before transferring onto wire racks to cool completely. **MAKES 26**
+ Liquid glucose is available from the baking aisle of most supermarkets.
++ As the mixture cools it will thicken. If it becomes too thick to work with, simply warm it a little in a saucepan over low heat.
Tip: Keep crisps in an airtight container, between sheets of non-stick baking paper, for up to 5 days.

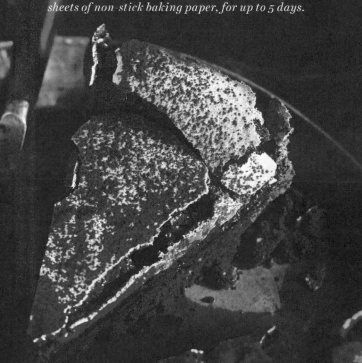

chocolate meringue cake

240g dark chocolate, chopped
180g unsalted butter, chopped
2 eggs
4 eggs, extra, separated
½ cup (90g) light brown sugar
1 teaspoon vanilla extract
⅓ cup (50g) plain (all-purpose) flour, sifted
½ teaspoon baking powder, sifted
⅓ cup (40g) almond meal (ground almonds)
1 cup (220g) caster (superfine) sugar
1 teaspoon white vinegar
3 teaspoons cornflour (cornstarch), sifted
¼ cup (25g) cocoa powder, sifted,
   plus extra for dusting

Preheat oven to 160°C (325°F). Line a 24cm round springform tin with non-stick baking paper. Place the chocolate and butter in a medium saucepan over low heat and stir until melted and smooth. Allow to cool slightly.

Place the eggs, extra yolks, brown sugar and vanilla in the bowl of an electric mixer and whisk for 3–4 minutes or until pale and thick. Add the chocolate mixture, the flour, baking powder and almond meal and gently fold to combine. Pour into the tin and bake for 35–40 minutes. Allow to cool in the tin slightly.

Increase the oven temperature to 180°C (350°F). Place the extra eggwhites in a cleaned bowl of the electric mixer and whisk on high speed until soft peaks form. Add the sugar, 1 tablespoon at a time, whisking for 30 seconds before adding more. Scrape down the sides of the bowl, add the vinegar and whisk for 2–3 minutes or until the meringue is thick and glossy. Add the cornflour and cocoa and fold to combine.

Spoon the meringue mixture onto the cake and spread evenly. Return the cake to the oven for 20–25 minutes or until the meringue is golden and crisp. Allow to cool in the tin for 15–20 minutes. Gently run a knife around the inside edge of the tin and remove the ring. Allow to cool to room temperature before refrigerating for 2 hours.

Place the cake on a cake stand or plate and dust with the extra cocoa to serve. **SERVES 8-10**
Note: Don't be worried if the cake cracks or collapses a little – it's supposed to look a bit rustic.

chocolate meringue cake

QUICK

chocolate coconut cups
chocolate shortbread slice
salted chocolate peanut butter cups
chocolate-dipped dried orange slices
cheat's hazelnut chocolate fudge
chocolate ice-cream pie
chocolate butterscotch swirls
crispy chocolate coconut bars
cheat's chocolate and pear crumbles
raspberry and coconut chocolate buttons
raspberry and chocolate brownie trifles
raspberry and turkish delight rocky road
peanut butter brownie ice-cream bars
magic chocolate molten puddings
no bake chocolate and walnut brownies
one-bowl chocolate and coconut muffins

FIX

chocolate coconut cups

1¼ cups (95g) shredded coconut
¼ cup (60ml) melted coconut oil*
1½ tablespoons light agave syrup*
80g dark chocolate, chopped
½ cup (125ml) coconut milk

Lightly grease 12 x 1½-tablespoon-capacity mini muffin tins. Place the coconut, coconut oil and agave in a small bowl and mix to combine. Press into the base and sides of the tins, using the back of a spoon, and freeze for 10 minutes or until firm.

Place the chocolate and coconut milk in a small saucepan over low heat and stir until melted and smooth. Pour into the coconut cases and freeze for 15 minutes or until set.

Remove the coconut cups from the tins to serve. MAKES 12
Tip: Keep these treats refrigerated or frozen in an airtight container for up to 1 week.

chocolate shortbread slice

⅓ cup (80ml) single (pouring) cream*
400g dark chocolate, chopped
100g unsalted butter, chopped
175g store-bought plain shortbread biscuits
cocoa powder, for dusting

Line an 8cm x 20cm loaf tin with non-stick baking paper. Place the cream, chocolate and butter in a medium saucepan over low heat and stir until melted and smooth. Pour one-third of the chocolate mixture into the tin.

Arrange half the shortbread biscuits in the tin. Pour half the remaining chocolate mixture over the shortbread. Repeat with the remaining shortbread and chocolate and smooth the top. Refrigerate for 3–4 hours or until set.

Remove the slice from the tin and dust with cocoa. Slice, using a hot knife, to serve. SERVES 8–10

salted chocolate peanut butter cups

½ cup (140g) smooth peanut butter
¼ cup (60ml) melted coconut oil*
100g dark chocolate, melted
2 teaspoons melted coconut oil*, extra
black sea salt flakes*, to serve

Line 12 x 1-tablespoon capacity mini muffin tins with paper cases. Place the peanut butter and coconut oil in a small saucepan over low heat and stir until melted and smooth. Divide between the tins and freeze for 15–20 minutes or until firm.

While the peanut butter cups are freezing, place the chocolate in a small bowl, add the extra coconut oil and mix until smooth.

Spoon the chocolate mixture into the cups, sprinkle with salt and return to the freezer for 10–15 minutes or until firm. Remove from the tin to serve. MAKES 12
Tip: These peanut butter cups are best stored in the refrigerator until ready to serve.

chocolate-dipped dried orange slices

100g dark chocolate, melted
1 teaspoon vegetable oil
20 store-bought dried orange slices+

Line 2 large trays with non-stick baking paper. Place the chocolate and oil in a small bowl and mix to combine.

Dip the orange slices halfway into the chocolate, allowing the excess to drip off, and place on the trays. Refrigerate for 10 minutes or until set. MAKES 20
+ You can buy dried orange slices at delicatessens and specialty grocers.
Tip: Keep the orange slices refrigerated in an airtight container for up to 2 weeks.

cheat's hazelnut chocolate fudge

350g dark chocolate, chopped
395g can sweetened condensed milk
2 tablespoons single (pouring) cream*
2 teaspoons vanilla extract
1½ cups (210g) hazelnuts, roasted and chopped

Line a 20cm square slice tin with non-stick baking paper. Place the chocolate, condensed milk, cream and vanilla in a medium saucepan over medium heat. Cook, stirring, for 5–6 minutes or until melted and smooth.

Add half the hazelnuts and stir to combine. Pour into the tin. Top with the remaining hazelnuts and refrigerate for 2 hours or until set. Remove the fudge from the tin and slice into pieces to serve. MAKES 20

chocolate ice-cream pie

250g store-bought plain chocolate biscuits, finely crushed
100g unsalted butter, melted
1 litre store-bought chocolate ice-cream, softened
2 cups (500ml) single (pouring) cream*

Place the crushed biscuits and butter in a medium bowl and mix well to combine. Reserve and set aside 2 tablespoons of the crumb mixture. Press the remaining mixture into the base of an 18cm round (1-litre-capacity) pie tin and freeze for 10 minutes or until firm.

Spoon the ice-cream into the base of the pie and smooth into an even layer. Freezer for 1–2 hours or until firm.

Place the cream in the bowl of an electric mixer and whisk until soft peaks form.

Spoon the cream over the pie and sprinkle with the reserved crumb mixture. Serve immediately. SERVES 8-10

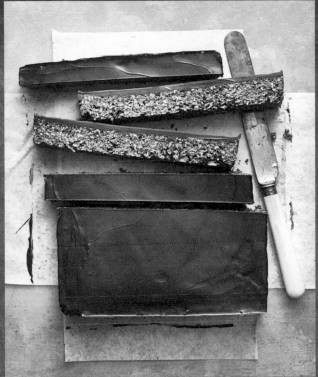

chocolate butterscotch swirls

1 cup (250ml) single (pouring) cream*
½ cup (125g) mascarpone
¼ cup (40g) icing (confectioner's) sugar, sifted
2 teaspoons vanilla extract
100g dark chocolate, melted
¼ cup (60ml) butterscotch schnapps
2 tablespoons store-bought chocolate-coated
    coffee beans, crushed
store-bought biscotti, to serve

Place the cream, mascarpone, sugar and vanilla in a
medium bowl and whisk until soft peaks form.

Place the chocolate and schnapps in a small bowl and
whisk to combine. Add the chocolate mixture to the
cream mixture and gently stir to create a swirled effect.

Divide between 4 x 1-cup-capacity (250ml) serving
glasses. Sprinkle with the crushed coffee beans and
serve with biscotti. MAKES 4

crispy chocolate coconut bars

150g milk chocolate, chopped
75g unsalted butter, chopped
¼ cup (90g) golden syrup
3 cups (90g) puffed brown rice*
1 cup (75g) shredded coconut
200g dark chocolate, melted
1 teaspoon vegetable oil

Line a 20cm square slice tin with non-stick baking paper.
Place the milk chocolate, butter and golden syrup in a small
saucepan over low heat and stir until melted and smooth.
Add the puffed rice and coconut and mix to combine. Press
into the base of the tin, using the back of a spoon.

Place the chocolate and oil in a small bowl and mix to
combine. Pour the chocolate mixture over the crispy base
and smooth the top. Refrigerate for 2 hours or until firm.

Remove from the tin and slice into bars to serve. MAKES 18

cheat's chocolate and pear crumbles

1kg Packham pears (about 5 pears), peeled and chopped
200g dark chocolate, grated
½ cup (125ml) maple syrup
¼ cup (60ml) single (pouring) cream*
2 cups (260g) store-bought granola

Preheat oven to 180°C (350°F). Place the pear, chocolate, maple syrup and cream in a large bowl and mix to combine.

Divide the mixture between 4 x 1½-cup-capacity (375ml) ovenproof dishes. Top with the granola. Place on an oven tray, cover with aluminium foil and bake for 25 minutes. Remove the foil and bake for a further 5 minutes or until golden, before serving. MAKES 4

raspberry and coconut chocolate buttons

200g dark chocolate, melted
1 teaspoon vegetable oil
¼ cup (10g) coconut flakes
2 tablespoons freeze-dried raspberries, crushed+

Line 2 large trays with non-stick baking paper. Place the chocolate and oil in a small bowl and mix to combine.

Spoon the chocolate onto the trays in 10cm rounds. Sprinkle with the coconut and crushed raspberries. Refrigerate for 30 minutes or until set. MAKES 8
+ *Freeze-dried raspberries are available from gourmet food stores and specialty grocers.*
Tip: Keep these buttons refrigerated in an airtight container for up to 1 week.

raspberry and chocolate brownie trifles

1 cup (240g) sour cream*
½ cup (125ml) single (pouring) cream*
¼ cup (55g) caster (superfine) sugar
1 teaspoon vanilla extract
4 store-bought chocolate brownies (400g),
    halved horizontally
cocoa powder, for dusting
125g raspberries, to serve
store-bought ginger syrup*, to serve

Place the sour cream, cream, sugar and vanilla in a
medium bowl and whisk until soft peaks form.
    Place the brownie bases onto serving plates. Top with
the cream mixture and sandwich with the brownie tops.
Dust with cocoa and sprinkle with raspberries. Drizzle
the trifles with ginger syrup to serve. SERVES 4

raspberry and turkish delight rocky road

400g dark chocolate, melted
1 tablespoon vegetable oil
2 cups (500g) store-bought Turkish delight (lokum),
    roughly chopped
½ cup (15g) freeze-dried raspberries, plus extra,
    crushed to serve[+]
2 tablespoons edible dried rose petals[+]

Line a 20cm square slice tin with non-stick baking paper.
Place the chocolate and oil in a large bowl and mix well to
combine. Add the Turkish delight and raspberries and mix
to combine. Spread into the tin and sprinkle with the extra
crushed raspberries and the rose petals. Refrigerate for
1 hour or until set.
    Remove from the tin and slice into pieces to serve. MAKES 20
+ Edible dried rose petals (pesticide-free) and freeze-dried
raspberries are available from delicatessens, specialty food
stores and select grocers.
Tip: Keep this rocky road refrigerated in an airtight
container for up to 1 week.

peanut butter brownie ice-cream bars

800g store-bought chocolate brownies (about 8 brownies)
1 cup (280g) smooth peanut butter
2 litres store-bought vanilla ice-cream, softened

Line a 20cm x 30cm slice tin with non-stick baking paper.
Place the brownies and half the peanut butter in a food
processor and pulse until finely chopped and just combined.
   Press half the mixture into the base of the tin, using the
back of a spoon. Scoop the ice-cream into the tin and spoon
the remaining peanut butter on top. Spread gently to create
a swirled effect. Top with the remaining brownie mixture,
pressing to secure, and freeze for 3 hours or until firm.
   Remove from the tin and slice into bars to serve. MAKES 15
Tip: Keep these ice-cream bars frozen for up to 2 weeks.

magic chocolate molten puddings

2 eggs
2 egg yolks, extra
1½ cups (450g) store-bought dulce de leche* or thick caramel
⅓ cup (35g) cocoa powder, sifted, plus extra for dusting

Preheat oven to 220°C (425°F). Place the eggs and
extra yolks in the bowl of an electric mixer and whisk
for 5 minutes or until thick and pale. Add the dulce de
leche and whisk until just combined. Add the cocoa
and gently fold to combine.
   Lightly grease 4 x 1-cup-capacity (250ml) metal
dariole (pudding) moulds and place on an oven tray.
Divide the mixture between the moulds and bake for
12 minutes or until set on top but still slightly soft in
the middle. Allow to stand for 1 minute.
   Using a small knife, loosen the edges and invert the
puddings onto serving plates. Dust with extra cocoa
to serve. MAKES 4

no-bake chocolate and walnut brownies

18 soft fresh dates (360g), pitted
1 cup (100g) cocoa powder, plus extra for dusting
¼ cup (60ml) maple syrup
1½ cups (240g) almonds
60g unsalted butter, melted
2¼ cups (335g) raisins
¾ cup (75g) walnuts

Line a 20cm square slice tin with non-stick baking paper.
Place the dates, cocoa, maple syrup, almonds and butter
in a food processor. Process for 3–4 minutes or until well
combined. Add the raisins and walnuts and process to
combine. Press into the tin, using the back of a spoon.
Refrigerate for 2 hours or until firm.

Remove the brownie from the tin and cut into squares.
Dust with cocoa to serve. MAKES 16

one-bowl chocolate and coconut muffins

2 cups (300g) self-raising (self-rising) flour
1 cup (175g) light brown sugar
½ cup (40g) desiccated coconut
¼ cup (25g) cocoa powder, sifted
1 cup (250ml) milk
½ cup (125ml) vegetable oil
2 eggs, lightly beaten
2 teaspoons vanilla extract
200g dark chocolate, chopped

Preheat oven to 180°C (350°F). Line 12 x ½-cup-capacity
(125ml) muffin tins with paper cases. Place the flour, sugar,
coconut and cocoa in a large bowl and mix to combine. Add
the milk, oil, eggs, vanilla and chocolate and mix until just
combined. Spoon into the tins and bake for 20 minutes or
until cooked when tested with a skewer.

Allow to cool in the tins for 5 minutes before placing
onto a wire rack to cool completely. MAKES 12

FRESH AND LIGHT

—

My mantra for bringing a bit more balance into my kitchen is simply to use more fresh produce. I love that even when it comes to chocolate, I can do just that. With dark raw cacao as the base, these recipes celebrate the tropical cacao bean (chocolate does grow on trees!) and give treats a clever superfood boost.

flourless cacao cake

flourless cacao cake

1 cup (250ml) melted coconut oil*
1 cup (100g) raw cacao or cocoa powder*,
  plus extra for dusting
½ cup (175g) rice malt syrup*
6 eggs, separated
1¼ cups (200g) rapadura sugar*
1 cup (120g) almond meal (ground almonds)

Preheat oven to 180°C (350°F). Line a 22cm round springform tin with non-stick baking paper. Place the coconut oil, cacao and rice malt syrup in a small saucepan over medium heat and cook, stirring, for 2–3 minutes or until smooth. Set aside to cool.

Place the egg yolks and half the sugar in the bowl of an electric mixer and whisk for 2–3 minutes or until thick and pale. Add the cacao mixture and gently fold to combine. Add the almond meal and mix to combine.

Place the eggwhites in a clean bowl of the electric mixer and whisk until stiff peaks form. Gradually add the remaining sugar and whisk until thick and glossy.

Add the eggwhite mixture to the cacao mixture and gently fold until just combined. Pour into the tin and bake for 25 minutes or until firm at the edges but with a slight wobble in the centre. Allow to cool a little in the tin before refrigerating for 2–3 hours or until chilled.

Remove from the tin and place on a cake stand or serving plate. Dust with extra cacao to serve. SERVES 6–8

cacao cupcakes with ricotta maple frosting

¾ cup (90g) almond meal (ground almonds)
1 cup (160g) rapadura sugar*
½ cup (80g) wholemeal (whole-wheat) plain (all-purpose) flour*
½ cup (50g) raw cacao or cocoa powder[+]
½ teaspoon baking powder
¼ teaspoon bicarbonate of (baking) soda
125g unsalted butter, melted
2 eggs
¾ cup (180ml) buttermilk
2 teaspoons vanilla bean paste or vanilla extract
¼ teaspoon fine sea salt
ricotta maple frosting
1 cup (240g) fresh firm ricotta
¼ cup (60ml) maple syrup, plus extra to serve (optional)
2 teaspoons vanilla bean paste or vanilla extract
¼ cup (25g) raw cacao or cocoa powder[+]

Preheat oven to 160°C (325°F). Line 12 x ½-cup-capacity (125ml) cupcake tins with paper cases. Place the almond meal, sugar, flour, cacao, baking powder, bicarbonate of soda, butter, eggs, buttermilk, vanilla and salt in the bowl of an electric mixer and beat for 1–2 minutes or until smooth. Spoon into the tins and bake for 22–25 minutes or until cooked when tested with a skewer. Place on a wire rack to cool completely.

To make the ricotta maple frosting, place the ricotta, maple syrup, vanilla and cacao in a food processor and process for 1 minute, scraping down the sides of the bowl, until smooth and glossy.

Spread the frosting over the cooled cupcakes and refrigerate until ready to serve. Drizzle with extra maple syrup to serve. MAKES 12

+ Available in nibs and powder form, raw cacao comes from the same tropical cacao beans as regular cocoa, but is derived via cold pressing. This means it can retain more antioxidants and enzymes. Rich, dark and pleasantly bitter, find raw cacao in supermarkets and health food stores.

cacao cupcakes with ricotta maple frosting

goji coconut bliss balls

raw lamingtons with blackberry jam

3 cups (480g) cashews
1½ cups (120g) desiccated coconut
¾ cup (180ml) coconut cream
¼ cup (60ml) melted coconut oil*
¼ cup (90g) honey
3 cups (225g) shredded coconut
blackberry chia jam
250g blackberries
1½ tablespoons honey
1 tablespoon lemon juice
1 tablespoon water
1 tablespoon black chia seeds*
chocolate icing
¼ cup (60ml) coconut cream
½ cup (50g) raw cacao or cocoa powder*
½ cup (125ml) melted coconut oil*
2 tablespoons honey

goji coconut bliss balls

½ cup (70g) dried goji berries+
1 cup (160g) almonds
2 cups (150g) shredded coconut
¼ cup (50g) white chia seeds*
10 soft fresh dates (200g), pitted
½ cup (50g) raw cacao or cocoa powder*
¼ cup (60ml) maple syrup
150g 70% dark chocolate, melted
¼ cup (35g) pistachios, finely chopped

Place the goji berries in a small heatproof bowl, cover with boiling water and allow to soak for 20 minutes. Drain well, squeezing out as much liquid as possible.

Place the goji berries, almonds, coconut, chia seeds, dates, cacao and maple syrup in a food processor and process, scraping down the sides of the bowl, for 4 minutes or until the mixture comes together.

Line a large tray with non-stick baking paper. Roll 1-tablespoon portions of the mixture into balls. Dip 1 bliss ball into the chocolate, allowing the excess to drip off. Place on the tray and sprinkle with the pistachios. Repeat with the remaining bliss balls, chocolate and pistachios. Refrigerate for 20 minutes or until set. MAKES 28
+ *Goji berries, with origins in Chinese medicine, are still thought of by many today as a superfood. Sweet-yet-tart in flavour and pink in colour, they're available dried from the health food aisle of supermarkets.*

Line a 20cm x 30cm slice tin with non-stick baking paper. Place the cashews in a food processor and process until finely chopped. Add the desiccated coconut, coconut cream, coconut oil and honey and pulse until the mixture comes together. Press evenly into the base of the tin using the back of a spoon. Refrigerate for 1 hour or until firm.

To make the blackberry chia jam, place the blackberries, honey, lemon juice, water and chia seeds in a small saucepan over medium heat. Bring to a simmer and cook, stirring, for 12–15 minutes or until thickened. Place in a medium bowl and refrigerate for 15 minutes or until cold.

Line a tray with non-stick baking paper. Remove the cashew slice from the tin and, using a large serrated knife, cut it in half horizontally. Spread 1 half with the jam and sandwich with the remaining half. Place on the tray and freeze for 15 minutes or until the jam is firm.

To make the chocolate icing, place the coconut cream, cacao, coconut oil and honey in a small bowl and whisk to combine.

Place the shredded coconut in a medium shallow bowl. Remove the lamington from the freezer and cut into 3cm squares, trimming any excess. Dip 1 square into the chocolate icing and roll in the shredded coconut to coat. Repeat with the remaining squares. Serve the lamingtons immediately or refrigerate until ready to serve. MAKES 15

raw lamingtons with blackberry jam

raw cacao, coconut and walnut cake

raw cacao, coconut and walnut cake

3 cups (300g) walnuts
⅓ cup (55g) sultanas
15 soft fresh dates (300g), pitted
½ cup (50g) raw cacao or cocoa powder[+]
⅓ cup (80ml) melted coconut oil*
1 cup (90g) rolled oats
2 teaspoons vanilla extract
¼ cup (20g) shredded coconut, toasted
cacao nibs, crushed to serve[+]

Line an 18cm round cake tin with non-stick baking paper.
Place the walnuts and sultanas in a large heatproof bowl
and cover with boiling water. Allow to soak for 10 minutes.
Drain well and place in a food processor. Add the dates
and process for 2 minutes or until smooth. Add the cacao
powder, coconut oil, oats, vanilla and coconut and process
for 1 minute or until combined. Press the mixture into
the base of the tin, using the back of a spoon, and smooth
the top. Refrigerate for 2 hours or until firm.

Remove the cake from the tin and place it on a cake
stand or plate. Top with the cacao nibs to serve. SERVES 12–14
+ *Available in nibs and powder form, raw cacao comes
from the same tropical cacao beans as regular cocoa, but is
derived via cold pressing. This means it can retain more
antioxidants and enzymes. Rich, dark and pleasantly
bitter, find cacao in supermarkets and health food stores.
Note: Keep this cake refrigerated in an airtight container
for up to 3 days.*

raw chocolate-glazed turkish delight doughnuts

1⅓ cups (215g) almonds
⅓ cup (45g) pistachios
2 tablespoons raw cacao or cocoa powder*
2 tablespoons psyllium husks*
¼ cup (60ml) maple syrup
12 soft fresh dates (240g), pitted
2 tablespoons dried goji berries*
200g 70% dark chocolate, melted
1 teaspoon rosewater
edible dried rose petals, to serve[+]
freeze-dried raspberries, crushed to serve[+]
pistachios, extra, finely chopped to serve

Line a tray with non-stick baking paper. Place the almonds,
pistachios, cacao, psyllium husks, maple syrup, dates and
goji berries in a food processor and process for 2 minutes
or until the mixture comes together. Roll 2-tablespoon
portions of the mixture into balls, flatten slightly and,
using your finger, make a hole through the centre. Place
on the tray and refrigerate for 20 minutes.

Place the chocolate in a small bowl, add the rosewater
and mix to combine. Dip the top of each doughnut in the
chocolate and return to the tray. Sprinkle 4 of the doughnuts
with rose petals, 4 with crushed raspberries and 4 with
chopped pistachios. Refrigerate for 5 minutes or until set,
before serving. MAKES 12
+ *Edible dried rose petals (pesticide-free) and freeze-dried
raspberries are available from delicatessens, specialty food
stores and select grocers.
Tip: Keep doughnuts refrigerated in an airtight container
for up to 1 week.*

raw chocolate-glazed
turkish delight doughnuts

chocolate-coated raw cookies
with raspberry and coconut filling

chocolate-coated raw cookies with raspberry and coconut filling

125g raspberries
1 tablespoon white chia seeds*
200g 70% dark chocolate, melted
2 teaspoons melted coconut oil*
oat cookies
¾ cup (60g) rolled oats
¾ cup (120g) almonds
2 tablespoons natural almond butter*
½ cup (75g) raisins
1 tablespoon maple syrup
coconut filling
¾ cup (60g) desiccated coconut
½ cup (125ml) coconut cream
1 tablespoon coconut oil*

To make the oat cookies, line a large tray with non-stick baking paper. Place the oats, almonds, almond butter, raisins and maple syrup in a food processor and process for 2–3 minutes or until the mixture comes together. Turn out the dough and roll out between 2 sheets of non-stick baking paper to 4mm thick. Refrigerate for 10 minutes or until firm. Remove the top sheet of paper and, using a 5.5cm round cookie cutter, cut 20 rounds from the dough, re-rolling if necessary. Place the rounds on the tray and refrigerate until needed.

Place the raspberries in a small bowl and crush with a fork. Add the chia seeds, mix to combine, and set aside for 30 minutes or until thickened.

To make the coconut filling, place the coconut, coconut cream and coconut oil in a blender and blend until well combined and fluffy.

Top 1 of the oat cookies with 1 teaspoon of the raspberry mixture and 2 teaspoons of the coconut filling. Sandwich with another oat cookie. Return to the tray. Repeat with the remaining cookies, jam and filling. Refrigerate for 20 minutes or until firm.

Place the chocolate and coconut oil in a small bowl and mix to combine. Dip 1 of the cookies in the chocolate, shaking off any excess, and return to the tray. Repeat with the remaining cookies and chocolate. Refrigerate for 10 minutes or until just set, before serving. MAKES 10
Tip: Keep these cookies refrigerated in an airtight container for up to 3 days.

cacao buckwheat crackles

¼ cup (25g) raw cacao or cocoa powder*
½ cup (180g) honey
1 teaspoon vanilla bean paste or vanilla extract
⅓ cup (80ml) melted coconut oil*
2 tablespoons tahini*
1 cup (30g) puffed brown rice*
¾ cup (150g) raw buckwheat[+]
1 cup (80g) flaked almonds, toasted
½ cup (40g) shredded coconut
2 tablespoons white chia seeds*

Place the cacao, honey, vanilla, coconut oil and tahini in a medium saucepan over low heat. Cook, stirring, for 3 minutes or until melted. Remove from the heat and add the puffed rice, buckwheat, almonds, coconut and chia seeds. Mix well to combine.

Line 2 large trays with non-stick baking paper. Shape ¼-cup (60ml) portions of the mixture into balls and place on the trays. Flatten slightly and freeze for 30 minutes or until set, before serving. MAKES 12
+ *Buckwheat is the seed of a plant related to rhubarb. Loved for its wholesome benefits and nutty flavour, the little pyramid-shaped kernels are light brown or green in colour. Buy raw buckwheat in the health food aisle of most supermarkets and at health food stores. Tip: Keep these crackles in the fridge or freezer in an airtight container for up to 2 weeks.*

cacao buckwheat crackles

raw peppermint slice

raw peppermint slice

2 cups (160g) desiccated coconut
2 tablespoons rice malt syrup*
⅔ cup (160ml) coconut cream
2 teaspoons peppermint extract
100g raw organic 70% dark chocolate[+]
2 teaspoons vegetable oil
coconut base
10 soft fresh dates (200g), pitted
¾ cup (120g) almonds
⅓ cup (20g) desiccated coconut

To make the coconut base, line a 20cm square slice tin with non-stick baking paper. Place the dates, almonds and coconut in a food processor and process for 1–2 minutes or until the mixture just comes together. Press into the base of the tin, using the back of a spoon, and refrigerate for 20 minutes.

Place the coconut, rice malt syrup, coconut cream and peppermint in a food processor and process for 3–4 minutes, scraping down the sides of the bowl, until smooth. Spread the peppermint mixture evenly over the base. Refrigerate for 40 minutes or until set.

Place the chocolate in a heatproof bowl over a saucepan of simmering water (the bowl shouldn't touch the water) and stir until melted. Remove from the heat, add the oil and mix to combine. Spread the chocolate over the peppermint layer and smooth the top. Refrigerate for 1 hour or until set.

Remove the slice from the tin and, using a hot knife, cut it into bars. Refrigerate until ready to serve. MAKES 20
+ *Raw organic chocolate is available at health food stores and specialty grocers. If you can't find it, you can use 70% dark chocolate. To keep the chocolate raw while melting, use a sugar (candy) thermometer to ensure it stays under 42°C (107°F).*
Tip: Keep this slice refrigerated in an airtight container for up to 2 weeks.

chocolate mousse slice

1½ cups (135g) rolled oats
1 cup (80g) desiccated coconut
1 cup (120g) almond meal (ground almonds)
15 soft fresh dates (300g), pitted
80g unsalted butter, melted
½ cup (50g) raw cacao or cocoa powder,
    plus extra for dusting[+]
chocolate mousse topping
2 x 400ml cans coconut cream, refrigerated overnight[++]
⅓ cup (35g) raw cacao or cocoa powder, sifted[+]
¼ cup (40g) icing (confectioner's) sugar, sifted

Preheat oven to 160°C (325°F). Line a 20cm x 30cm slice tin with non-stick baking paper. Place the oats, coconut, almond meal, dates, butter and cacao in a food processor and process for 3–4 minutes or until the mixture comes together. Press into the base of the tin, using the back of a spoon, and smooth the top. Bake for 20 minutes or until firm. Set aside in the tin to cool completely.

To make the chocolate mousse topping, scoop the firm coconut cream from the top of the cans into the bowl of an electric mixer, discarding the liquid. Add the cacao and sugar and whisk for 1 minute or until combined and firm.

Spread the mousse topping onto the cooled base and refrigerate for 1 hour or until set.

Remove from the tin, dust with extra cacao and slice to serve. MAKES 20
+ *Available in nibs and powder form, raw cacao comes from the same tropical cacao beans as regular cocoa, but is derived via cold pressing. This means it can retain more antioxidants and enzymes. Rich, dark and pleasantly bitter, find raw cacao in supermarkets and health food stores.*
++ *Refrigerate the coconut cream for at least 6 hours or overnight to allow the cream to separate, and don't shake before opening the cans.*
Tip: Keep this slice refrigerated in an airtight container for up to 5 days.

chocolate mousse slice

caramel, toffee and coffee

Smooth glossy caramel, with its velvety texture and mellow sweetness, gives its golden crown to so many of our beloved puddings and treats – not to mention fudgy slices and crunchy toffees. In this same kingdom of luscious, syrupy desserts also belongs its deeper, darker and more grown-up cousin – coffee.

steamed sticky date pudding with spiced rum and maple glaze

steamed sticky date pudding with spiced rum and maple glaze

15 soft fresh dates (300g), pitted
1 teaspoon bicarbonate of (baking) soda
½ cup (125ml) boiling water
60g unsalted butter, chopped and softened
¾ cup (135g) dark brown sugar
1 teaspoon vanilla extract
4 eggs
¾ cup (110g) self-raising (self-rising) flour, sifted
¾ cup (90g) almond meal (ground almonds)
1 teaspoon mixed spice
spiced rum and maple glaze
½ cup (125ml) maple syrup
½ cup (125ml) spiced rum
1 teaspoon vanilla extract

Line a 1.75-litre-capacity metal pudding bowl with non-stick baking paper. Place the dates, bicarbonate of soda and water in a large heatproof jug and allow to soften for 10 minutes. Using a hand-held stick blender, blend until smooth. Place the butter, sugar and vanilla in the bowl of an electric mixer and beat on high speed for 4–5 minutes or until pale and creamy. Add the eggs, 1 at a time, beating well after each addition. Add the flour, almond meal, mixed spice and the date mixture and beat on low speed until just combined. Spoon into the pudding bowl. Top with a round of non-stick baking paper. Cover the top of the bowl with aluminium foil and tie with kitchen string to secure.

Place the bowl in a large saucepan over low heat and fill with boiling water until it reaches three-quarters of the way up the sides of the bowl. Cover the saucepan with a tight-fitting lid and cook for 2 hours, adding more boiling water if needed. Carefully remove the bowl from the saucepan and allow to stand for 15 minutes.

While the pudding is standing, make the spiced rum and maple glaze. Place the maple syrup, rum and vanilla in a small saucepan over high heat. Bring to the boil and cook, stirring, for 5–6 minutes or until thickened and reduced.

Turn the pudding out onto a cake stand or plate and spoon the glaze over to serve. SERVES 6–8

salted caramel brownie squares

150g dark chocolate, chopped
200g unsalted butter, chopped
1½ cups (265g) light brown sugar
3 eggs
¾ cup (110g) plain (all-purpose) flour, sifted
2 tablespoons cocoa powder, sifted
sea salt flakes, for sprinkling
caramel
¾ cup (180ml) single (pouring) cream*
90g unsalted butter, chopped
1½ cups (330g) caster (superfine) sugar
½ cup (125ml) water

Preheat oven to 160°C (325°F). Line a 20cm x 30cm slice tin with non-stick baking paper. Place the chocolate and butter in a small saucepan over low heat and cook, stirring, until melted and smooth. Place the sugar, eggs, flour and cocoa in a large bowl. Whisk to combine. Add the chocolate mixture and whisk until well combined. Pour the mixture into the tin. Bake for 30–35 minutes or until cooked when tested with a skewer. Allow to cool in the tin for 10 minutes. Refrigerate for 30 minutes or until cooled completely.

To make the caramel, place the cream and butter in a small saucepan over medium heat and cook, stirring, until the butter is melted. Set aside. Place the sugar and water in a medium saucepan over high heat and stir to dissolve the sugar. Bring to the boil and cook, without stirring, until dark golden and the temperature reaches 175°C (347°F) on a sugar (candy) thermometer⁺. Remove from the heat and carefully add the cream mixture in a thin, steady stream, stirring to combine. Place the pan over low heat and cook, stirring, for 5 minutes or until the caramel has thickened slightly. Pour the caramel over the cooled brownie and refrigerate for 4–5 hours or until firm.

Remove the slice from the tin and cut into pieces. Refrigerate until ready to serve. Sprinkle with salt just before serving. MAKES 20

+ Sugar (candy) thermometers are available at kitchen shops and some supermarkets – they take the guesswork out of heating syrups and creams for sweet treats like these. Tip: Once the syrup begins to caramelise, you can swirl the pan to even out the colour of the caramel and prevent the edges from darkening. Use a wet pastry brush to gently wipe any sugar crystals that may appear on the side of the saucepan. This will stop the caramel from crystallising.

salted caramel brownie squares

caramel popcorn, salted almond and malt cookies

caramel popcorn, salted almond and malt cookies

⅔ cup (120g) light brown sugar
½ cup (110g) white (granulated) sugar
100g unsalted butter, softened
1 teaspoon vanilla extract
1 egg
1 cup (150g) plain (all-purpose) flour, sifted
¼ teaspoon baking powder
¼ cup (30g) malted milk powder, sifted
1 teaspoon sea salt flakes
2 cups (75g) store-bought caramel popcorn
1 cup (160g) salted roasted almonds, chopped
dark hot chocolate, to serve

Preheat oven to 160°C (325°F). Line 2 large baking trays with non-stick baking paper. Place both the sugars, the butter and vanilla in the bowl of an electric mixer and beat on high speed for 5 minutes or until pale and creamy. Scrape down the sides of the bowl, add the egg and beat until well combined. Add the flour, baking powder, milk powder and salt and beat until just combined. Add the popcorn and almonds and fold to combine.

Shape 2-tablespoon portions of the dough into balls and place on the trays, flattening slightly and allowing room to spread. Bake for 15–18 minutes or until the cookies are golden. Allow to cool on the trays before serving with hot chocolate. MAKES 16

cocoa-dusted coffee cookies

120g unsalted butter, chopped and softened
1½ cups (265g) light brown sugar
⅓ cup (115g) golden syrup
1 egg
1 teaspoon vanilla extract
2¼ cups (335g) plain (all-purpose) flour
¼ teaspoon bicarbonate of (baking) soda
1 tablespoon finely ground coffee beans
½ cup (50g) cocoa powder, sifted

Preheat oven to 180°C (350°F). Line 3 large baking trays with non-stick baking paper. Place the butter, sugar and golden syrup in the bowl of an electric mixer and beat on high speed for 3 minutes or until pale and fluffy. Add the egg and vanilla and beat to combine. Add the flour, bicarbonate of soda and coffee and beat until just combined.

Roll 2-teaspoon portions of the dough into balls and place on the trays. Bake for 10–12 minutes or until golden brown. Transfer to a wire rack to cool for 10 minutes. Place the cocoa and cookies in a medium bowl and toss to coat. Return to the wire rack to cool completely, before serving. MAKES 38

cocoa-dusted coffee cookies

coffee cheesecake with coffee syrup

coffee cheesecake with coffee syrup

225g store-bought plain chocolate biscuits
½ cup (50g) hazelnut meal (ground hazelnuts)
60g unsalted butter, melted
1 tablespoon coffee beans, finely crushed
2 cups (500ml) single (pouring) cream*, whipped
filling
1⅓ cups (295g) caster (superfine) sugar
1⅓ cups (320g) cream cheese, chopped and softened
2 cups (480g) fresh firm ricotta
5 eggs, at room temperature
1½ tablespoons cornflour (cornstarch)
1 teaspoon vanilla extract
⅓ cup (80ml) coffee liqueur
coffee syrup
¼ cup (60ml) coffee liqueur
¼ cup (55g) caster (superfine) sugar
2 tablespoons water

Preheat oven to 150°C (300°F). Line a 20cm round springform tin with non-stick baking paper. Place the biscuits, hazelnut meal and butter in a food processor. Process into coarse crumbs. Add the coffee beans and pulse to combine. Press the mixture into the base of the tin with the back of a spoon. Refrigerate for 15 minutes.

To make the filling, place the sugar, cream cheese and ricotta in the cleaned food processor and process until smooth. Add the eggs and process until combined. Place the cornflour, vanilla and liqueur in a small bowl and mix to combine. Add the liqueur mixture to the ricotta mixture and process to combine. Pour into the tin and tap gently to remove any air bubbles. Place on an oven tray and bake for 1 hour or until golden and just set. Turn the oven off. Allow the cake to cool in the oven with the door closed for 30 minutes. Remove from the oven and cool completely.

While the cake is cooling, make the coffee syrup. Place the liqueur, sugar and water in a small saucepan over medium heat. Bring to a simmer and cook for 5 minutes or until thickened. Allow to cool completely.

Carefully remove the cheesecake from the tin and place on a cake stand or plate. Top with the whipped cream and drizzle with the coffee syrup to serve. **SERVES 8–10**

upside-down maple pecan tarts

2 cups (240g) pecans
100g unsalted butter, chopped
1 cup (250ml) maple syrup
¼ cup (60ml) water
1 teaspoon vanilla extract
½ teaspoon mixed spice
2 sheets frozen butter puff pastry, thawed

Preheat oven to 200°C (400°F). Divide the pecans between 4 x 12cm (1¾-cup-capacity) heavy-based ovenproof frying pans (skillets), arranging them evenly to cover the bases.

Place the butter, maple syrup, water, vanilla and mixed spice in a large non-stick frying pan over high heat. Bring to the boil and cook, whisking occasionally, for 2–3 minutes or until slightly reduced. Carefully divide the syrup mixture between the skillets.

Using a plate as a guide, cut 4 x 12cm circles from the pastry. Top each tart with a pastry round and gently tuck the edges in to enclose. Using a small sharp knife, cut a cross into the centre of each round. Place the skillets on a large oven tray and bake for 20–25 minutes or until puffed and golden brown. Allow the tarts to cool for 30 seconds+ before turning out onto plates to serve. **MAKES 4**
+ It's best to only leave the tarts in the skillets for 30 seconds after baking – any longer and the sugar will harden, making it difficult to turn them out neatly.

upside-down maple pecan tarts

caramel gingerbread cakes

caramel gingerbread cakes

60g unsalted butter
¼ cup (90g) golden syrup
¼ cup (90g) treacle*
1½ cups (225g) plain (all-purpose) flour
1¼ teaspoons baking powder
1 teaspoon ground ginger
1 teaspoon mixed spice
½ cup (90g) dark brown sugar
1 egg
⅓ cup (80ml) milk
store-bought thick caramel or dulce de leche*, to serve
store-bought granola, to serve

Preheat oven to 180°C (350°F). Grease 2 x 12cm x 16cm
(1-litre-capacity) heavy-based ovenproof frying pans
(skillets). Place the butter, golden syrup and treacle in a
large saucepan over medium heat and cook, stirring, for
2–3 minutes or until melted and smooth. Remove from
the heat, add the flour, baking powder, ginger, mixed spice,
sugar, egg and milk and whisk until smooth. Divide the
mixture between the skillets and place on a large oven tray.
Bake for 18–20 minutes or until golden and cooked when
tested with a skewer. Allow to cool in the skillets.

Spread the cakes with caramel, sprinkle with granola
and slice to serve. **SERVES 6–8**

caramel affogatos with cinnamon churros

500ml store-bought caramel ice-cream
4 x 60ml (double) shots hot espresso coffee
cinnamon churros
1 teaspoon ground cinnamon
1 cup (220g) white (granulated) sugar
100g unsalted butter, chopped
1 cup (250ml) water
1 cup (150g) plain (all-purpose) flour
3 eggs
vegetable oil, for deep-frying

To make the cinnamon churros, place the cinnamon and
sugar in a shallow tray and mix to combine. Place the butter
and water in a medium saucepan over high heat and bring
to the boil. Reduce the heat to low, add the flour and beat
with a wooden spoon for 2 minutes or until the mixture is
smooth and comes away from the sides of the pan. Remove
from the heat and add the eggs, 1 at a time, beating well after
each addition and until the mixture is glossy and smooth.
Fill a large saucepan half-full with the oil and place over
medium heat until the temperature reaches 180°C (350°F)
on a deep-frying thermometer. Spoon the churro mixture
into a piping bag fitted with a 1cm star-shaped nozzle. In
batches, pipe 4cm lengths of the mixture into the oil, using
kitchen scissors to snip them. Cook, turning occasionally,
for 2–3 minutes or until golden. Remove with a slotted
spoon and drain on absorbent kitchen paper. While the
churros are still hot, toss them in the cinnamon sugar and
thread them onto small metal skewers.

Place scoops of the ice-cream into 4 x 2-cup-capacity
(500ml) serving glasses. Top with churros and serve with
the coffee. **SERVES 4**

caramel affogatos with cinnamon churros

s'more caramel slice

s'more caramel slice

250g store-bought plain sweet malt biscuits
125g unsalted butter, melted
½ cup (125ml) warm water
2 tablespoons gelatine powder*
1½ cups (330g) caster (superfine) sugar
⅔ cup (230g) liquid glucose*
½ cup (125ml) water, extra
1 teaspoon vanilla extract
200g dark chocolate, chopped
1 tablespoon vegetable oil
1 cup (300g) store-bought thick caramel or dulce de leche*

Line a 20cm x 30cm slice tin with non-stick baking paper.
Place the biscuits in a food processor and process into fine
crumbs. Add the butter and process until combined. Using
the back of a spoon, press the mixture into the base of the
tin. Set aside in the refrigerator.

Place the warm water in the bowl of an electric mixer,
sprinkle with the gelatine and stir to combine. Set aside for
5 minutes or until the gelatine is absorbed. Place the sugar,
glucose and extra water in a small saucepan over medium
heat and cook, stirring, until the sugar has dissolved.
Increase the heat to high and bring to the boil. Cook,
without stirring, for 5-7 minutes or until the temperature
reaches 115°C (240°F) on a sugar (candy) thermometer. In
a thin, steady stream, gradually pour the hot sugar syrup
into the gelatine mixture, beating on high speed. Add the
vanilla and beat for 3-4 minutes or until the mixture is
thick and fluffy. Working quickly, spoon the mixture into
the tin, smoothing it over the biscuit base with a greased
spatula. Refrigerate for 10 minutes or until just firm.

Place the chocolate and oil in a heatproof bowl over a
saucepan of simmering water (the bowl shouldn't touch
the water) and stir until melted and smooth. Allow to
cool for 10 minutes.

Spread the caramel evenly over the marshmallow layer.
Refrigerate for 10 minutes. Top the slice with the chocolate,
spread evenly and refrigerate for a further 20 minutes or
until firm. Use a hot sharp knife to cut the slice into bars
to serve. MAKES 8

*Tip: You can keep this slice refrigerated, in an airtight
container, for up to 1 week.*

molten dulce de leche lava cakes

2 eggs
2 egg yolks, extra
1 teaspoon vanilla extract
1½ cups (450g) store-bought dulce de leche* or thick caramel
¼ cup (35g) plain (all-purpose) flour, sifted
store-bought vanilla ice-cream, to serve

Preheat oven to 220°C (425°F). Grease 4 x 1-cup-capacity
(250ml) metal dariole (pudding) moulds. Place the eggs,
extra yolks and vanilla in the bowl of an electric mixer and
whisk for 4–5 minutes or until very thick and pale. Add the
dulce de leche and whisk on low speed until just combined.
Add the flour and gently fold to combine. Divide the mixture
between the moulds. Place on an oven tray and bake for
10–12 minutes or until golden but slightly soft in the centre.
Allow to cool in the moulds for 1 minute.

Gently run a small knife around the inside edge of the
moulds. Invert the cakes onto serving plates. Top with
ice-cream and serve immediately. SERVES 4

molten dulce de leche lava cakes

coffee and brown sugar tray cake

coffee and brown sugar tray cake

1 cup (175g) dark brown sugar
2 teaspoons ground cinnamon
2½ cups (375g) self-raising (self-rising) flour, sifted
1½ cups (330g) caster (superfine) sugar
4 eggs
1½ cups (375ml) milk
250g unsalted butter, melted
2 teaspoons vanilla extract
1 tablespoon good-quality instant coffee granules
60g unsalted butter, extra, melted

Preheat oven to 160°C (325°F). Line a 20cm x 30cm slice tin with non-stick baking paper. Place the brown sugar and cinnamon in a small bowl and mix to combine. Set aside.

Place the flour, sugar, eggs, milk, butter and vanilla in a large bowl and whisk until smooth. Pour half the mixture into the tin. Sprinkle with the coffee and half the brown sugar mixture. Top with the remaining cake mixture and spread evenly. Sprinkle with the remaining brown sugar mixture. Pour the extra butter over. Bake for 50–55 minutes or until cooked when tested with a skewer. Allow to cool in the tin for 5 minutes, before slicing to serve. SERVES 8–10

chocolate salted caramel cookies

200g unsalted butter, melted and cooled
1 cup (175g) light brown sugar
¾ cup (165g) white (granulated) sugar
1 egg
1 egg yolk, extra
2 teaspoons vanilla extract
¼ teaspoon baking powder
½ teaspoon bicarbonate of (baking) soda
1 teaspoon water
2 cups (300g) plain (all-purpose) flour
¼ teaspoon table salt
⅓ cup (35g) cocoa powder
2 tablespoons milk
300g 70% dark chocolate, chopped
⅔ cup (200g) store-bought thick caramel or dulce de leche*
sea salt flakes, for sprinkling

Preheat oven to 160°C (325°F). Line 2 large baking trays with non-stick baking paper. Place the butter and both the sugars in the bowl of an electric mixer and beat on medium speed for 6–8 minutes or until sandy in texture. Add the egg, extra yolk and vanilla, increase the speed to high and beat for 2 minutes or until pale and creamy. Place the baking powder, bicarbonate of soda and water in a small bowl and mix to combine. Add the baking powder mixture, flour, table salt, cocoa, milk and chocolate to the butter mixture and beat on low speed until just combined.

Working in batches, shape ¼-cup (60ml) portions of the dough into balls and place on the trays, allowing room to spread+. Bake for 18–20 minutes or until golden brown and firm to the touch. Allow to cool on the trays for 10 minutes, before transferring to wire racks to cool completely. Repeat with the remaining dough to make a total of 15 cookies.

Spread cookies with the caramel and sprinkle with sea salt to serve. MAKES 15

+ *This recipe makes 15 large cookies. To make regular-sized cookies, simply shape 2-tablespoon portions of the dough into balls and place onto the trays, allowing room to spread. Bake for 14–16 minutes.*
Tip: You can store these cookies, without the caramel and sea salt, in an airtight container for up to 4 days.

chocolate salted caramel cookies

banana maple toffee cookies

banana maple toffee cookies

200g unsalted butter, melted and cooled
1 cup (175g) light brown sugar
¾ cup (165g) white (granulated) sugar
1 egg
1 egg yolk, extra
2 teaspoons vanilla extract
¼ teaspoon baking powder
½ teaspoon bicarbonate of (baking) soda
1 teaspoon water
2 cups (300g) plain (all-purpose) flour
1 teaspoon ground cinnamon
¼ teaspoon table salt
1½ cups (160g) dried banana chips, crushed
maple toffee
1 cup (250ml) maple syrup
¼ cup (45g) light brown sugar

Preheat oven to 160°C (325°F). Line 2 large baking trays with non-stick baking paper. Place the butter and both the sugars in the bowl of an electric mixer and beat on medium speed for 6–8 minutes or until sandy in texture. Add the egg, extra yolk and vanilla, increase the speed to high and beat for 2 minutes or until pale and creamy. Place the baking powder, bicarbonate of soda and water in a small bowl and mix to combine. Add the baking powder mixture, the flour, cinnamon and salt to the butter mixture and beat on low speed until just combined.

Working in batches, shape ¼-cup (60ml) portions of the dough into balls and place on the trays, allowing room to spread⁺. Sprinkle with the banana chips, gently pressing into the dough. Bake for 18–20 minutes or until golden and firm to the touch. Allow to cool on the trays for 10 minutes, before transferring to wire racks to cool completely. Repeat with the remaining dough to make a total of 15 cookies.

While the cookies are cooling, make the maple toffee. Place the maple syrup and sugar in a small saucepan over low heat. Cook, stirring, for 6–8 minutes or until syrupy. Set aside to cool completely.

Drizzle cookies with the maple toffee to serve. **MAKES 15**
+ *This recipe makes 15 large cookies. To make regular-sized cookies, simply shape 2-tablespoon portions of the dough into balls and place onto the trays, allowing room to spread. Top with the banana chips and bake for 14–16 minutes.*
Tip: Store cookies in an airtight container for up to 4 days.

caramel and cardamom kisses

1¼ cups (185g) self-raising (self-rising) flour, sifted
¾ cup (165g) caster (superfine) sugar
¼ teaspoon ground cardamom
2 eggs
¾ cup (180ml) milk
125g unsalted butter, melted
1 teaspoon vanilla extract
2 eggwhites, extra
1 cup (300g) store-bought thick caramel or dulce de leche*

Preheat oven to 180°C (350°F). Lightly grease 12 x 1½-tablespoon-capacity non-stick patty tins. Place the flour, sugar, cardamom, eggs, milk, butter and vanilla in a large bowl and whisk until smooth. Place the eggwhites in the bowl of an electric mixer and whisk until stiff peaks form. Add the eggwhite to the flour mixture and gently fold to combine.

Place 1 tablespoon of the mixture into each patty tin. Bake for 8–10 minutes or until golden and cooked when tested with a skewer. Turn out the cakes onto a wire rack and allow to cool completely. Repeat with the remaining mixture, re-greasing the tins, to make a total of 36 cakes.

Spread half the cooled cakes with the caramel and sandwich with the remaining cakes to serve. **MAKES 18**

caramel and cardamom kisses

chocolate peppermint caramels

chocolate peppermint caramels

1¼ cups (310ml) double (thick) cream*
2½ cups (550g) white (granulated) sugar
100g unsalted butter, chopped
2 teaspoons vanilla extract
1 cup (350g) golden syrup
½ teaspoon peppermint extract
100g dark chocolate, melted

Line a 20cm square slice tin with non-stick baking paper. Place the cream, sugar, butter, vanilla, golden syrup and peppermint in a large saucepan over high heat and bring to the boil, stirring to dissolve the sugar. Reduce the heat to medium and cook, without stirring, for 10–15 minutes or until the temperature reaches 124°C (255°F) on a sugar (candy) thermometer+. Allow to cool for 5 minutes. Pour into the tin and allow to set, at room temperature, for 8 hours or overnight until firm.

Remove the caramel from the tin and drizzle with the chocolate. Allow to set. Slice into pieces to serve++. **MAKES 20**
+ *Sugar (candy) thermometers are available at kitchen shops and some supermarkets. They take the guesswork out of heating creams and syrups for sweet treats like these.*
++ *If the caramel is a little too soft to cut, refrigerate it for 10 minutes to firm it up slightly.*
Note: If making the caramels a few days ahead, slice them and store in an airtight container between sheets of non-stick baking paper. Serve at room temperature.

salted peanut caramels

1¼ cups (310ml) double (thick) cream*
2½ cups (550g) white (granulated) sugar
100g unsalted butter, chopped
2 teaspoons vanilla extract
1 cup (350g) golden syrup
3 cups (420g) roasted salted peanuts

Line a 20cm square slice tin with non-stick baking paper. Place the cream, sugar, butter, vanilla and golden syrup in a large saucepan over high heat and bring to the boil, stirring to dissolve the sugar. Reduce the heat to medium and cook, without stirring, for 10–15 minutes or until the temperature reaches 124°C (255°F) on a sugar (candy) thermometer+. Allow to cool for 5 minutes. Add the peanuts and mix to combine. Pour into the tin and allow to set, at room temperature, for 8 hours or overnight until firm.

Remove the caramel from the tin and slice into pieces to serve++. **MAKES 20**
+ *Sugar (candy) thermometers are available at kitchen shops and some supermarkets. They take the guesswork out of heating creams and syrups for sweet treats like these.*
++ *If the caramel is a little too soft to cut, refrigerate it for 10 minutes to firm it up slightly.*
Note: If making the caramels a few days ahead, slice them and store in an airtight container between sheets of non-stick baking paper. Serve at room temperature.

salted peanut caramels

cardamom and pistachio caramels

cardamom and pistachio caramels

1¼ cups (310ml) double (thick) cream*
2½ cups (550g) white (granulated) sugar
100g unsalted butter, chopped
2 teaspoons vanilla extract
1 cup (350g) golden syrup
8 cardamom pods
1½ cups (210g) pistachios

Line a 20cm square slice tin with non-stick baking paper. Place the cream, sugar, butter, vanilla and golden syrup in a large saucepan over high heat and bring to the boil, stirring to dissolve the sugar. Reduce the heat to medium and cook, without stirring, for 10–15 minutes or until the temperature reaches 124°C (255°F) on a sugar (candy) thermometer[+]. Allow to cool for 5 minutes.

Place the cardamom pods in a mortar and crack them open using a pestle. Remove and discard the green shells and crush the black seeds until fine.

Add the cardamom and pistachios to the caramel and mix to combine. Pour into the tin and allow to set, at room temperature, for 8 hours or overnight until firm. Slice into pieces to serve[++]. MAKES 20

+ *Sugar (candy) thermometers are available at kitchen shops and some supermarkets. They take the guesswork out of heating creams and syrups for sweet treats like these.*
++ *If the caramel is a little too soft to cut, refrigerate it for 10 minutes to firm it up slightly.*
Note: If making the caramels a few days ahead, slice them and store in an airtight container, between sheets of non-stick baking paper. Serve at room temperature.

caramel pecan brownies

225g unsalted butter, chopped
200g dark chocolate, chopped
200g 70% dark chocolate, chopped
4 eggs
1 cup (220g) white (granulated) sugar
1 cup (175g) light brown sugar
2 teaspoons vanilla extract
1 cup (150g) plain (all-purpose) flour, sifted
1 cup (120g) pecans, chopped, plus 48 extra for decorating
1 cup (300g) store-bought thick caramel or dulce de leche*

Preheat oven to 180°C (350°F). Line a 20cm x 30cm slice tin with non-stick baking paper. Place the butter and both the chocolates in a medium saucepan over low heat and stir until melted and smooth. Place the eggs, both the sugars and the vanilla in a large bowl and whisk to combine. Add the chocolate mixture and whisk until combined. Add the flour and chopped pecans and mix until well combined. Pour into the tin and bake for 35–40 minutes or until fudgy when tested with a skewer. Allow to cool in the tin completely.

Remove the brownie from the tin and spread with the caramel. Top with the extra pecans, pressing in gently to secure. Refrigerate for 30 minutes or until firm. Slice into pieces to serve. MAKES 24

caramel pecan brownies

caramel swirl meringue cake

caramel swirl meringue cake

½ cup (125ml) milk
3 eggwhites, at room temperature
1 teaspoon vanilla extract
¼ cup (60ml) amaretto or almond liqueur
1¼ cups (185g) plain (all-purpose) flour, sifted
2 teaspoons baking powder, sifted
¾ cup (165g) caster (superfine) sugar
100g unsalted butter, softened
caramel swirl meringue
75ml eggwhite (about 2 eggs), at room temperature[+]
½ cup (110g) caster (superfine) sugar
½ teaspoon white vinegar
½ teaspoon cornflour (cornstarch)
1 teaspoon water
1 tablespoon store-bought thick caramel or dulce de leche*

Preheat oven to 160°C (325°F). Line a lightly greased 18cm round cake tin with 2 long strips of non-stick baking paper, overlapping them in a criss-cross at the base and ensuring there is excess overhanging. Line the base and sides of the tin, leaving 2cm paper above the rim. Set aside.

Place the milk, eggwhites, vanilla and liqueur in a medium bowl and whisk to combine. Place the flour, baking powder and sugar in the bowl of an electric mixer and beat on low speed until combined. Add the butter and beat until the mixture resembles fine breadcrumbs. Gradually add the milk mixture, increase the speed to medium and beat for 1–2 minutes or until combined. Pour into the tin and bake for 50 minutes or until cooked when tested with a skewer. Set aside to cool in the tin slightly.

To make the caramel swirl meringue, place the eggwhite in a clean bowl of the electric mixer and whisk on high speed until stiff peaks form. Add the sugar, 1 tablespoon at a time, whisking for 30 seconds before adding more. Whisk for a further 6 minutes or until thick and glossy. Scrape down the sides of the bowl and add the vinegar and cornflour. Whisk for 2 minutes or until combined. Spoon the meringue on top of the cake. Place the water and caramel in a bowl and mix to combine. Spoon the caramel onto the meringue, gently mixing to create a swirled effect.

Bake for 40 minutes or until the top of the meringue is dry to the touch. Allow to cool completely in the tin.

Use the strips of baking paper to carefully lift the cake out of the tin and onto a cake stand or plate to serve. SERVES 6
+ *It's best to measure eggwhites carefully for meringue.*

mocha swirl ice-creams

1 tablespoon good-quality instant coffee granules
1 tablespoon light brown sugar
¼ cup (60ml) maple syrup
750ml (525g) store-bought dark chocolate ice-cream,
    roughly chopped[+]
360g white chocolate, melted
¼ cup (60ml) vegetable oil
100g milk chocolate, melted

Place the coffee, sugar and maple syrup in a small saucepan over low heat. Stir to dissolve the coffee and sugar and bring to a simmer. Cook, stirring, for 2 minutes or until thickened slightly. Set aside to cool.

Place the ice-cream in the bowl of an electric mixer and beat on low speed until softened. Add the coffee syrup and gently fold in to create a swirled effect. Spoon into 8 x ⅓-cup-capacity (80ml) popsicle moulds, insert the sticks and freeze for 8 hours or overnight.

Line a large tray with non-stick baking paper. Run the moulds under hot water for 10 seconds to help remove the popsicles. Place on the tray and freeze until needed.

Place the white chocolate and 2 tablespoons of the oil in a small bowl and mix until smooth. Place the milk chocolate and remaining oil in a separate bowl and mix until smooth. Allow to cool to room temperature. Pour both the chocolate mixtures into a large bowl at the same time, without mixing them together. Working quickly, dip the popsicles in the chocolate mixture, creating a swirled effect. Serve immediately or freeze until ready to serve. MAKES 8
+ *Because all store-bought ice-creams vary, for this recipe we've given a volume and weight suggestion. Use the volume measurement to help you purchase enough ice-cream at the supermarket. At home, weigh the ice-cream before you begin and you'll end up with 8 perfectly sized popsicles.*
Tip: Keep these ice-creams in the freezer for up to 2 days.

mocha swirl ice-creams

candied almond ice-creams

candied almond ice-creams

½ cup (110g) caster (superfine) sugar
¼ cup (60ml) water
¾ cup (120g) almonds
625ml (440g) store-bought vanilla ice-cream,
    roughly chopped[+]
400g milk chocolate, melted
2 tablespoons vegetable oil

Line a baking tray with non-stick baking paper. Place the sugar and water in a medium saucepan over low heat and cook, stirring, until the sugar has dissolved. Increase the heat to high, add the almonds and cook, stirring occasionally, for 6–8 minutes or until golden. Pour onto the tray and allow to set at room temperature. Roughly chop and set aside.

Place the ice-cream in the bowl of an electric mixer and beat on low speed until softened. Add ⅓ cup (60g) of the chopped candied almonds and mix to combine. Spoon into 6 x ⅓-cup-capacity (80ml) popsicle moulds, insert the sticks and freeze for 8 hours or overnight.

Line a large tray with non-stick baking paper. Run the moulds under hot water for 10 seconds to help remove the popsicles. Place on the tray and freeze until needed.

Place the chocolate and oil in a medium bowl and mix until smooth. Allow to cool to room temperature. Working quickly, dip each popsicle in the chocolate mixture and return to the tray. Sprinkle immediately with the remaining candied almonds to serve, or freeze until ready to serve. MAKES 6
+ *Because all store-bought ice-creams vary, for this recipe we've given a volume and weight suggestion. Use the volume measurement to help you purchase enough ice-cream at the supermarket. At home, weigh the ice-cream before you begin and you'll end up with 6 perfectly sized popsicles. Tip: Keep these ice-creams in the freezer for up to 2 days.*

salted caramel crunch ice-creams

¼ cup (55g) caster (superfine) sugar
¼ cup (10g) puffed brown rice*
625ml (440g) store-bought vanilla ice-cream,
    roughly chopped[+]
⅓ cup (100g) store-bought thick caramel or dulce de leche*
200g 70% dark chocolate, melted
1 tablespoon vegetable oil
sea salt flakes, for sprinkling

Line a baking tray with non-stick baking paper. Place the sugar in a small saucepan over medium heat. Cook for 12–14 minutes or until deep golden in colour, swirling the pan occasionally. Working quickly, add the puffed rice, fold to combine and pour the mixture onto the tray. Allow to set at room temperature. Finely chop and set aside.

Place the ice-cream in the bowl of an electric mixer and beat on low speed until softened. Add the caramel and the crunchy puffed rice. Gently fold to create a swirled effect. Spoon into 6 x ⅓-cup-capacity (80ml) popsicle moulds, insert sticks and freeze for 8 hours or overnight.

Line a large tray with non-stick baking paper. Run the moulds under hot water for 10 seconds to help remove the popsicles. Place on the tray and freeze until needed.

Place the chocolate and oil in a medium bowl and mix until smooth. Allow to cool to room temperature. Working quickly, dip half of each popsicle into the chocolate mixture and return to the tray. Sprinkle immediately with salt to serve, or freeze until ready to serve. MAKES 6
+ *Because all store-bought ice-creams vary, for this recipe we've given a volume and weight suggestion. Use the volume measurement to help you purchase enough ice-cream at the supermarket. At home, weigh the ice-cream before you begin and you'll end up with 6 perfectly sized popsicles. Tip: Keep these ice-creams in the freezer for up to 2 days.*

salted caramel crunch ice-creams

tiramisu sponge cake

tiramisu sponge cake

½ cup (75g) plain (all-purpose) flour
1 teaspoon baking powder
2 tablespoons cocoa powder, plus extra for dusting
4 eggs
½ cup (110g) caster (superfine) sugar
2 teaspoons good-quality instant coffee granules
1 teaspoon boiling water
50g unsalted butter, melted and cooled
¼ cup (60ml) coffee liqueur
mascarpone cream
3 cups (750g) mascarpone
¾ cup (180ml) single (pouring) cream*
½ cup (80g) icing (confectioner's) sugar, sifted
1 teaspoon vanilla extract

Preheat oven to 180°C (350°F). Line 2 x 18cm round cake tins with non-stick baking paper. Sift the flour, baking powder and cocoa together into a medium bowl 3 times.

Place the eggs and sugar in the bowl of an electric mixer and whisk on high speed for 12–15 minutes or until pale, thick and tripled in volume. Place the coffee and water in a small bowl and mix until smooth. In 2 batches, sift the flour mixture into the egg mixture and, using a large metal spoon, gently fold to combine. Add the butter and coffee mixture and fold to combine. Divide the mixture between the tins. Bake for 15–18 minutes or until the cakes are springy to the touch and the edges have come away from the sides of the tins. Turn out onto wire racks and allow to cool completely.

To make the mascarpone cream, place the mascarpone, cream, sugar and vanilla in a clean bowl of the electric mixer and whisk until soft peaks form.

Using a large serrated knife, carefully cut the cakes in half horizontally. Brush the cut sides of each cake with the liqueur. To assemble, place 1 of the sponge halves on a cake stand or plate. Spread with 1 cup (250ml) of the mascarpone cream. Repeat the layering 3 more times with the cake and mascarpone cream. Spread the sides with the remaining mascarpone cream. Dust with extra cocoa to serve. SERVES 8

mocha meringue cake

2 teaspoons good-quality instant coffee granules
½ teaspoon boiling water
1 tablespoon cornflour (cornstarch)
1 cup (100g) hazelnut meal (ground hazelnuts)
150ml eggwhite (about 4 eggs), at room temperature
1½ cups (240g) icing (confectioner's) sugar, sifted, plus extra for dusting
mocha mousse
½ cup (125ml) single (pouring) cream*
¼ cup (15g) good-quality instant coffee granules
300g white chocolate, finely chopped
100g dark chocolate, finely chopped
4 egg yolks
2 eggwhites
1½ cups (375ml) double (thick) cream*, whipped

Preheat oven to 120°C (250°F). Line 2 baking trays with non-stick baking paper. Draw a 21cm circle on each sheet and turn the paper over, to avoid marks transferring.

Place the coffee and water in a small bowl, mix to dissolve and set aside. Place the cornflour and hazelnut meal in a small bowl, mix to combine and set aside.

Place the eggwhite in the bowl of an electric mixer and whisk on high speed until stiff peaks form. Add the sugar, 1 tablespoon at a time, whisking for 30 seconds before adding more. Scrape down the sides of the bowl and whisk for a further 2–3 minutes or until the mixture is thick and glossy. Add the cornflour mixture and coffee mixture and whisk until just combined. Divide the mixture evenly between the trays, spreading it within the circles. Bake for 1 hour or until crisp and dry to the touch. Turn the oven off. Allow to cool in the oven with the door closed for 2 hours.

To make the mousse, place the single cream and coffee in a large heatproof bowl over a saucepan of simmering water (the bowl shouldn't touch the water). Whisk to dissolve the coffee. Add the chocolates, whisking until melted. Allow to cool slightly. Add the egg yolks and whisk to combine. Place the eggwhites in a clean bowl of the electric mixer and whisk to soft peaks. Gently fold into the mousse. Add the whipped cream and fold to combine. Refrigerate for 15 minutes.

Line a 24cm round springform tin with non-stick baking paper. Place 1 meringue in the tin. Top with the mousse and the remaining meringue. Refrigerate for 3–4 hours or until set. Remove from the tin and place on a cake stand or plate. Dust with extra icing sugar to serve. SERVES 8-10

mocha meringue cake

date and walnut cake with butterscotch toffee icing

date and walnut cake with butterscotch toffee icing

10 soft fresh dates (200g), pitted and roughly chopped
½ teaspoon bicarbonate of (baking) soda
¼ cup (60ml) boiling water
¼ cup (60ml) butterscotch schnapps
6 eggs, separated
¾ cup (135g) light brown sugar
2 tablespoons finely grated orange rind
4½ cups (540g) walnut meal (ground walnuts)
butterscotch toffee icing
1 cup (220g) caster (superfine) sugar
¼ cup (60ml) water
80g unsalted butter, chopped
¼ cup (60ml) single (pouring) cream*
2 tablespoons butterscotch schnapps

Preheat oven to 160°C (325°F). Line a 24cm round springform tin with non-stick baking paper. Place the date, bicarbonate of soda, water and schnapps in a medium bowl and mash with a fork to combine. Transfer to a small food processor and process until well combined.

Place the egg yolks, ¼ cup (45g) of the sugar and the orange rind in the bowl of an electric mixer and whisk on high speed for 7 minutes or until pale and thick. Add the date mixture and walnut meal and fold to combine.

Place the eggwhites in a clean bowl of the electric mixer and whisk on high speed until stiff peaks form. Gradually add the remaining ½ cup (110g) sugar and whisk until thick. Scrape down the sides of the bowl and whisk for a further 2–3 minutes or until thick and glossy. Fold the eggwhite mixture into the date mixture in 2 batches. Pour into the tin. Bake for 1 hour 10 minutes – 1 hour 20 minutes or until just a few crumbs are attached when tested with a skewer. Allow to cool completely in the tin.

To make the butterscotch toffee icing, place the sugar and water in a small saucepan over medium heat, stirring to dissolve the sugar. Increase the heat to high and bring to the boil. Cook, without stirring, for 7–8 minutes or until the temperature reaches 160°C (325°F) on a sugar (candy) thermometer[+]. Remove from the heat, add the butter, cream and schnapps and carefully stir to combine. Return to high heat and stir until smooth. Allow to cool at room temperature.

Turn out the cake onto a cake stand or plate and spread with the icing to serve. **SERVES 8–10**
+ You can find sugar (candy) thermometers at kitchen shops.

chocolate tiramisu pie

250g store-bought plain chocolate biscuits
100g unsalted butter, melted
600g dark chocolate, chopped
½ cup (125ml) espresso coffee
1¼ cups (310ml) single (pouring) cream*
cocoa powder, for dusting
whipped mascarpone
1½ cups (375ml) single (pouring) cream*
¾ cup (180g) mascarpone

Place the biscuits and butter in a food processor and process until finely crushed. Press into the base and sides of a 25cm (1.5-litre-capacity) oval-shaped dish, using the back of a spoon. Refrigerate for 10 minutes or until firm.

Place the chocolate in the cleaned food processor and pulse until finely chopped. Place the coffee and cream in a small saucepan over high heat until almost boiling. Remove from the heat, add the chocolate and allow to stand for 5 minutes. Stir until melted and smooth. Pour into the dish over the biscuit base and refrigerate for 3–4 hours or until set.

To make the whipped mascarpone, place the cream and mascarpone in the bowl of an electric mixer and whisk until soft peaks form. Spoon into a piping bag fitted with a 1.5cm round nozzle. Pipe the mascarpone mixture onto the surface of the ganache. Dust the pie with cocoa to serve. **SERVES 10–12**

chocolate tiramisu pie

tiramisu cheesecakes

tiramisu cheesecakes

2½ teaspoons gelatine powder*
½ cup (125ml) hot espresso coffee
2 cups (500g) cream cheese, softened
1 cup (220g) caster (superfine) sugar
3 cups (750ml) single (pouring) cream*
1 cup (240g) sour cream*
2 tablespoons icing (confectioner's) sugar, sifted
½ cup (125ml) maple syrup
54 store-bought mini sponge finger biscuits
cocoa powder, for dusting

Line 6 x 7.5cm round pastry rings⁺ with non-stick baking paper, leaving 2cm paper above the rim. Line a baking tray with non-stick baking paper and place the rings on the tray.

Place the gelatine and half the coffee in a small bowl and mix to combine. Set aside for 5 minutes or until the gelatine is absorbed. Place the cream cheese and caster sugar in the bowl of an electric mixer and whisk on medium speed for 3–4 minutes or until smooth. Add the gelatine mixture and 1 cup (250ml) of the single cream and whisk for 1 minute or until thickened. Divide the mixture between the pastry rings, smooth the tops and refrigerate for 1–2 hours or until set.

Place the sour cream, icing sugar and the remaining single cream in a clean bowl of the electric mixer and whisk on high speed until soft peaks form. Place the maple syrup and the remaining coffee in a small saucepan over high heat. Bring to the boil and cook for 4–5 minutes or until thickened slightly. Allow to cool to room temperature.

Place the cheesecakes onto serving plates and remove the pastry rings and paper. Press the biscuits around the side of each cake. Spoon the cream mixture and coffee syrup over the cakes and dust with cocoa to serve. MAKES 6
+ *We used 4cm-deep pastry rings for this recipe. They're available from kitchenware shops and some supermarkets. You can also use crumpet rings.*

sticky date meringue cake

5 soft fresh dates (100g), pitted and roughly chopped
½ teaspoon bicarbonate of (baking) soda
⅓ cup (80ml) boiling water
50g unsalted butter, softened
½ teaspoon vanilla extract
½ cup (90g) light brown sugar
1 tablespoon finely grated orange rind
2 eggs, at room temperature
⅔ cup (100g) self-raising (self-rising) flour, sifted
¼ cup (30g) almond meal (ground almonds)
1½ tablespoons golden syrup
¼ cup (35g) slivered pistachios
150ml eggwhite (about 4 eggs), at room temperature, extra⁺
1 cup (220g) caster (superfine) sugar
1 teaspoon white vinegar
1 tablespoon cornflour (cornstarch)
icing (confectioner's) sugar, for dusting

Preheat oven to 160°C (325°F). Line a 24cm round springform tin with non-stick baking paper. Place the dates, bicarbonate of soda and water in a medium bowl. Set aside for 15 minutes to soak. Using a hand-held stick blender, blend until smooth.

Place the butter, vanilla, sugar and orange rind in the bowl of an electric mixer and beat on high speed for 10–12 minutes or until pale and creamy. Scrape down the sides of the bowl and add the eggs, 1 at a time, beating well after each addition. Add the flour, date mixture, almond meal, golden syrup and pistachios and beat until well combined. Spoon into the tin and bake for 30–35 minutes or until cooked when tested with a skewer. Allow to cool in the tin.

Increase the oven temperature to 180°C (350°F). Place the eggwhite in a clean bowl of the electric mixer and whisk on high speed until stiff peaks form. Add the sugar, 1 tablespoon at a time, whisking for 30 seconds before adding more. Whisk for a further 6 minutes or until stiff and glossy. Scrape down the sides of the bowl, add the vinegar and cornflour and whisk for 2 minutes to combine.

Spread the meringue over the top of the cake and bake for 15–20 minutes or until the meringue is just golden and dry to the touch. Allow the cake to stand at room temperature for 15 minutes. Gently run a knife around the inside edge of the tin and remove the ring. Allow to cool slightly. Refrigerate for 2 hours. Dust with icing sugar to serve. SERVES 8-10
+ *It's best to measure the eggwhites – egg sizes do vary.*

sticky date meringue cake

salted caramel swirl meringues

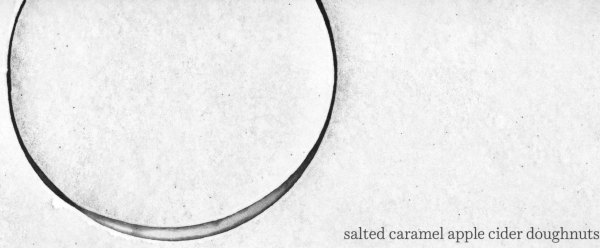

salted caramel apple cider doughnuts

½ cup (125ml) apple cider or sparkling apple juice
1 teaspoon vanilla bean paste or vanilla extract
2¼ cups (335g) plain (all-purpose) flour, plus extra for dusting
⅓ cup (75g) caster (superfine) sugar
2 teaspoons dry yeast
4 egg yolks
50g unsalted butter, softened
¼ cup (60ml) double (thick) cream*
1½ cups (450g) store-bought thick caramel or dulce de leche*
2 teaspoons smoked sea salt flakes[+]

salted caramel swirl meringues

150ml eggwhite (about 4 eggs), at room temperature[+]
1 cup (220g) caster (superfine) sugar
1 teaspoon white vinegar
2 tablespoons store-bought thick caramel or dulce de leche*
sea salt flakes, for sprinkling

Preheat oven to 150°C (300°F). Place the eggwhite in the bowl of an electric mixer and whisk on high speed until stiff peaks form. Gradually add the sugar, 1 tablespoon at a time, whisking for 30 seconds before adding more. Whisk for a further 6 minutes or until stiff and glossy. Scrape down the sides of the bowl, add the vinegar and whisk for 2 minutes.

Line 2 large baking trays with non-stick baking paper. Draw 4 x 10cm circles on each sheet and turn the paper over, to avoid marks transferring. Divide the meringue mixture between the trays, spooning it within the circles. Top each with 1 teaspoon of the caramel and swirl the mixture using a palette knife, spreading it to the edge of each circle. Sprinkle with the salt, reduce the oven temperature to 120°C (250°F) and bake for 30 minutes or until crisp to the touch. Turn the oven off and allow the meringues to cool in the oven with the door closed for 30 minutes, before serving. MAKES 8
+ Making meringue is a science – be sure to measure the eggwhites carefully, remembering egg sizes do vary.

Place the cider and vanilla in a small saucepan over medium heat and cook until just warm. Place the flour, sugar and yeast in the bowl of an electric mixer fitted with a dough hook and beat on medium speed until combined. Add the cider mixture and egg yolks and beat until just combined. Add the butter and cream and beat for 6–8 minutes or until a smooth sticky dough forms. Place the dough in a lightly greased bowl, cover with a clean damp tea towel and set aside in a warm place for 1 hour – 1 hour 30 minutes or until the dough has doubled in size.

Line a large baking tray with non-stick baking paper. Roll out the dough on a lightly floured surface to 1.5cm thick. Using an 8.5cm round cookie cutter, lightly dusted in flour, cut 6 rounds from the dough. Arrange on the tray, allowing room to spread. Using a 4cm round cookie cutter, lightly dusted in flour, cut and remove the centre of each round. Set aside at room temperature for 30 minutes or until risen.

Preheat oven to 180°C (350°F). Bake the doughnuts for 8–10 minutes or until golden brown and puffed. Allow to cool completely on the trays. Spread the doughnuts with the caramel and sprinkle with the salt to serve. MAKES 6
+ Smoked salt is cold-smoked, giving it a subtle woody flavour and colour. Find it in gourmet food stores, or substitute with regular sea salt flakes.
Note: These doughnuts are best eaten on the day they are made.

salted caramel apple cider doughnuts

QUICK

—

quick honey toffee sauce
salted chocolate caramel tarts
choc-toffee pretzel bark
caramel coffee bliss balls
quick caramel sauce
caramelised brioche with ice-cream and honeycomb
one-bite salted caramel french toasts
peanut butter and caramel fudge
chocolate tiramisu mousse
banoffee wafer sandwiches
coffee cream puffs
caramelised fig meringues
irish coffee affogatos
cheat's caramel-filled peanut cookies
iced coffee cubes
quick coffee caramel sauce

—

FIX

quick honey toffee sauce

125g unsalted butter, chopped
½ cup (110g) caster (superfine) sugar
¼ cup (90g) honey
1 teaspoon vanilla bean paste or vanilla extract
¼ cup (60ml) milk

Place the butter, sugar, honey and vanilla in a medium saucepan over medium heat and stir until the butter is melted. Cook for a further 12 minutes. Remove from the heat, add the milk and mix to combine. Allow to cool slightly before serving. MAKES 1½ CUPS

Tips: Serve this toffee sauce warm with your favourite desserts. If you're not using it right away, simply seal it in a jar and refrigerate for up to 1 week. Reheat the sauce over medium heat to serve.

salted chocolate caramel tarts

⅔ cup (200g) store-bought thick caramel or dulce de leche*
4 x 8cm round store-bought pastry cases
100g dark chocolate, melted
1 teaspoon vegetable oil
sea salt flakes, for sprinkling

Divide the caramel between the tart shells and spread until smooth. Place the chocolate and oil in a small bowl and mix to combine. Spoon the chocolate mixture over the caramel and smooth the tops. Refrigerate for 15 minutes or until just set. Sprinkle with salt to serve. MAKES 4

choc-toffee pretzel bark

1 cup (220g) raw caster (superfine) sugar
100g dark chocolate, grated
1 cup (50g) store-bought mini pretzels*
¼ cup (40g) roasted almonds, chopped

Preheat oven to 200°C (400°F). Line a large baking tray
with non-stick baking paper. Sprinkle the sugar evenly
over the tray. Bake for 15 minutes or until melted and
golden. Allow to cool for 1 minute.

Sprinkle the chocolate over the sugar and gently spread
to create a smooth thin layer. Top with the pretzels and
chopped almonds. Refrigerate for 10 minutes or until set.
Break into pieces to serve. SERVES 4–6

caramel coffee bliss balls

18 soft fresh dates (360g), pitted
1½ cups (240g) almonds
¼ cup (25g) cocoa powder
2 tablespoons tahini*
1 teaspoon vanilla extract
¼ cup (50) store-bought chocolate-coated
    coffee beans, finely chopped

Place the dates, almonds, cocoa, tahini and vanilla
in a food processor and process for 2–3 minutes or
until the mixture comes together.

Spread the chopped coffee beans on a tray. Shape
1-tablespoon portions of the date mixture into balls.
Roll each bliss ball in the coffee beans to coat, pressing
to secure. Refrigerate until firm. MAKES 20
*Tip: Keep these bliss balls refrigerated in an airtight
container for up to 2 weeks.*

quick caramel sauce

1½ cups (375ml) single (pouring) cream*
1½ cups (265g) light brown sugar
90g unsalted butter, chopped

Place the cream, sugar and butter in a medium saucepan over medium heat and stir until the butter is melted. Cook for a further 8–10 minutes or until thickened slightly. Allow to cool a little before serving. **MAKES 2 CUPS**
Tip: Serve this caramel sauce warm with your favourite desserts. If you're not using it right away, simply seal it in a jar and refrigerate for up to 1 week. Reheat the sauce over medium heat to serve.

caramelised brioche with ice-cream and honeycomb

2 tablespoons white (granulated) sugar
4 small store-bought brioche rolls
20g unsalted butter, melted
250ml store-bought vanilla ice-cream
80g store-bought chocolate-coated honeycomb, chopped

Place the sugar on a small plate. Using a serrated knife, trim and discard the top-thirds of the rolls. Brush the cut surfaces with the butter and press into the sugar.
Place a medium non-stick frying pan over medium heat. Add the brioche, sugar-side down, and cook for 1–2 minutes or until golden and caramelised.
Place the rolls onto serving plates and top each with a scoop of the ice-cream. Sprinkle with the honeycomb and serve immediately. **SERVES 4**
Tip: To make brioche ice-cream sandwiches, halve each roll, caramelise both the cut sides and fill, instead of top, with the ice-cream and honeycomb.

one-bite salted caramel french toasts

1 baguette, sliced into 16 thin rounds
½ cup (150g) store-bought thick caramel or dulce de leche*
2 eggs
⅓ cup (80ml) milk
2 tablespoons icing (confectioner's) sugar, sifted
20g unsalted butter, for frying
sea salt flakes, to serve

Spread 8 of the baguette slices with the caramel and sandwich with the remaining slices. Place the eggs, milk and sugar in a medium bowl and whisk to combine. Dip the sandwiches into the egg mixture, allowing them to soak in the liquid for 1–2 seconds.

Melt half the butter in a medium non-stick frying pan over medium heat. Add half the sandwiches and cook for 1–2 minutes each side or until golden brown. Repeat with the remaining butter and sandwiches.

Stack the warm toasts on serving plates and sprinkle with salt to serve. SERVES 4

peanut butter and caramel fudge

150g unsalted butter, chopped
⅓ cup (80ml) single (pouring) cream*
1⅓ cups (370g) smooth peanut butter
1 teaspoon vanilla extract
2½ cups (400g) icing (confectioner's) sugar, sifted
⅓ cup (100g) store-bought thick caramel or dulce de leche*
50g dark chocolate, melted

Line a 20cm square tin with non-stick baking paper. Place the butter, cream, peanut butter and vanilla in a medium saucepan over medium heat. Cook, stirring, for 2–3 minutes or until smooth and the mixture just begins to bubble.

Place the sugar in a large bowl. Add the peanut butter mixture and stir until well combined. Add the caramel and gently fold to create a swirled effect. Pour into the tin and smooth the top. Refrigerate for 1 2 hours or until set.

Remove the fudge from the tin and drizzle with the chocolate. Refrigerate for 10 minutes or until set. Cut into squares to serve. MAKES 20
Tip: Keep this fudge refrigerated in an airtight container for up to 1 week.

chocolate tiramisu mousse

2 tablespoons espresso coffee
1¼ cups (310ml) single (pouring) cream*
50g dark chocolate, finely chopped
½ cup (125g) mascarpone
¼ cup (40g) icing (confectioner's) sugar, sifted
8 mini store-bought sponge finger biscuits
50g dark chocolate, extra, melted
cocoa powder, for dusting

Place the coffee, ½ cup (125ml) of the cream and the chopped chocolate in a small saucepan over medium heat and stir until melted and smooth. Transfer to the bowl of an electric mixer. Allow to cool slightly. Add the mascarpone, the remaining cream and the sugar. Whisk on high speed until stiff peaks form. Spoon into 4 x 1-cup-capacity (250ml) serving bowls and refrigerate for 20 minutes.

Line a tray with non-stick baking paper. Dip the biscuits halfway into the chocolate, place on the tray and refrigerate for 10 minutes or until set.

Dust the mousse with the cocoa and serve with the chocolate-dipped biscuits. SERVES 4
+ *You can keep this mousse refrigerated for up to 3 days.*

banoffee wafer sandwiches

1 cup (250ml) single (pouring) cream*
⅓ cup (100g) store-bought thick caramel or dulce de leche*
8 large store-bought sweet wafer biscuits+
1 small banana, peeled and thinly sliced
cocoa powder, for dusting

Place the cream in the bowl of an electric mixer and whisk on high speed until soft peaks form. Add the caramel and gently fold to create a swirled effect.

Place 4 of the wafers onto serving plates. Top each with caramel cream and banana. Sandwich with the remaining biscuits. Dust with cocoa to serve. MAKES 4
+ *Find large round wafer biscuits at supermarkets and delicatessens.*

coffee cream puffs

1 sheet frozen butter puff pastry, thawed
1 cup (250ml) double (thick) cream*
¼ cup (60ml) single (pouring) cream*
¼ cup (60ml) espresso coffee, cooled
¼ cup (40g) icing (confectioner's) sugar
cocoa powder, for dusting

Preheat oven to 200°C (400°F). Line 2 baking trays
with non-stick baking paper. Cut 9 x 8cm squares from
the pastry and place on the trays. Bake for 12 minutes
or until puffed and golden. Set aside to cool completely.

While the pastry is cooling, place both the creams,
the coffee and sugar in a medium bowl and whisk until
soft peaks form.

Slice each pastry puff in half. Spoon the coffee cream
onto 9 of the pastries and top with the remaining puffs.
Place on serving plates and dust with cocoa to serve. MAKES 9

caramelised fig meringues

2 figs, halved lengthways
2 teaspoons light brown sugar
¾ cup (180ml) single (pouring) cream*
4 store-bought meringues
⅓ cup (100g) store-bought thick caramel or dulce de leche*

Sprinkle the cut side of the figs with the sugar. Place
a small non-stick frying pan over high heat. Add the
figs, sugar-side down, and cook for 1–2 minutes or
until golden and caramelised. Allow to cool slightly.

Place the cream in a medium bowl and whisk until
soft peaks form.

Spoon the cream onto the meringues and top with
the caramel and figs to serve. MAKES 4

irish coffee affogatos

⅓ cup (80ml) whiskey
2 tablespoons maple syrup
500ml store-bought vanilla ice cream
2 tablespoons store-bought chocolate-coated
    coffee beans, finely chopped
4 x 30ml shots hot espresso coffee, to serve

Place the whiskey and maple syrup in a small jug
and stir to combine. Divide the mixture between
4 x 1½-cup-capacity (375ml) serving glasses. Top
each glass with 2 scoops of the ice-cream. Sprinkle
with the chopped coffee beans and serve with the
coffee. MAKES 4

cheat's caramel-filled peanut cookies

16 store-bought peanut snap biscuits
100g 70% dark chocolate, melted
⅔ cup (200g) store-bought thick caramel or dulce de leche*

Line 2 trays with non-stick baking paper. Divide the
biscuits between the trays. Drizzle with the chocolate
and refrigerate for 10 minutes or until set.
    Spread the underside of 8 of the biscuits with the
caramel and sandwich with the remaining biscuits
to serve. MAKES 8

iced coffee cubes

½ cup (125ml) hot espresso coffee
2 teaspoons vanilla extract
1 tablespoon caster (superfine) sugar
1½ cups (375ml) water
3 cups (750ml) milk, to serve

Place the coffee, vanilla and sugar in a large jug and
mix well to dissolve the sugar. Add the water and mix
to combine. Pour into an ice-cube tray and freeze for
6 hours or overnight until solid.

Divide the cubes between 4 x 2-cup-capcity (500ml)
serving glasses. Top with the milk to serve. SERVES 4

quick coffee caramel sauce

1 cup (250ml) single (pouring) cream*
1 cup (175g) light brown sugar
60g unsalted butter, chopped
⅓ cup (80ml) espresso coffee

Place the cream, sugar and butter in a medium saucepan
over medium heat and stir until the butter is melted. Cook
for a further 12–15 minutes or until thickened slightly.
Remove from the heat, add the coffee and mix to combine.
Allow to cool a little before serving. MAKES 1½ CUPS
*Tip: Serve this sauce warm with your favourite desserts.
If you're not using it right away, simply seal it in a jar
and refrigerate it for up to 1 week. Reheat the sauce over
medium heat to serve.*

syrupy coffee and date upside-down cake

FRESH AND LIGHT

—

Caramel, coffee and toffee treats lend themselves particularly well to healthy change-ups. My secrets are to use naturally sweet dates for their rich and fudgy texture, and darker unrefined sugars for their caramelly warmth. With plenty of nuts and raw cacao swapped in, it's indulgence, but not as you know it.

syrupy coffee and date upside-down cake

18 soft fresh dates (360g), pitted and halved[+]
¼ cup (60ml) hot espresso coffee
⅓ cup (80ml) boiling water
¼ cup (40g) rapadura sugar*
1 teaspoon vanilla extract
1¼ cups (200g) wholemeal (whole-wheat) self-raising
　(self-rising) flour*
½ cup (60g) almond meal (ground almonds)
2 eggs
½ cup (125ml) milk
⅓ cup (80ml) grapeseed oil
1 tablespoon maple syrup
⅓ cup (55g) rapadura sugar*, extra

Preheat oven to 160°C (325°F). Line a 20cm round cake tin with non-stick baking paper. Arrange the dates, cut-side down, evenly over the base of the tin. Place the coffee, water, sugar and vanilla in a medium jug and stir to dissolve the sugar. Pour the coffee mixture over the dates.

Place the flour, almond meal, eggs, milk, oil, maple syrup and the extra sugar in a large bowl and whisk to combine. Pour the mixture over the dates. Bake for 40–45 minutes or until cooked when tested with a skewer. Allow the cake to cool in the tin for 30 minutes.

Invert the cake tin onto a cake stand or plate. Carefully remove the tin and slice to serve. SERVES 8–10
+ *A high source of soluble dietary fibre, dates are great for digestion. They're also known to be high in bone-strengthening vitamins. Fresh dates are sold loose with their seeds intact, in supermarkets and greengrocers.*

caramel cheesecake

15 soft fresh dates (300g), pitted
2 cups (480g) fresh firm ricotta
1 cup (280g) natural Greek-style (thick) yoghurt
3 eggs
¼ cup (55g) raw caster (superfine) sugar
1 teaspoon vanilla extract
1 teaspoon finely grated lemon rind
2 teaspoons cornflour (cornstarch)
2 teaspoons water
almond base
¾ cup (120g) almonds
6 soft fresh dates (120g), pitted
⅓ cup (60g) white rice flour*
2 tablespoons light-flavoured extra virgin olive oil
caramel sauce
½ cup (125ml) coconut milk
¼ cup (35g) coconut sugar*
1 teaspoon vanilla extract

Preheat oven to 150°C (300°F). Line a 20cm round springform tin with non-stick baking paper. Place the dates in a small bowl and cover with boiling water. Set aside for 10 minutes.

While the dates are soaking, make the almond base. Place the almonds, dates, flour and oil in a food processor and process for 1–2 minutes or until the mixture comes together. Using the back of a spoon, press the mixture into the base of the tin. Bake for 30 minutes or until golden.

Drain the dates and place in a food processor. Add the ricotta, yoghurt, eggs, sugar, vanilla and lemon rind. Place the cornflour and water in a small bowl, mix to combine and add to the food processor. Process for 1–2 minutes or until smooth. Pour the ricotta mixture over the almond base. Bake for 35 minutes or until just set (the centre will still have a slight wobble). Allow the cake to cool in the tin for 2 hours before refrigerating until chilled.

While the cheesecake is cooling, make the caramel sauce. Place the coconut milk, sugar and vanilla in a small saucepan over high heat and bring to the boil. Reduce the heat to medium and cook for 5 minutes. Allow to cool completely.

Remove the cheesecake from the tin and place on a cake stand or plate. Top with the caramel sauce to serve. SERVES 8–10

caramel cheesecake

banoffee cheesecake

banoffee cheesecake

1 cup (160g) almonds
6 soft fresh dates (120g), pitted
1 tablespoon raw cacao or cocoa powder*
⅓ cup (60g) white rice flour*
2 tablespoons light-flavoured extra virgin olive oil
2 teaspoons vanilla extract
2 bananas, peeled and halved lengthways
natural Greek-style (thick) yoghurt, to serve
chocolate cheesecake filling
2 cups (480g) fresh firm ricotta
1 cup (280g) natural Greek-style (thick) yoghurt
3 eggs
⅔ cup (90g) coconut sugar+
⅓ cup (35g) raw cacao or cocoa powder*, plus extra to serve
2 teaspoons cornflour (cornstarch)
2 teaspoons water
coconut caramel sauce
½ cup (70g) coconut sugar+
2 tablespoons coconut milk
1 teaspoon vanilla extract

Preheat oven to 150°C (300°F). Line a 20cm round springform tin with non-stick baking paper. Place the almonds, dates, cacao, flour, oil and vanilla in a food processor and process for 1–2 minutes or until the mixture comes together. Using the back of a spoon, press the mixture into the base and sides of the tin. Bake for 20 minutes or until dry to the touch.

To make the cheesecake filling, place the ricotta, yoghurt, eggs, sugar and cacao in the cleaned food processor. Place the cornflour and water in a small bowl, mix to combine and add to the processor. Process for 1–2 minutes or until smooth.

Pour the filling over the base and bake for 35 minutes or until just set (the centre will still have a slight wobble). Allow to cool in the tin for 2 hours. Refrigerate until chilled.

While the cheesecake is cooling, make the coconut caramel sauce. Place the sugar, coconut milk and vanilla in a small saucepan over high heat and bring to the boil. Reduce the heat to medium and cook for 2 minutes. Allow to cool completely.

Remove the cheesecake from the tin and place on a cake stand or plate. Top with the banana, coconut caramel sauce, yoghurt and extra cacao to serve. **SERVES 8-10**
+ *From the flowers of the coconut palm, coconut sugar is available to buy in the health food aisle of supermarkets and specialty grocers.*

peanut butter fudge

1 cup (280g) smooth natural peanut butter+
⅔ cup (160ml) melted coconut oil*
½ cup (180g) honey
2 teaspoons vanilla extract

Line a 10cm x 20cm loaf tin with non-stick baking paper. Place the peanut butter, oil, honey and vanilla in a medium saucepan over low heat and cook, stirring, for 3–4 minutes or until melted. Pour the mixture into the tin and refrigerate for 4 hours or until set.

Remove the fudge from the tin and slice into pieces. Refrigerate until ready to serve. **MAKES 10**
+ *Regular peanut butter can contain extra sodium, oils and sugar, so it's a good idea to use a natural variety where possible. Find it in the health food section of supermarkets or have it made fresh at health food stores. Tip: Keep this fudge refrigerated in an airtight container for up to 2 weeks.*

peanut butter fudge

raw caramel peanut crunch bars

raw caramel peanut crunch bars

20 soft fresh dates (400g), pitted
⅓ cup (95g) smooth natural peanut butter*
2 teaspoons vanilla extract
1 cup (30g) puffed brown rice*
½ cup (70g) unsalted peanuts, roughly chopped
80g raw organic 70% dark chocolate+

Line a 10cm x 20cm loaf tin with non-stick baking paper. Place the dates, peanut butter and vanilla in a food processor and process for 2–4 minutes or until the mixture comes together into a paste. Transfer to a large bowl, add the puffed rice and peanuts and mix to combine. Using the back of a spoon, press the mixture into the base of the tin++.

Place the chocolate in a heatproof bowl over a saucepan of simmering water (the bowl shouldn't touch the water) and stir until melted. Pour the chocolate over the slice and spread evenly. Refrigerate for 20–30 minutes or until set.

Remove the slice from the tin and cut into bars using a hot knife. Refrigerate until ready to serve. **MAKES 20**
+ *Raw organic chocolate is available at health food stores and specialty grocers. If you can't find it, simply use 70% dark chocolate. To keep the chocolate raw while melting, use a sugar (candy) thermometer to ensure it stays under 42°C (107°F).*
++ *If the mixture is sticky, grease the spoon in a little melted coconut oil to help you spread and smooth it.*
Tip: Keep bars refrigerated in an airtight container for up to 2 weeks.

ginger and date tiramisu

12 store-bought ginger nut (ginger snap) biscuits, crushed
1 cup (280g) natural Greek-style (thick) yoghurt
coffee syrup
1 cup (250ml) espresso coffee
½ cup (125ml) maple syrup+
date caramel
12 soft fresh dates (240g), pitted
¾ cup (180ml) maple syrup+
2 tablespoons water

To make the coffee syrup, place the coffee and maple syrup in a small saucepan over high heat and bring to the boil. Reduce the heat to medium and cook for 10–12 minutes or until thickened slightly. Allow to cool a little before refrigerating until chilled.

To make the date caramel, place the dates and maple syrup in a food processor and process for 2–3 minutes or until smooth. Add the water and pulse to combine.

Divide three-quarters of the crushed biscuits between 6 x 1-cup-capacity (250ml) serving glasses. Spoon three-quarters of the yoghurt between the glasses. Top with the coffee syrup and date caramel. Finish with the remaining yoghurt and crushed biscuits to serve. **MAKES 6**
+ *Naturally derived from the sap of the maple tree, pure maple syrup (not to be confused with maple-flavoured syrup) is a lovely, rich way to sweeten, plus it retains a few more antioxidants and minerals than other refined sugars.*

ginger and date tiramisu

raw caramel slice

raw caramel slice

⅓ cup (35g) raw cacao or cocoa powder*
¼ cup (60ml) melted coconut oil*
½ cup (180g) rice malt syrup*
lmond base
¾ cup (120g) almonds
⅓ cup (25g) desiccated coconut
5 soft fresh dates (120g), pitted
¼ cup (60ml) melted coconut oil*
date caramel
12 soft fresh dates (240g), pitted
⅓ cup (105g) natural almond butter*
2 tablespoons maple syrup
2 teaspoons vanilla bean paste or vanilla extract
¼ teaspoon sea salt flakes

To make the almond base, line a 20cm square slice tin with non-stick baking paper. Place the almonds, coconut, dates and oil in a food processor. Process for 1–2 minutes or until the mixture resembles fine breadcrumbs. Using the back of a spoon, press the mixture into the base of the tin and refrigerate for 30 minutes or until set.

To make the date caramel, place the dates, almond butter, maple syrup, vanilla and salt in the cleaned food processor and process for 1–2 minutes or until smooth. Spread over the base and refrigerate until needed.

Place the cacao, oil and rice malt syrup in a medium heatproof bowl over a saucepan of simmering water (the bowl shouldn't touch the water) and stir for 2–3 minutes or until smooth. Pour the cacao mixture over the caramel and refrigerate for 2 hours. Freeze for 30 minutes or until set.

Remove from the tin and cut into bars to serve. **MAKES 10**
Note: This caramel slice needs to be served chilled. If you prefer a harder set, keep it in the freezer until ready to serve.

raw chia caramel pecan pies

1¾ cups (210g) pecans
1 teaspoon raw cacao or cocoa powder*
40g unsalted butter, melted
¼ cup (20g) psyllium husks*
½ cup (60g) pecans, extra, chopped
maple syrup, to serve
chia caramel
1 tablespoon white chia seeds*
½ cup (125ml) water
¼ cup (35g) raisins
6 soft fresh dates (120g), pitted
1 teaspoon vanilla bean paste or vanilla extract
¼ teaspoon mixed spice
½ cup (60g) pecans

Line each of 6 x ¾-cup-capacity (180ml) Texas muffin tins with 2 strips of non-stick baking paper. Place the pecans, cacao, butter and psyllium in a food processor and process until finely chopped. Divide the mixture between the tins and, using the back of a spoon, press firmly into the bases and sides. Refrigerate for 20 minutes or until set.

To make the chia caramel, place the chia and water in a small bowl and allow to soak for 10 minutes. Transfer the chia mixture to the cleaned food processor and add the raisins, dates, vanilla and mixed spice. Process for 5 minutes or until smooth. Add the pecans and process for 1 minute.

Spoon the caramel into each case and smooth the tops. Sprinkle with the extra chopped pecans and refrigerate for 30 minutes or until set.

Remove the pies from the tins and drizzle with the maple syrup to serve. **MAKES 6**
+ Available from the health food aisle of supermarkets, psyllium husks are rich in fibre. They're often used in gluten-free baking recipes as a binding ingredient.

raw chia caramel pecan pies

chocolate and peanut butter date fudge

chocolate and peanut butter date fudge

16 soft fresh dates (320g), pitted
⅓ cup (95g) smooth natural peanut butter*
2 teaspoons vanilla bean paste or vanilla extract
80g 70% dark chocolate
1 teaspoon sea salt flakes (optional), to serve+

Line a 10cm x 20cm loaf tin with non-stick baking paper.
Place the dates, peanut butter and vanilla in a food
processor and process for 2–3 minutes or until smooth and
the mixture comes together. Using the back of a spoon,
press the mixture into the tin and smooth the surface++.

Place the chocolate in a heatproof bowl over a saucepan
of simmering water (the bowl shouldn't touch the water)
and stir until melted. Pour the chocolate over the fudge
and smooth the top. Sprinkle with the salt and freeze for
30 minutes or until firm.

Remove the fudge from the tin and use a hot knife to cut
it into pieces to serve. MAKES 32
+ *We used regular and black sea salt flakes, available at
most supermarkets and grocers. You can use either or both.*
++ *If the mixture is sticky, grease the spoon in a little
melted coconut oil to help you spread and smooth it.*
*Tip: Keep this fudge refrigerated in an airtight container
for up to 2 weeks.*

cacao caramel bites

30 soft fresh dates (600g), pitted
¼ cup (80g) natural hazelnut butter+
2 teaspoons vanilla bean paste or vanilla extract
2 tablespoons melted coconut oil*
¼ cup (25g) raw cacao or cocoa powder*
100g 70% dark chocolate
¼ cup (45g) raw cacao nibs*

Line a 10cm x 20cm loaf tin with non-stick baking paper.
Place the dates, hazelnut butter, vanilla, oil and cacao in a
food processor and process for 3–4 minutes or until smooth.
Using the back of a spoon, press the mixture into the tin
and smooth the surface++. Freeze for 4 hours or until firm.

Line a tray with non-stick baking paper. Place the
chocolate in a heatproof bowl over a saucepan of simmering
water (the bowl shouldn't touch the water) and stir until
melted and smooth.

Remove the slice from the tin and cut into 14 bars. Using
a fork, dip each bar into the chocolate, allowing any excess
to drip off. Place on the tray and sprinkle with the cacao
nibs. Refrigerate for 30 minutes or until set. MAKES 14
+ *Find hazelnut butter, or spread, in the health food aisle
of the supermarket. You could use almond or macadamia
butter here, too, just stick to natural nut spreads to skip
out on unwanted oils, sodium and sugar.*
++ *If the mixture is sticky, grease the spoon in a little
melted coconut oil to help you spread and smooth it.*
*Tip: Keep these bites refrigerated in an airtight container
for up to 3 weeks (for a firmer caramel) or at room
temperature for up to 1 week (for a softer caramel).*

cacao caramel bites

CHAPTER

———

sugar and spice

———

THREE

A pinch of cinnamon here and a dusting of fine sugar there – it's often the little details that make baking so enchanting. Think of adding warming nutmeg or a sprinkle of ground ginger, even chai tea to treats. Among these dreamy ideas you will also find plenty of my most favourite spice that makes all things nice – vanilla.

vanilla almond cake
with tarragon and mint

vanilla almond cake with tarragon and mint

6 eggs
1½ cups (330g) caster (superfine) sugar
1 tablespoon vanilla extract
225g unsalted butter, melted
1½ cups (225g) self-raising (self-rising) flour, sifted
1½ cups (180g) almond meal (ground almonds)
2 teaspoons finely chopped tarragon leaves
¾ cup (180ml) single (pouring) cream*
¼ cup (60g) sour cream*
2 tablespoons icing (confectioner's) sugar, sifted,
    plus extra for dusting
⅓ cup mint leaves, to serve

Preheat oven to 160°C (325°F). Line a deep 20cm round cake tin with non-stick baking paper. Place the eggs, caster sugar, vanilla, butter, flour, almond meal and tarragon in a large bowl and whisk until smooth. Pour the mixture into the tin and bake for 1 hour – 1 hour 10 minutes or until cooked when tested with a skewer. Allow to cool in the tin for 10 minutes before turning out onto a wire rack to cool completely.

Place the single cream, sour cream and icing sugar in the bowl of an electric mixer and whisk on high speed until soft peaks form.

Using a large serrated knife, evenly trim and discard the top of the cake. Cut the cake in half horizontally. Place the top-half of the cake on a cake stand or plate and spread with the cream mixture. Top with the remaining cake[+]. Arrange the mint leaves on the cake and dust with extra icing sugar to serve. SERVES 8–10
+ *For best presentation, use the base of the cake as the top. This will ensure the surface is smooth, even and golden.*

lavender and honey madeleines

½ cup (75g) plain (all-purpose) flour, sifted
½ teaspoon baking powder, sifted
⅓ cup (75g) caster (superfine) sugar
1 teaspoon edible dried lavender[+]
2 eggs
80g unsalted butter, melted
1 tablespoon honey
1 teaspoon vanilla bean paste or vanilla extract
lavender sugar
½ cup (110g) white (granulated) sugar
2 teaspoons edible dried lavender[+]

Preheat oven to 180°C (350°F). To make the lavender sugar, place the sugar and lavender in a medium bowl and rub with your fingertips to combine. Set aside.

Lightly grease 12 x 1½-tablespoon-capacity madeleine tins[++]. Place the flour, baking powder, sugar, lavender, eggs, butter, honey and vanilla in a large bowl and whisk until smooth. Spoon the mixture into the tins and bake for 8–10 minutes or until puffed and golden.

Remove the madeleines from the tins and, while still warm, add them to the lavender sugar and gently toss to coat. Place onto wire racks to cool before serving. MAKES 12
+ *Edible dried lavender (pesticide-free) is available at health food stores, specialty grocers and tea shops.*
++ *You can find madeleine tins at kitchen supply stores and online.*

lavender and honey madeleines

crème fraîche-glazed cinnamon scrolls

crème fraîche-glazed cinnamon scrolls

1¼ teaspoons dry yeast
⅓ cup (80ml) lukewarm milk
¼ cup (55g) caster (superfine) sugar
3¼ cups (485g) plain (all-purpose) flour, plus extra for dusting
¼ teaspoon table salt
⅓ cup (80g) crème fraîche*
2 eggs
125g unsalted butter, melted
½ cup (90g) light brown sugar
2 teaspoons ground cinnamon, plus extra for dusting
50g unsalted butter, melted, extra
crème fraîche glaze
1 cup (160g) icing (confectioner's) sugar, sifted
¼ cup (60g) crème fraîche*
2 teaspoons milk

Place the yeast, milk and 2 teaspoons of the caster sugar in a small bowl and mix to combine. Set aside in a warm place for 5 minutes or until foamy. Place the flour, salt, crème fraîche, eggs, butter, the remaining 2½ tablespoons of caster sugar and the yeast mixture in the bowl of an electric mixer with a dough hook attached. Beat on low speed for 5 minutes or until the dough is smooth and elastic. Place in a lightly greased bowl, cover with plastic wrap and set aside in a warm place for 1 hour or until the dough has doubled in size.

Place the brown sugar and cinnamon in a small bowl. Mix to combine and set aside. Lightly grease 2 x 14cm round heavy-based ovenproof frying pans (skillets).

Cut the dough in half. Roll out 1 half on a lightly floured surface to make a 20cm x 30cm rectangle. Brush with half the extra butter and sprinkle with half the cinnamon sugar. Cut into 5 x 4cm x 30cm strips. Roll up 1 strip tightly into a round. Place on top of the next strip and roll up again. Repeat until you have 1 large scroll. Place the scroll into a pan. Repeat with the remaining dough, butter, cinnamon sugar and pan. Cover both pans with plastic wrap. Set aside in a warm place for 25–30 minutes or until doubled in size.

Preheat oven to 180°C (350°F). Place pans on an oven tray. Bake for 23–25 minutes or until golden and cooked through.

To make the crème fraîche glaze, place the sugar, crème fraîche and milk in a small bowl and mix for 1–2 minutes or until well combined and slightly thickened.

While the scrolls are still warm, drizzle with the crème fraîche glaze and allow to set. Dust with extra cinnamon to serve. **SERVES 8**

soft vanilla sponge cake

12 eggwhites, at room temperature
1 teaspoon cream of tartar
¾ cup (165g) caster (superfine) sugar
2 teaspoons vanilla extract
1 cup (150g) plain (all-purpose) flour
½ cup (110g) caster (superfine) sugar, extra
icing (confectioner's) sugar, for dusting

Preheat oven to 180°C (350°F). Place the eggwhites and cream of tartar in the bowl of an electric mixer and whisk on high speed until soft peaks form. Gradually add the caster sugar and vanilla and whisk until thick and glossy.

Sift the flour and extra caster sugar into a medium bowl. Sift for a second time over the eggwhite mixture and gently fold to combine.

Spoon the mixture into an ungreased 2.5-litre-capacity Bundt tin and smooth the top. Bake for 35 minutes or until the cake comes away from the sides of the tin. Invert the tin and set aside for 1 hour or until cooled completely.

Using a butter knife, loosen the edges of the cake from the tin and turn out onto a cake stand or serving plate. Dust with icing sugar to serve. **SERVES 10**

soft vanilla sponge cake

spiced vanilla biscuits

spiced vanilla biscuits

125g unsalted butter, softened
¾ cup (135g) light brown sugar
1 egg
¼ cup (90g) honey
1 teaspoon vanilla bean paste or vanilla extract
2¼ cups (335g) plain (all-purpose) flour, sifted
¼ teaspoon bicarbonate of (baking) soda, sifted
½ teaspoon ground cinnamon
¼ teaspoon ground allspice
1½ teaspoons ground ginger
2 vanilla beans, sliced lengthways into quarters
2 cups (320g) icing (confectioner's) sugar mixture, sifted
2 tablespoons boiling water

Preheat oven to 160°C (325°F). Place the butter and sugar in the bowl of an electric mixer and beat on high speed for 6–8 minutes or until light and fluffy. Add the egg, honey and vanilla bean paste and beat until smooth. Add the flour, bicarbonate of soda, cinnamon, allspice and ginger and beat until just combined. Refrigerate for 30 minutes.

Line 2 large baking trays with non-stick baking paper. Roll 1-tablespoon portions of the dough into balls. Place on the trays, allowing room to spread. Bake for 16 minutes or until golden. Allow to cool completely on the trays.

Line a small baking tray with non-stick baking paper. Place the vanilla beans on the tray and bake for 15 minutes or until dry and crisp. Allow to cool. Place in a small food processor and process until fine.

Place the icing sugar mixture and water in a bowl and mix until smooth. Dip the biscuits in the icing, place on a wire rack set above a tray and immediately sprinkle with the ground vanilla. Allow to set before serving. MAKES 26
Tip: Keep biscuits in an airtight container for up to 1 week.

almond and date scones with whipped butter

3½ cups (525g) self-raising (self-rising) flour, plus extra for dusting
1 cup (120g) almond meal (ground almonds)
1 teaspoon baking powder
¾ cup (165g) caster (superfine) sugar
10 soft fresh dates (200g), pitted and roughly chopped
75g unsalted butter, melted
1¼ cups (310ml) unsweetened almond milk*, plus extra for brushing
½ cup (80g) almonds, chopped
100g unsalted butter, extra, softened

Preheat oven to 180°C (350°F). Line a 20cm x 30cm slice tin with non-stick baking paper. Place the flour, almond meal, baking powder, sugar and date in a large bowl and mix to combine. Add the melted butter and, using a butter knife, gently mix to combine. Make a well in the centre. Add the almond milk. Lightly mix until just combined. Turn out the dough onto a well-floured surface and gently bring together using floured hands. Flatten into a rough 1.5cm-thick round and, using a 5.5cm cookie cutter, cut 15 rounds from the dough, re-rolling as necessary.

Arrange the scones to fit snugly in the tin and brush with extra almond milk. Sprinkle with the chopped almonds and bake for 25–30 minutes or until golden.

While the scones are baking, place the extra butter in the bowl of an electric mixer and whisk on medium speed for 1–2 minutes or until pale and creamy.

Halve the warm scones and spread with the whipped butter to serve. MAKES 15
Tips: Dip the cookie cutter in a little flour to release the scones more easily into the tray. For even edges, push the cutter straight down when cutting the scones and try to avoid twisting as you remove it.

almond and date scones
with whipped butter

almond syrup cake

almond syrup cake

3 eggs
¾ cup (165g) caster (superfine) sugar
1 teaspoon vanilla extract
1 cup (150g) self-raising (self-rising) flour, sifted
1 cup (120g) almond meal (ground almonds), sifted
75g unsalted butter, melted
1 tablespoon finely grated lemon rind
2 tablespoons amaretto or almond liqueur
½ cup (40g) flaked almonds
amaretto syrup
1 cup (250ml) water
1 cup (220g) caster (superfine) sugar
1 vanilla bean, split and seeds scraped
¼ cup (60ml) amaretto or almond liqueur

Preheat oven to 160°C (325°F). Line a 24cm round springform tin with non-stick baking paper. Place the eggs, sugar and vanilla extract in the bowl of an electric mixer and whisk for 12–15 minutes or until pale and tripled in volume. Add the flour, almond meal, butter, lemon rind and liqueur and gently fold to combine. Pour the mixture into the tin and spread evenly. Sprinkle with the flaked almonds and bake for 30–35 minutes or until cooked when tested with a skewer. Allow to cool completely in the tin.

While the cake is cooling, make the amaretto syrup. Place the water, sugar, vanilla bean and seeds and liqueur in a small saucepan over medium heat and stir to combine. Bring to the boil and cook for 10–12 minutes or until reduced. Allow the syrup to cool slightly and discard the vanilla pod.

Remove the cake from the tin and place on a cake stand or plate. Drizzle with the amaretto syrup to serve. **SERVES 6-8**

spiced layered apple cake

1½ cups (330g) white (granulated) sugar
2 tablespoons finely grated lemon rind
1 teaspoon ground cinnamon
2 vanilla beans, split and seeds scraped
2kg Granny Smith (green) apples (about 12 apples)
2 tablespoons lemon juice

Preheat oven to 180°C (350°F). Line a 20cm round springform tin with non-stick baking paper, placing an extra layer of paper on the base. Line a baking tray with non-stick baking paper and place the tin on the tray[+].

Place the sugar, lemon rind, cinnamon and vanilla seeds in a medium bowl and use your fingertips to combine.

Peel the apples and rub all over with the lemon juice[++]. Using a mandolin slicer, finely slice the apples to 2mm thick.

Line the base of the tin with 1 layer of apple slices, placing each slice over half the previous slice. Sprinkle evenly with 2 tablespoons of the sugar mixture. Repeat the layering with the remaining apple and sugar mixture. Bake for 50 minutes. Press down gently on the cake, using the back of a large spoon, and cover tightly with aluminium foil. Bake for a further 35–45 minutes or until the apple is very soft and the top layer is caramelised. Allow to cool slightly in the tin.

Place a sheet of non-stick baking paper over the tin and place a slightly smaller plate or cake tin on top of the cake. Weigh down with cans of beans or tomatoes and refrigerate for 2–3 hours or until cool and firm.

Run a small knife around the edge of the cake. Carefully remove from the tin and place on a cake stand or plate. Serve chilled with double (thick) cream, if you like. **SERVES 8**
+ *The apple will release quite a lot of juice as it's baking, so it's a good idea to double-line the tin and place it on a lined tray, to catch any spills.*
++ *The lemon juice helps prevent the apples from browning.*

spiced layered apple cake

almond pancakes with spiced almond butter and maple syrup

almond pancakes with spiced almond butter and maple syrup

1½ cups (225g) self-raising (self-rising) flour
1 cup (120g) almond meal (ground almonds)
½ teaspoon bicarbonate of (baking) soda
½ cup (110g) raw caster (superfine) sugar
4 eggs, separated
1½ cups (375ml) unsweetened almond milk*
vegetable oil, for brushing
maple syrup, to serve
spiced almond butter
2 cups (320g) roasted almonds
¼ teaspoon sea salt flakes
2 tablespoons vegetable oil
2 teaspoons mixed spice
2 teaspoons vanilla bean paste or vanilla extract

To make the spiced almond butter, place the almonds and salt in a small food processor and process for 1–2 minutes or until coarsely ground. Add the oil, mixed spice and vanilla and process for 3–4 minutes or until well combined. Transfer to a small bowl and refrigerate for 1 hour.

Place the flour, almond meal, bicarbonate of soda and sugar in a large bowl and whisk to combine. Make a well in the centre, add the egg yolks and almond milk and whisk to combine. Place the eggwhites in the bowl of an electric mixer and whisk until soft peaks form. In 2 batches, add the eggwhite to the flour mixture and gently fold to combine.

Heat a large non-stick frying pan over medium heat. Reduce the heat to low and brush the pan with oil. Add ¼-cup (60ml) portions of the batter to the pan in batches, re-greasing as necessary, and cook for 2–3 minutes each side or until puffed and golden. Remove from the pan and keep warm.

Divide the pancakes between serving plates and top with the spiced almond butter and maple syrup to serve. SERVES 4

carrot cake with cream cheese icing

5 eggs, at room temperature
1½ cups (265g) light brown sugar
1 teaspoon vanilla extract
½ cup (125ml) vegetable oil
3½ cups (420g) almond meal (ground almonds)
1 teaspoon ground cinnamon
1 teaspoon ground ginger
¼ teaspoon ground nutmeg
1 teaspoon baking powder
2⅔ cups (320g) grated carrot (about 3 carrots)
1 cup (75g) shredded coconut
½ cup (70g) slivered almonds, toasted
½ cup (80g) dried currants
cream cheese icing
250g cream cheese, chopped
⅓ cup (55g) icing (confectioner's) sugar mixture, sifted
1 tablespoon lemon juice

Preheat oven to 160°C (325°F). Line a 24cm round springform tin with non-stick baking paper and set aside.

Place the eggs, sugar and vanilla in the bowl of an electric mixer and whisk for 15 minutes or until thick and tripled in volume. Place the oil, almond meal, cinnamon, ginger, nutmeg, baking powder, carrot, coconut, almonds and currants in a large bowl and mix to combine. Add the egg mixture and fold to combine. Bake for 1 hour 20 minutes – 1 hour 25 minutes or until just a few crumbs are attached when tested with a skewer. Allow to cool completely in the tin. Refrigerate for 2–3 hours or until firm.

To make the cream cheese icing, place the cream cheese and icing sugar in the bowl of an electric mixer and beat for 5 minutes. Scrape down the sides of the bowl, add the lemon juice and beat for a further 1 minute or until smooth.

Run a small knife around the edge of the cake and remove the tin. Place on a cake stand or plate and spread with the icing to serve. SERVES 8–10

carrot cake with cream cheese icing

angel food cake with white chocolate ganache

angel food cake with white chocolate ganache

12 eggwhites, at room temperature
1 teaspoon cream of tartar
¾ cup (165g) caster (superfine) sugar
1 teaspoon vanilla extract
1 cup (150g) plain (all-purpose) flour
½ cup (110g) caster (superfine) sugar, extra
1¼ cups (300ml) single (pouring) cream*, whipped
white chocolate ganache
2⅓ cups (600ml) single (pouring) cream*
375g white chocolate buttons

Preheat oven to 180°C (350°F). Place the eggwhites and cream of tartar in the bowl of an electric mixer and whisk on high speed until soft peaks form. Gradually add the sugar and vanilla and whisk until thick and glossy.

Sift the flour and extra sugar into a medium bowl. Sift for a second time, then sift for a third time over the eggwhite mixture. Gently fold to combine. Spoon the mixture into an ungreased 21cm round angel food cake tin and smooth the top with a palette knife. Bake for 30 minutes or until the cake comes away from the sides of the tin. Invert the tin and set aside for 1 hour or until cooled completely.

To make the white chocolate ganache, place half the cream in a medium saucepan over high heat and bring to the boil. Add the chocolate and stir until melted and smooth. Refrigerate until cold. Place the remaining cream in a clean bowl of the electric mixer and whisk on high speed until stiff peaks form. Add the cooled ganache and whisk until just thickened.

Using a butter knife, loosen the edge of the cake from the tin and twist the centre funnel to remove it. Using a large serrated knife, slice the cake horizontally into 4 layers. Place 1 layer on a cake stand or plate and top with 1¼ cups (310ml) of the ganache. Repeat with the remaining cake layers and ganache. Using a palette knife, spread the top and sides of the cake with the whipped cream to serve. SERVES 12-16

almond doughnut cookies

1 cup (120g) almond meal (ground almonds)
1⅔ cups (270g) icing (confectioner's) sugar, sifted
¾ cup (100g) plain (all-purpose) flour, sifted
½ teaspoon baking powder, sifted
5 eggwhites
½ cup (125ml) vegetable oil
icing (confectioner's) sugar, extra, for dusting

Preheat oven to 120°C (250°F). Grease 10 x ½-cup-capacity (125ml) mini Bundt tins. Place the almond meal, sugar, flour, baking powder, eggwhites and oil in a large bowl and whisk to combine. Spoon 2-tablespoon portions of the mixture into each tin. Bake for 30 minutes or until cooked when tested with a skewer. Using a butter knife, loosen the edges of the cookies and turn out immediately onto a wire rack to cool.

Dust with extra icing sugar to serve. MAKES 10

almond doughnut cookies

baked ricotta and cinnamon cheesecakes

baked ricotta and cinnamon cheesecakes

1½ cups (360g) fresh firm ricotta
125g cream cheese, softened
¼ cup (55g) caster (superfine) sugar
1 teaspoon vanilla extract
1 egg
2 teaspoons cornflour (cornstarch)
¼ teaspoon ground cinnamon
icing (confectioner's) sugar, for dusting
freshly grated nutmeg, for dusting
pastry
150g unsalted butter, softened
¾ cup (165g) caster (superfine) sugar
1 egg
1 egg yolk, extra
⅓ cup (80ml) single (pouring) cream*
1 teaspoon vanilla extract
3 cups (450g) plain (all-purpose) flour, sifted
1½ teaspoons baking powder, sifted

Preheat oven to 160°C (325°F). To make the pastry, place the butter and sugar in the bowl of an electric mixer and beat for 5–6 minutes or until pale and creamy. Add the egg and extra yolk and beat until well combined. Add the cream, vanilla, flour and baking powder. Beat until just combined. Turn out onto a lightly floured surface and gently knead to form a smooth dough. Roll out the dough between 2 sheets of non-stick baking paper to 4mm thick. Place on a large baking tray and refrigerate for 10 minutes or until firm.

Using a plate as a guide, cut out 6 x 14cm rounds from the pastry. Use them to line 6 x 8cm fluted loose-based tart tins, trimming any excess pastry. Prick the bases with a fork, return to the tray and refrigerate for 5–10 minutes. Re-roll the excess pastry to 4mm thick and refrigerate for 10 minutes or until firm. Cut out 6 x 10cm rounds from the pastry and refrigerate until needed. Bake the pastry cases for 8–10 minutes or until light golden brown.

Place the ricotta, cream cheese, sugar and vanilla in the bowl of an electric mixer. Beat on high speed for 2 minutes or until smooth. Add the egg, cornflour and cinnamon and beat until well combined. Divide the mixture between the cases and top each with a pastry round. Press the edges well to seal, trimming any excess pastry. Bake for 15–20 minutes or until golden brown. Allow to cool completely in the tins.

Remove the cheesecakes from the tins and dust with icing sugar and nutmeg to serve. MAKES 6

earl grey doughnuts with brown butter glaze

½ cup (125ml) sparkling clear lemonade
1 teaspoon earl grey tea leaves
1 teaspoon vanilla bean paste or vanilla extract
2¼ cups (335g) plain (all-purpose) flour, plus extra for dusting
⅓ cup (75g) caster (superfine) sugar
2 teaspoons dry yeast
4 egg yolks
50g unsalted butter, softened
¼ cup (60ml) double (thick) cream*
2 tablespoons coffee sugar or Demerara sugar+
brown butter glaze
40g unsalted butter, chopped
2 cups (320g) icing (confectioner's) sugar, sifted
¼ cup (60ml) boiling water

Place the lemonade, tea and vanilla in a small saucepan over medium heat until just warm. Place the flour, caster sugar and yeast in the bowl of an electric mixer fitted with a dough hook and beat on medium speed until combined. Add the warm lemonade mixture and egg yolks and beat until just combined. Add the butter and cream and beat on medium speed for 6–8 minutes or until a smooth dough forms. Place the dough in a lightly greased bowl, cover with a clean damp tea towel and set aside in a warm place for 1 hour – 1 hour 30 minutes or until doubled in size.

Line a baking tray with non-stick baking paper. Roll out the dough on a lightly floured surface to 1.5cm thick. Using an 8.5cm round cookie cutter, lightly dusted in flour, cut 6 rounds from the dough. Place on the tray, allowing room to spread. Using a 4cm round cutter, lightly dusted in flour, cut and remove the centre of each round. Set aside at room temperature for 30 minutes or until risen.

Preheat oven to 180°C (350°F). Bake the doughnuts for 8–10 minutes or until golden brown and puffed.

While the doughnuts are baking, make the brown butter glaze. Place the butter in a small non-stick frying pan over medium heat and stir until melted. Cook for 3 minutes or until golden brown with a nutty fragrance. Transfer to a medium bowl, add the sugar and water and mix to combine.

While the doughnuts are still warm, dip the top half of each doughnut into the glaze and place on a wire rack. Sprinkle with the coffee sugar and allow to stand for 10 minutes or until set, before serving. MAKES 6
+ *Coffee sugar has large granules, making it a lovely crunchy topping for desserts. Find it in most supermarkets.*

earl grey doughnuts with brown butter glaze

buttermilk and ricotta pikelets

buttermilk and ricotta pikelets

2½ cups (375g) plain (all-purpose) flour
2 teaspoons bicarbonate of (baking) soda
1 cup (220g) caster (superfine) sugar
3 eggs
1¾ cups (430ml) buttermilk
1 tablespoon malt vinegar
¾ cup (180g) fresh firm ricotta
20g unsalted butter, melted
fresh honeycomb, to serve[+]

Place the flour, bicarbonate of soda, sugar and eggs in a large bowl and whisk to combine. Place the buttermilk and vinegar in a small bowl and mix to combine. Add the milk mixture to the flour mixture and whisk to combine. Add the ricotta and fold to combine.

Heat a large non-stick frying pan over medium heat and brush with butter. Add 1-tablespoon portions of the batter to the pan in batches, re-greasing as needed, and cook for 2 minutes each side or until golden and cooked through. Remove from the pan and keep warm.

Serve pikelets warm with honeycomb. MAKES 25
+ *Buy fresh honeycomb from some greengrocers and health food stores. Use regular honey if unavailable.*

date doughnuts with spiced sugar

9 soft fresh dates (180g), pitted and chopped
¼ cup (60ml) boiling water
1¼ cups (185g) self-raising (self-rising) flour, sifted
¾ cup (165g) caster (superfine) sugar
2 eggs
¾ cup (180ml) milk
125g unsalted butter, melted
1 teaspoon vanilla extract
spiced sugar
½ cup (110g) white (granulated) sugar
½ teaspoon ground cinnamon
¼ teaspoon ground nutmeg

Preheat oven to 160°C (325°F). Grease 6 x ⅓-cup-capacity (80ml) doughnut tins. Place the date and water in a small bowl and allow to soak for 5 minutes or until softened. Mash the date until smooth, using a fork.

Place the flour, sugar, eggs, milk, butter, vanilla and the date mixture in a large bowl and whisk until smooth. Pour half the mixture into the tins and bake for 12–14 minutes or until golden brown and cooked when tested with a skewer. Turn out onto a wire rack to cool. Repeat with the remaining batter, re-greasing the tins, to make a total of 12 doughnuts.

To make the spiced sugar, place the sugar, cinnamon and nutmeg in a large bowl and mix to combine.

Toss the doughnuts in the spiced sugar to serve. MAKES 12

date doughnuts with spiced sugar

sticky ginger puddings

sticky ginger puddings

1¼ cups (185g) self-raising (self-rising) flour, sifted
¾ cup (165g) caster (superfine) sugar
1 teaspoon ground ginger
2 eggs
¾ cup (180ml) milk
125g unsalted butter, melted
1 teaspoon vanilla extract
¼ cup (55g) glacé ginger, finely chopped
2 tablespoons ginger syrup*
½ cup (90g) dark brown sugar
1 cup (250ml) boiling water

Preheat oven to 180°C (350°F). Place the flour, caster sugar, ginger, eggs, milk, butter, vanilla and glacé ginger in a large bowl and whisk until smooth. Divide the mixture between 3 x 2-cup-capacity (500ml) ovenproof pudding bowls+ and place on a large oven tray.

Place the ginger syrup, brown sugar and water in a small bowl and mix to combine. Gently spoon the syrup over the puddings and bake for 30–35 minutes or until cooked when tested with a skewer.

Spoon the pudding into serving bowls and serve warm with vanilla ice-cream, if you like. **SERVES 6**
+ *If you prefer, you can make 1 large pudding. Use a 1.5-litre-capacity ovenproof pudding bowl and bake for 45 minutes or until cooked when tested with a skewer.*

ginger molasses cookies

200g unsalted butter, melted and cooled
1 cup (175g) light brown sugar
¾ cup (165g) white (granulated) sugar
1 egg
1 egg yolk
2 teaspoons vanilla extract
¼ teaspoon baking powder
½ teaspoon bicarbonate of (baking) soda
1 teaspoon water
2 cups (300g) plain (all-purpose) flour
2 teaspoons ground ginger
1 tablespoon finely grated ginger
2 tablespoons molasses*
¼ teaspoon table salt
½ cup (110g) crystallised ginger, chopped
½ cup (110g) coffee sugar or Demerara sugar+

Preheat oven to 160°C (325°F). Line 2 large baking trays with non-stick baking paper. Place the butter and brown and white sugars in the bowl of an electric mixer and beat on medium speed for 6–8 minutes or until sandy in texture. Add the egg, egg yolk and vanilla, increase the speed to high and beat for 2 minutes or until pale and creamy. Place the baking powder, bicarbonate of soda and water in a small bowl and mix to combine. Add the baking powder mixture, the flour, ground ginger, grated ginger, molasses and salt to the butter mixture and beat on low speed to just combine. Add the crystallised ginger and fold to combine. Refrigerate the cookie dough for 30–45 minutes or until slightly firm.

Place the coffee sugar in a small bowl. Shape ¼-cup (60ml) portions of the dough into balls and toss in the sugar to coat++. Working in batches, place the rounds on the trays, allowing room to spread. Bake for 20 minutes or until golden and firm to the touch. Allow to cool on trays for 10 minutes before transferring onto wire racks to cool completely. Repeat with the remaining dough to make a total of 15 cookies. **MAKES 15**
+ *Coffee sugar has large granules, making it a lovely crunchy topping for sweet treats. Find it in most supermarkets.*
++ *This recipe makes 15 large cookies. To make regular-sized cookies, simply shape 2-tablespoon portions of the dough into*

ginger molasses cookies

granola and maple
bourbon raisin cookies

granola and maple bourbon raisin cookies

1 cup (150g) raisins
¾ cup (180ml) bourbon
1 cup (250ml) maple syrup
200g unsalted butter, melted and cooled
1 cup (175g) light brown sugar
¾ cup (165g) white (granulated) sugar
1 egg
1 egg yolk, extra
2 teaspoons vanilla extract
¼ teaspoon baking powder
½ teaspoon bicarbonate of (baking) soda
1 teaspoon water
2 cups (300g) plain (all-purpose) flour
¼ teaspoon table salt
1½ cups (150g) store-bought fruit-free granola,
    plus extra for sprinkling

Preheat oven to 160°C (325°F). Place the raisins, bourbon and maple syrup in a small saucepan over high heat and bring to a simmer. Cook for 12 minutes or until the mixture is thick and glossy. Set aside to cool slightly.

Line 2 large baking trays with non-stick baking paper. Place the butter and both the sugars in the bowl of an electric mixer and beat on medium speed for 6–8 minutes or until sandy in texture. Add the egg, extra yolk and vanilla, increase the speed to high and beat for 2 minutes or until pale and creamy. Place the baking powder, bicarbonate of soda and water in a small bowl and mix to combine. Add the baking powder mixture, the flour and salt to the butter mixture and beat on low speed until combined. Add the granola and the raisin mixture and beat until just combined. Working in batches, shape ¼-cup (60ml) portions of the dough into balls and place on the trays, allowing room to spread+. Top with extra granola and bake for 20 minutes or until golden brown and firm to the touch. Allow to cool on the trays for 10 minutes before transferring onto wire racks to cool completely. Repeat with the remaining dough to make a total of 15 cookies. MAKES 15

+ This recipe makes 15 large cookies. To make regular-sized cookies, shape 2-tablespoon portions of the dough into balls. Place on trays with room to spread and bake for 14–16 minutes.

carrot cake muffins with spiced honey glaze

13 soft fresh dates (260g), pitted and chopped
½ cup (125ml) boiling water
2½ cups (375g) self-raising (self-rising) flour
½ cup (110g) caster (superfine) sugar
¼ cup (20g) desiccated coconut
2 teaspoons mixed spice
2 eggs, lightly beaten
2 teaspoons vanilla extract
½ cup (125ml) milk
½ cup (125ml) light-flavoured extra virgin olive oil
2 cups (240g) finely grated carrot (about 2 carrots)
250g cream cheese, softened
2 tablespoons caster (superfine) sugar, extra
spiced honey glaze
½ cup (180g) honey
1 tablespoon water
½ teaspoon mixed spice

Preheat oven to 180°C (350°F). Grease 12 x ½-cup-capacity (125ml) muffin tins. Place the date and water in a medium bowl and allow to soak for 5–10 minutes or until combined.

Place the flour, sugar, coconut and mixed spice in a large bowl and mix to combine. Add the egg, vanilla, milk, oil, carrot and the date mixture. Using a butter knife, gently mix until just combined.

Divide half the muffin mixture between the tins, filling them halfway. Place the cream cheese and extra sugar in a medium bowl and mix to combine. Spoon 1 tablespoon of the cream cheese mixture into each tin and top with the remaining muffin mixture. Bake for 20 minutes or until cooked when tested with a skewer. Allow to cool in the tins for 2 minutes before placing on a wire rack to cool completely.

While the muffins are baking, make the spiced honey glaze. Place the honey and water in a small non-stick frying pan over high heat and cook for 3 minutes or until syrupy. Add the mixed spice and stir to combine.

Pour the warm glaze over the muffins to serve. MAKES 12

carrot cake muffins with spiced honey glaze

bourbon sugar and pretzel truffles

bourbon sugar and pretzel truffles

¾ cup (180ml) single (pouring) cream*
600g dark chocolate, finely chopped
2 cups (100g) store-bought pretzels*, crushed
½ teaspoon sea salt flakes
⅓ cup (80ml) bourbon
bourbon sugar
1 cup (220g) Demerara sugar*
2 tablespoons bourbon

Place the cream in a small saucepan over high heat and bring to the boil. Place the chocolate in a medium heatproof bowl and top with the cream. Place the bowl over a saucepan of simmering water (the bowl shouldn't touch the water) and, using a metal spoon, stir until melted and smooth. Add the crushed pretzels, salt and bourbon and mix well to combine. Allow to stand at room temperature for 10 minutes. Refrigerate for 2–3 hours or until just set.

While the mixture is cooling, make the bourbon sugar. Preheat oven to 160°C (325°F). Line a large baking tray with non-stick baking paper. Place the sugar and bourbon in a small bowl and mix to combine. Spread in an even layer on the tray and bake for 30 minutes or until golden and crisp. Allow to cool completely before crushing into fine crumbs.

Roll 1-teaspoon portions of the truffle mixture into balls and press in the bourbon sugar to coat. Place the truffles on the tray and refrigerate for 30 minutes or until firm. MAKES 60

brûlée black rice pudding with coconut gelato

1½ cups (300g) black rice
3 cups (750ml) water
½ cup (125ml) coconut cream
½ cup (100g) grated dark palm sugar⁺
½ cup (75g) white (granulated) sugar
store-bought coconut gelato, to serve

Place the rice and water in a medium saucepan over high heat and bring to the boil. Reduce the heat to low, cover with a tight-fitting lid and cook for 18–20 minutes or until almost tender and most of the water has been absorbed. Add the coconut cream and palm sugar. Cover and cook for a further 10–12 minutes or until thickened and the rice is soft. Divide between 6 x 1-cup-capacity (250ml) serving bowls. Sprinkle with the white sugar and, using a small kitchen blowtorch, caramelise the tops. Allow to set for 3–4 minutes or until the sugar is hard.

Top with scoops of gelato and serve immediately. SERVES 6
+ Often used in Asian desserts, palm sugar is produced by tapping the sap of palm trees. It's then allowed to crystallise and is sold in cubes or round blocks, for grating or shaving. Find it in supermarkets and Asian food stores. You can use dark brown sugar if palm sugar is unavailable.

brûlée black rice pudding with coconut gelato

spiced chai bundt cake

spiced chai bundt cake

1 tablespoon loose-leaf chai tea
2 tablespoons boiling water
2½ cups (375g) self-raising (self-rising) flour
1½ cups (330g) caster (superfine) sugar
2 teaspoons mixed spice
4 eggs
1½ cups (375ml) milk
250g unsalted butter, melted
2 teaspoons vanilla extract

Preheat oven to 180°C (350°F). Grease a 3-litre-capacity Bundt tin. Place the chai and water in a small bowl, mix to combine and allow to stand for 5 minutes.

Place the flour, sugar, mixed spice, eggs, milk, butter, vanilla and the tea mixture in a large bowl and whisk until smooth. Pour into the tin and bake for 30–35 minutes or until cooked when tested with a skewer. Invert onto a wire rack and allow to cool in the tin for 10 minutes. Remove the tin gently and allow to cool completely.

Place on a cake stand or plate and slice to serve. SERVES 8–10

burnt butter and salted maple sticky buns

1¼ teaspoons dry yeast
⅔ cup (160ml) lukewarm milk
2½ tablespoons maple syrup
3¼ cups (485g) plain (all-purpose) flour, plus extra for dusting
¼ teaspoon table salt
2 eggs, lightly beaten
125g unsalted butter, melted
1 tablespoon black sea salt flakes*
maple glaze
⅔ cup (160ml) maple syrup
⅔ cup (120g) light brown sugar
150g unsalted butter, chopped
burnt butter filling
125g unsalted butter, chopped
¾ cup (135g) light brown sugar
2 teaspoons ground allspice

Place the yeast, milk and 2 teaspoons of the maple syrup in a small bowl and mix to combine. Set aside in a warm place for 5 minutes or until the surface is foamy. Place the flour, table salt, egg, butter, the remaining 2 tablespoons of maple syrup and the yeast mixture in the bowl of an electric mixer with a dough hook attached. Beat on low speed for 5 minutes or until the dough is smooth and elastic. Place in a lightly greased bowl, cover with a clean damp tea towel and set aside in a warm place for 1 hour or until doubled in size.

To make the maple glaze, place the maple syrup, sugar and butter in a small saucepan over low heat and stir until melted and smooth. Pour half the glaze into a 20cm x 30cm slice tin. Reserve and set aside the remaining glaze.

To make the burnt butter filling, place the butter in a small non-stick frying pan over high heat and stir until melted. Bring to a simmer and cook for 2–3 minutes or until golden brown with a nutty fragrance. Transfer to a medium bowl, add the sugar and allspice and mix to combine.

Roll out the dough on a lightly floured surface to make a 25cm x 60cm rectangle. Spread with the filling, leaving a 1cm border. Starting from 1 long edge, roll up the dough tightly to enclose. Trim the edges. Slice into 12 even pieces. Arrange the buns in the tin on top of the glaze. Cover with a damp tea towel. Set aside for 1 hour or until doubled in size.

Preheat oven to 180°C (350°F). Bake the sticky buns for 25–30 minutes or until golden brown and cooked through. Gently warm the remaining glaze over low heat. Pour over the buns and sprinkle with the salt to serve. MAKES 12

burnt butter and salted maple sticky buns

miso-glazed doughnuts

miso-glazed doughnuts

¾ cup (180ml) lukewarm milk
3 teaspoons dry yeast
¼ cup (55g) caster (superfine) sugar
2 cups (300g) plain (all-purpose) flour, plus extra for dusting
2 egg yolks
25g unsalted butter, softened
vegetable oil, for deep-frying
1 tablespoon black sesame seeds
miso glaze
2 cups (320g) icing (confectioner's) sugar, sifted
30g unsalted butter, melted
¼ cup (60ml) boiling water
1 tablespoon white miso paste*

Place the milk, yeast and 1 tablespoon of the caster sugar in a small bowl and mix to combine. Set aside in a warm place for 5–10 minutes or until the surface is foamy. Place the remaining 2 tablespoons of sugar, the flour, egg yolks, butter and the yeast mixture in the bowl of an electric mixer with a dough hook attached. Beat on low speed for 4–5 minutes or until the dough is smooth and elastic. Place in a lightly greased bowl, cover with a clean damp tea towel and set aside in a warm place for 45 minutes or until doubled in size.

Line a baking tray with non-stick baking paper. Turn out the dough on a lightly floured surface and knead for 5 minutes or until smooth and elastic. Roll out to 1cm thick. Using an 8cm round cookie cutter, lightly dusted in flour, cut 8 rounds from the dough. Place on the tray, allowing room to spread. Using a 3cm round cutter, lightly dusted in flour, cut and remove the centre of each round. Cover the tray loosely with plastic wrap and set aside in a warm place for 30 minutes or until the doughnuts have doubled in size.

To make the miso glaze, place the sugar, butter, water and miso in a medium bowl and whisk to combine.

Half-fill a large, deep saucepan with oil and place over medium heat until the temperature reaches 180°C (350°F) on a deep-frying thermometer. Deep-fry the doughnuts, in batches, for 30 seconds each side or until golden brown. Drain on absorbent kitchen paper. While the doughnuts are still hot, carefully dip each side in the miso glaze. Working quickly, sprinkle with the sesame seeds and place on a wire rack to set, before serving. MAKES 8

Tip: You can also deep-fry the 'holes' of the doughnuts to make mini doughnut rounds. Because they're smaller, you only need to cook them for 20 seconds each side.

mixed spice and raspberry slice

2½ cups (375g) self-raising (self-rising) flour
½ cup (90g) dark brown sugar
½ cup (110g) caster (superfine) sugar
1 teaspoon mixed spice
2 teaspoons ground ginger
2 teaspoons finely grated ginger
2 eggs, lightly beaten
2 teaspoons vanilla extract
½ cup (125ml) buttermilk
½ cup (125ml) vegetable oil
250g raspberries
200g dark chocolate, chopped
icing (confectioner's) sugar, for dusting

Preheat oven to 180°C (350°F). Line 2 x 15cm x 20cm slice tins with non-stick baking paper[+]. Place the flour, brown sugar, caster sugar, mixed spice, ground and fresh ginger in a large bowl. Add the egg, vanilla, buttermilk and oil and, using a butter knife, mix gently until just combined. Add the raspberries and chocolate and fold to combine. Divide the mixture between the tins and bake for 30 minutes or until cooked when tested with a skewer. Allow to cool in the tins for 10 minutes.

Dust with icing sugar and slice to serve. SERVES 8–10

+ If you prefer, you can use this recipe to make 1 larger slice – simply use a 20cm x 30cm slice tin.

mixed spice and raspberry slice

QUICK

ricotta hotcakes with spiced sugar
chocolate and pear sugared brioche pillows
whipped ricotta, orange and nutmeg cannoli
star anise and vanilla roasted plums
peach and raspberry brioche bake
cinnamon sugar crostini with ricotta
cheat's sugar cookies with jam and cream
coconut and strawberry filo tarts
fruit and nut bread and butter puddings
coconut chai granita
spiced cream and maple brioche trifles
cheat's ginger and caramel pecan pies
maple and cinnamon roasted pears
cinnamon brioche churros with caramel
cheat's custard tarts
chocolate and ginger truffles

FIX

ricotta hotcakes with spiced sugar

1 cup (150g) self-raising (self-rising) flour, sifted
½ teaspoon bicarbonate of (baking) soda, sifted
½ teaspoon baking powder, sifted
¾ cup (165g) caster (superfine) sugar
¾ cup (180ml) buttermilk
2 eggs, separated
¾ cup (180g) fresh firm ricotta
unsalted butter, melted for brushing
½ teaspoon mixed spice
lemon wedges, to serve

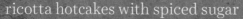

Place the flour, bicarbonate of soda, baking powder, ¼ cup (55g) of the sugar, the buttermilk and egg yolks in a large bowl and whisk until smooth. Place the eggwhites in the bowl of an electric mixer and whisk until stiff peaks form. Add the eggwhite and ricotta to the flour mixture and fold to combine.

   Heat a large non-stick frying pan over medium heat and brush with butter. Reduce the heat to low. Add 2-tablespoon portions of the batter in batches and cook for 2–3 minutes each side or until golden. Place the mixed spice and the remaining sugar in a small bowl and mix to combine.

   Serve hotcakes with the spiced sugar and lemon. MAKES 10

chocolate and pear sugared brioche pillows

¾ cup (90g) grated pear (about 1 pear)
60g dark chocolate, grated
1 teaspoon mixed spice
16 slices store-bought brioche loaf, crusts removed
2 tablespoons Demerara sugar*
60g unsalted butter, melted

Preheat oven to 220°C (425°F). Line a large baking tray with non-stick baking paper. Place the pear, chocolate and half the mixed spice in a bowl and mix to combine. Place 1-tablespoon portions of the pear mixture onto each of half the brioche slices. Top with the remaining brioche, pressing the edges to seal.

   Place the sugar and the remaining mixed spice in a small bowl. Brush each side of the parcels with butter and sprinkle with the spiced sugar. Place on the tray and bake for 6–8 minutes or until golden. Serve warm. MAKES 8

whipped ricotta, orange and nutmeg cannoli

1½ cups (360g) fresh firm ricotta
1 cup (250ml) double (thick) cream*
¼ cup (40g) icing (confectioner's) sugar, sifted,
    plus extra for dusting
1 teaspoon finely grated orange rind
½ teaspoon freshly grated nutmeg,
    plus extra for dusting
8 store-bought large cannoli shells

Place the ricotta, cream, sugar, orange rind and nutmeg
in a large bowl and whisk until stiff peaks form. Spoon
into a piping bag fitted with a 1.5cm star-shaped nozzle.
  Pipe the whipped ricotta into each cannoli shell and
place onto serving plates. Dust with extra icing sugar
and nutmeg to serve. MAKES 8

star anise and vanilla roasted plums

8 plums, halved and pitted
⅓ cup (75g) caster (superfine) sugar
4 star anise
1 vanilla bean, split and seeds scraped

Preheat oven to 240°C (465°F). Line a 20cm x 30cm baking
dish with non-stick baking paper. Place the plums, sugar,
star anise and the vanilla bean and seeds in the dish and
gently toss to combine. Bake for 15–20 minutes or until the
plums are caramelised.
  Spoon onto serving plates and top with double (thick)
cream to serve, if you like. SERVES 4

peach and raspberry brioche bake

⅓ cup (75g) caster (superfine) sugar
2 teaspoons vanilla extract
4 yellow peaches, cut into wedges
125g raspberries
50g unsalted butter, softened
6 thick slices store-bought brioche loaf

Preheat oven to 220°C (425°F). Line a 20cm x 30cm baking dish with non-stick baking paper. Place ¼ cup (55g) of the sugar, the vanilla, peach and raspberries in a large bowl and toss to combine.

Spread the butter onto 1 side of each of the brioche slices and sprinkle with the remaining 1 tablespoon of sugar. Arrange the brioche, sugar-side down, in the base of the dish. Top with the fruit mixture and bake for 30 minutes or until the fruit is blistered. SERVES 4

cinnamon sugar crostini with ricotta

¼ cup (55g) Demerara sugar*
1 teaspoon ground cinnamon, plus extra for dusting
12 thin baguette slices
50g unsalted butter, melted
1 cup (240g) fresh firm ricotta
¼ cup (40g) icing (confectioner's) sugar, sifted
mixed berries, to serve
freeze-dried raspberries*, crushed to serve

Preheat oven to 240°C (465°F). Line a baking tray with non-stick baking paper. Place the Demerara sugar and cinnamon on a small tray and mix to combine. Brush both sides of each baguette slice with butter and press each side into the sugar mixture to coat. Place on the tray and bake for 2 minutes each side.

Place the ricotta and icing sugar in a medium bowl and whisk until smooth. Divide between serving bowls and top with the berries and freeze-dried raspberries.

Dust the ricotta bowls with extra cinnamon and serve with the crostini. SERVES 4

cheat's sugar cookies with jam and cream

¼ cup (55g) white (granulated) sugar
½ teaspoon mixed spice
2 sheets frozen shortcrust pastry, thawed
1 egg, lightly beaten
½ cup (160g) store-bought raspberry jam
1 cup (250ml) single (pouring) cream*, whipped

Preheat oven to 180°C (350°F). Line 2 large baking trays with non-stick baking paper. Place the sugar and mixed spice in a small bowl and mix to combine. Using a 6cm round fluted cookie cutter, cut 20 rounds from the pastry. Brush the top of each round with egg and sprinkle with the spiced sugar. Place on the trays and bake for 8–10 minutes or until golden brown. Allow to cool on the trays.

Spoon jam and cream onto half the sugar cookies and sandwich with the remaining cookies to serve. MAKES 10

coconut and strawberry filo tarts

1½ cups (110g) shredded coconut
2 tablespoons honey
1 teaspoon vanilla bean paste or vanilla extract
5 sheets filo (phyllo) pastry
50g unsalted butter, melted
125g strawberries, hulled and sliced
2 teaspoons Demerara sugar*
icing (confectioner's) sugar, for dusting

Preheat oven to 200°C (400°F). Line a large baking tray with non-stick baking paper. Place the coconut, honey and vanilla in a small bowl and mix to combine.

Brush each sheet of pastry with butter and layer in a stack. Cut the stack into 6 equal rectangles. Divide the coconut mixture between the pastry rectangles, spreading to leave a 1cm border. Top each tart with strawberry slices, overlapping them slightly. Fold the edges of the pastry in and brush with butter. Sprinkle with the Demerara sugar and place on the tray. Bake for 12 minutes or until golden and the pastry is crisp. Allow to cool slightly on the tray.

Dust the tarts with icing sugar to serve. MAKES 6

fruit and nut bread and butter puddings

2 eggs
¼ cup (60ml) maple syrup, plus extra to serve
1 teaspoon vanilla extract
½ teaspoon ground cinnamon
1⅓ cups (330ml) single (pouring) cream*
6 slices store-bought fruit bread, quartered
1 tablespoon Demerara sugar*
½ cup (70g) hazelnuts, roughly chopped

Preheat oven to 180°C (350°F). Line 6 x ½-cup-capacity (125ml) muffin tins with paper cases. Place the eggs, maple syrup, vanilla and cinnamon in a large heatproof jug and whisk to combine. Place the cream in a small saucepan over medium heat until just boiling. Add to the jug and whisk to combine.

Divide the bread between the tins. Top with the cream mixture and sprinkle with the sugar and hazelnuts. Allow to soak for 5 minutes. Bake for 12–14 minutes or until golden and set.

Top puddings with extra maple syrup to serve. MAKES 6

coconut chai granita

3 cups (750ml) coconut milk
2 cups (500ml) water
¾ cup (270g) honey
½ cup (30g) loose-leaf chai tea

Place the coconut milk, water, honey and chai in a medium saucepan over medium heat and stir until just boiling. Reduce the heat to low and cook for 4 minutes. Strain the mixture through a fine sieve into a heatproof jug, discarding the solids, and pour into a 20cm x 30cm slice tin or metal container. Freeze for 4 hours or until firm.

Rake the granita into crystals with a fork to serve. SERVES 4-6

spiced cream and maple brioche trifles

4 thick slices store-bought brioche loaf, quartered
50g unsalted butter, melted
2 tablespoons white (granulated) sugar
½ teaspoon ground allspice, plus extra for dusting
1¼ cups (310ml) single (pouring) cream*
¼ cup (60ml) orange juice
¼ cup (60ml) maple syrup
¼ cup (20g) natural flaked almonds*, toasted

Preheat oven to 220°C (425°F). Line a baking tray with
non-stick baking paper. Brush the brioche pieces with
the butter. Sprinkle with the sugar and half the allspice.
Place on the tray and bake for 5 minutes.

Place the cream and the remaining allspice in a medium
bowl and whisk until soft peaks form. Place the orange juice
and maple syrup in a small jug and mix to combine.

Divide the cream and brioche between serving glasses
to create a layered effect and top with the almonds. Drizzle
with the maple orange syrup to serve. MAKES 4

cheat's ginger and caramel pecan pies

12 store-bought ginger nut (ginger snap) biscuits
⅓ cup (100g) store-bought thick caramel or
    dulce de leche*
12 pecans, toasted

Preheat oven to 180°C (350°F). Lightly grease
12 x 2-tablespoon-capacity patty tins. Place 1 biscuit
in each tin and bake for 2–3 minutes or until softened.
While still warm, gently press the biscuits to the shape
of the tins. Allow to cool completely in the tins.

Divide the caramel between the tart cases and
top with the pecans to serve. MAKES 12

maple and cinnamon roasted pears

9 small pears, halved+
⅓ cup (80ml) maple syrup
3 sticks cinnamon
50g unsalted butter, chopped

Preheat oven to 220°C (425°F). Place the pear, maple
syrup, cinnamon and butter in a medium roasting
pan. Cover tightly with aluminium foil and bake for
10 minutes. Remove the foil and bake for a further
15 minutes or until caramelised and soft.

Spoon onto serving plates and top with double
(thick) cream to serve, if you like. SERVES 6
+ *Williams and Corella pears are small, sweet and
lovely to roast. Although you don't eat the stalks of
the pears, it looks pretty to leave them on.*

cinnamon brioche churros with caramel

1 egg
2 tablespoons milk
⅔ cup (150g) white (granulated) sugar
1 teaspoon ground cinnamon
4 slices store-bought brioche loaf, crusts removed
   and cut into fingers
½ cup (150g) store-bought thick caramel or dulce de leche*

Preheat oven to 220°C (425°F). Line a large baking tray
with non-stick baking paper. Place the egg and milk in
a small bowl, whisk to combine and set aside. Place the
sugar and cinnamon on a small tray and mix to combine.

Brush each brioche finger with the egg mixture and roll
in the cinnamon sugar to coat. Place on the tray and bake
for 6 minutes or until golden and crisp. Allow to cool on
the tray for 2 minutes.

Serve the brioche churros with the caramel. SERVES 4

cheat's custard tarts

12 square wonton wrappers*
1 egg
3 egg yolks, extra
1 cup (240g) crème fraîche*
¼ teaspoon ground cinnamon
½ cup (110g) caster (superfine) sugar
1 teaspoon vanilla extract
¼ cup (90g) golden syrup

Preheat oven to 220°C (425°F). Line 12 x ½-cup-capacity (125ml) muffin tins with the wonton wrappers.

Place the egg, extra yolks, the crème fraîche, cinnamon, sugar and vanilla in a medium bowl and whisk to combine. Divide the mixture between the tins and bake for 10 minutes or until just blistered. Drizzle the tarts with half the golden syrup and bake for a further 2 minutes. Remove from the tins and place on a wire rack to cool. Refrigerate until cold.

Top tarts with the remaining golden syrup to serve. **MAKES 12**

chocolate and ginger truffles

¾ cup (180ml) single (pouring) cream*
600g dark chocolate, finely chopped
½ cup (110g) glacé ginger, chopped
cocoa powder, for dusting (optional)

Line a 20cm square slice tin with non-stick baking paper. Place the cream and chocolate in a large heatproof bowl over a saucepan of simmering water (the water shouldn't touch the bowl). Stir until melted and smooth. Add the ginger, mix to combine and pour into the tin. Refrigerate for 3 hours or until firm.

Remove the truffle from the tin, cut into pieces and toss in cocoa to coat. **MAKES 36**
Tip: Keep these truffles refrigerated in an airtight container for up to 2 weeks.

almond and nutmeg layer cake

FRESH AND LIGHT

——

I have all kinds of little tricks for keeping sweets a bit lighter when I'm baking. One of my favourites is to dial down their processed sugar, but boost their flavour using spices. Notes of creamy vanilla, warming cinnamon or exotic rosewater always give the illusion of indulgence, even in the most virtuous of treats!

almond and nutmeg layer cake

4 eggs, at room temperature
½ cup (110g) raw caster (superfine) sugar
1 cup (120g) almond meal (ground almonds), sifted
½ cup (80g) wholemeal (whole-wheat) self-raising
   (self-rising) flour*, sifted
½ teaspoon freshly grated nutmeg
50g unsalted butter, melted
1 tablespoon finely grated orange rind
honey orange syrup
½ cup (125ml) orange juice
¼ cup (90g) honey
ricotta icing
2 cups (480g) fresh firm ricotta
¼ cup (90g) honey
1 teaspoon vanilla bean paste or vanilla extract

Preheat oven to 160°C (325°F). Line a 20cm round cake tin with non-stick baking paper. Place the eggs and sugar in the bowl of an electric mixer and whisk on high speed for 8 minutes or until pale, thick and tripled in volume. Place the almond meal, flour and nutmeg in a medium bowl and mix to combine. Add the flour mixture to the egg mixture and gently fold until just combined. Add the butter and orange rind and gently fold to combine. Pour into the tin and bake for 30 minutes or until cooked when tested with a skewer. Turn the cake out onto a wire rack to cool completely.

To make the honey orange syrup, place the orange juice and honey in a small saucepan over medium heat and bring to the boil. Cook for 10–12 minutes or until thickened and syrupy. Refrigerate until cold.

To make the ricotta icing, place the ricotta, honey and vanilla in a clean bowl of the electric mixer and whisk on medium speed until smooth.

Using a large serrated knife, slice the cake in half horizontally. Place 1 half onto a cake stand or plate and spread with half the icing. Top with the remaining cake and spread with the remaining icing. Drizzle with the honey orange syrup to serve. SERVES 10–12

apple, berry, coconut and quinoa crumble

2 Granny Smith (green) apples (400g), peeled and chopped
4 cups (520g) frozen raspberries
½ cup (80g) dried currants
¼ teaspoon ground cardamom
¼ cup (90g) honey
¼ cup (60ml) coconut cream
quinoa, almond and chia crumble
1 cup (160g) almonds, chopped
½ cup (50g) quinoa flakes*
1 tablespoon light-flavoured extra virgin olive oil
2 tablespoons honey
2 tablespoons white chia seeds*

Preheat oven to 180°C (350°F). To make the quinoa, almond and chia crumble, place the almonds, quinoa, oil, honey and chia seeds in a medium bowl and mix well to combine.

Place the apple, raspberries, currants, cardamom and honey in a large saucepan over high heat and cook for 12 minutes, stirring occasionally, until slightly reduced.

Transfer the mixture to a 1-litre-capacity baking dish. Pour the coconut cream over the fruit mixture and top with the crumble. Place on an oven tray and bake for 15 minutes or until golden and crunchy. Serve with extra coconut cream, if you like. SERVES 4

apple, berry, coconut and quinoa crumble

ginger nut crunch bars

ginger nut crunch bars

3 cups (450g) cashews
⅓ cup (80ml) coconut cream
2 teaspoons finely grated ginger
1 teaspoon ground ginger
⅓ cup (80ml) maple syrup
coconut base
15 soft fresh dates (300g), pitted
1½ cups (135g) rolled oats
1 cup (200g) raw buckwheat*
1½ cups (120g) desiccated coconut
50g unsalted butter, chopped and melted
3 teaspoons finely grated ginger
buckwheat crumble
¾ cup (150g) raw buckwheat*
2 tablespoons maple syrup

Preheat oven to 160°C (325°F). Line a 20cm x 30cm slice tin with non-stick baking paper. Place the cashews in a large bowl, cover with boiling water and set aside to soak for 20 minutes.

To make the coconut base, place the dates, oats, buckwheat, coconut, butter and ginger in a food processor and process for 3–4 minutes or until the mixture comes together. Press into the base of the tin and smooth the top, using the back of a spoon. Bake for 20 minutes or until firm. Allow to cool completely in the tin.

Drain the cashews and place in the cleaned food processor. Add the coconut cream, grated ginger, ground ginger and maple syrup. Process, scraping down the sides occasionally, for 3–4 minutes or until smooth and creamy. Spread the cashew mixture over the cooled base and refrigerate for 2 hours or until set.

To make the buckwheat crumble, increase the oven temperature to 200°C (400°F). Line a baking tray with non-stick baking paper. Place the buckwheat and maple syrup on the tray and toss to combine. Bake for 10 minutes or until golden. Allow to cool completely.

Sprinkle the crumble over the slice and press gently to secure. Refrigerate for a further 1 hour or until set. Remove the slice from the tin and cut into bars to serve. MAKES 20
Tip: Keep this slice refrigerated in an airtight container for up to 10 days.

pistachio, rosewater and sour cherry squares

1 cup (140g) pistachios
1½ cups (140g) rolled oats
¾ cup (120g) cashews
6 soft fresh dates (120g), pitted
¼ cup (60ml) light-flavoured extra virgin olive oil
2 teaspoons rosewater⁺
2 teaspoons vanilla bean paste or vanilla extract
½ cup (70g) pistachios, extra, chopped
½ cup (75g) dried sour cherries, chopped
¼ cup (25g) rolled oats, extra
1 tablespoon honey

Preheat oven to 160°C (325°F). Line a 20cm square slice tin with non-stick baking paper. Place the pistachios, oats, cashews and dates in a food processor and process until finely chopped. Add the oil, rosewater and vanilla and process until well combined. Press the mixture into the base of the tin, using the back of a spoon.

Place the extra pistachio, the cherry, extra oats and the honey in a small bowl and mix to combine. Sprinkle onto the base and bake for 30 minutes or until golden brown. Allow to cool completely in the tin.

Remove the slice from the tin and, using a serrated knife, cut into squares to serve. MAKES 16
⁺ *Popular in Middle-Eastern treats for its sweet, aromatic flavour, find rosewater in the baking aisle of supermarkets.*
Tip: Keep this slice in an airtight container for up to 7 days.

pistachio, rosewater and sour cherry squares

carrot cake bliss balls

carrot cake bliss balls

3 cups (360g) pecans
20 soft fresh dates (400g), pitted
1 cup (120g) grated carrot (about 1 carrot)
1 teaspoon ground cinnamon
½ teaspoon ground nutmeg
½ teaspoon ground ginger
1⅓ cups (130g) LSA+

Place 1 cup (120g) of the pecans in a food processor and pulse until finely chopped. Place in a small bowl and set aside. Place the dates, carrot, cinnamon, nutmeg, ginger, LSA and the remaining 2 cups (240g) of pecans in the food processor and process for 1 minute or until the mixture comes together.

Shape 1-tablespoon portions of the mixture into balls and roll in the chopped pecans to coat. Refrigerate until ready to serve. MAKES 28

+ *LSA is a mix of ground linseeds, sunflower seeds and almonds. Find it in the health food aisle of supermarkets.*
Tip: Keep these bliss balls refrigerated in an airtight container for up to 2 weeks.

crunchy coconut, tahini and date fudge

20 soft fresh dates (400g), pitted
¼ cup (70g) tahini*
¼ cup (25g) raw cacao or cocoa powder*
1 teaspoon ground cinnamon
1 teaspoon vanilla extract
coconut topping
½ cup (40g) shredded coconut
2 tablespoons sesame seeds
2 tablespoons maple syrup

Preheat oven to 160°C (325°F). Line a 10cm x 20cm loaf tin with non-stick baking paper.

To make the coconut topping, line a baking tray with non-stick baking paper. Place the coconut, sesame seeds and maple syrup in a small bowl. Mix to combine and spread on the tray. Bake, stirring halfway, for 8 minutes or until golden. Set aside to cool completely.

Place the dates, tahini, cacao, cinnamon and vanilla in a food processor and process for 2 minutes or until smooth. Spoon the mixture into the tin and smooth the top. Sprinkle with the coconut topping and freeze for 2 hours or until firm.

Remove the fudge from the tin and cut into bars. Freeze until ready to serve. MAKES 16
Tip: Keep this fudge frozen in an airtight container for up to 2 weeks.

crunchy coconut, tahini and date fudge

almond milk crepes with whipped ricotta

almond milk crepes with whipped ricotta

1 cup (160g) wholemeal (whole-wheat) plain
  (all-purpose) flour*, sifted
¼ cup (30g) almond meal (ground almonds)
2¼ cups (560ml) unsweetened almond milk*
2 eggs
unsalted butter, melted for brushing
¼ cup (90g) honey, to serve
ground cinnamon, for dusting
whipped ricotta
2 cups (480g) fresh firm ricotta
1 teaspoon vanilla bean paste or vanilla extract

Place the flour and almond meal in a large bowl. Place
the almond milk and eggs in a medium jug and whisk to
combine. Gradually add the milk mixture to the flour
mixture, whisking until smooth. Cover the bowl with
plastic wrap and allow to stand for 20 minutes.

Heat a small non-stick frying pan over medium heat
and brush with the butter. Add ¼-cup (60ml) portions
of the batter to the pan at a time, re-greasing as needed,
and gently tilt to coat the base. Cook crepes for 4 minutes
each side. Remove from the pan and keep warm.

To make the whipped ricotta, place the ricotta and
vanilla in a medium bowl and whisk until smooth.

Top crepes with the whipped ricotta and drizzle with
the honey. Dust with cinnamon to serve. MAKES 10

chewy cinnamon and date cookies

18 soft fresh dates (360g), pitted and chopped
½ cup (80g) rapadura sugar⁺
125g unsalted butter
1 teaspoon bicarbonate of (baking) soda
1 cup (140g) wholemeal spelt flour*
1 cup (90g) rolled oats
2 teaspoons ground cinnamon
1 egg
1 teaspoon vanilla extract

Preheat oven to 160°C (325°F). Line 2 large baking trays
with non-stick baking paper. Place the date, sugar and
butter in a medium saucepan over medium heat and stir
until the butter is melted. Cook, stirring, for a further
5 minutes or until the date is soft. Remove from the heat,
add the bicarbonate of soda and mix to combine. Allow
to cool for 5 minutes.

Place the flour, oats, cinnamon, egg and vanilla in a
large bowl and mix to combine. Add the date mixture
and fold to combine. Shape 2-tablespoon portions of the
mixture into balls. Place on the trays and gently flatten
into 7cm rounds. Bake for 12–14 minutes or until golden.
Allow cookies to cool on the trays before serving. MAKES 15
+ *Rapadura sugar, or panela, is extracted from the pure
juice of cane sugar. It's evaporated over low heat, so it
retains more of the minerals and vitamins from the cane.
Find it in the health food aisle of major supermarkets
or in health food stores and specialty grocers.*

chewy cinnamon and date cookies

apple and ginger crumble muffins

apple and ginger crumble muffins

2¼ cups (290g) white spelt flour*
⅓ cup (75g) raw caster (superfine) sugar
¼ cup (30g) almond meal (ground almonds)
3 teaspoons baking powder
3 eggs, lightly beaten
¾ cup (180ml) light-flavoured extra virgin olive oil
½ cup (140g) natural Greek-style (thick) yoghurt
1 teaspoon vanilla bean paste or vanilla extract
1½ cups (345g) firmly packed grated
   Granny Smith (green) apple (about 2 apples)
2 tablespoons finely chopped glacé ginger
fresh honeycomb, to serve⁺
crunchy crumble topping
⅔ cup (60g) rolled oats
½ cup (80g) pepitas (pumpkin seeds)*
¼ cup (40g) sunflower seeds
¼ cup (90g) honey

Preheat oven to 180°C (350°F). Line 12 x ½-cup-capacity
(125ml) muffin tins with paper cases. To make the crunchy
crumble topping, place the oats, pepitas, sunflower seeds
and honey in a small bowl and mix to combine. Set aside.

Place the flour, sugar, almond meal and baking powder
in a large bowl. Mix to combine. Add the egg, oil, yoghurt,
vanilla, apple and ginger and mix until just combined.
Spoon the mixture into the tins and sprinkle with the
crumble topping. Bake for 20–25 minutes or until golden
and cooked when tested with a skewer. Allow to cool in
the tins for 5 minutes before placing onto a wire rack to
cool completely. Serve muffins with honeycomb. **MAKES 12**
*+ Buy fresh honeycomb from most greengrocers and
health food stores. Use regular honey if unavailable.*

orange and cinnamon syrup cake

2 medium oranges (500g), skin on
3 eggs
½ cup (80g) rapadura sugar⁺
1¼ cups (150g) almond meal (ground almonds)
½ cup (80g) buckwheat flour*
1 teaspoon baking powder
½ cup (40g) natural flaked almonds*, toasted
orange cinnamon syrup
2 cups (500ml) orange juice
⅓ cup (50g) rapadura sugar⁺
2 sticks cinnamon

Place the oranges in a small saucepan, cover with water
and weigh down with a small heatproof plate to submerge.
Bring to a simmer over high heat and cook for 1 hour or
until very soft. Drain and allow to cool slightly. Place the
oranges in a food processor and process until smooth.

Preheat oven to 180°C (350°F). Line a 20cm x 30cm slice
tin with non-stick baking paper. Place the eggs and sugar
in the bowl of an electric mixer and whisk on high speed
for 6–8 minutes or until thick and tripled in volume. Add
the orange puree, almond meal, flour and baking powder
and gently fold to combine. Pour into the tin and bake for
30 minutes or until cooked when tested with a skewer.

While the cake is baking, make the orange cinnamon
syrup. Place the orange juice, sugar and cinnamon in a
small saucepan over high heat and cook for 12–15 minutes
or until slightly reduced.

Remove and discard the cinnamon and pour half the
syrup over the hot cake in the tin. Allow to cool slightly.

Remove the cake from the tin, place on a serving plate
and top with the remaining syrup. Sprinkle with the
almonds to serve. **SERVES 8-10**
*+ Rapadura sugar, or panela, is extracted from the pure
juice of cane sugar. It's evaporated over low heat, so it
retains more of the minerals and vitamins from the cane.
Find it in the health food aisle of major supermarkets
or in health food stores and specialty grocers.*

orange and cinnamon syrup cake

fruit and berries

Baking with fruit is quite nostalgic for me. I've always loved the way it softens in the oven, giving jewel-like colours and sweet tartness to pies and desserts. Be it syrupy pear cakes, still warm from the tins, or a sugar-crusted berry tart, cooling on the windowsill, these rustic-style recipes will transport you right to the orchard itself.

blueberry and thyme tart

blueberry and thyme tart

⅓ cup (40g) almond meal (ground almonds)
375g blueberries
1 teaspoon finely grated lemon rind
⅓ cup (75g) caster (superfine) sugar
2 teaspoons cornflour (cornstarch)
1 teaspoon thyme leaves, plus extra sprigs to serve
20g unsalted butter, chopped
1 egg, lightly beaten
2 tablespoons raw or Demerara sugar*
pastry
1½ cups (225g) plain (all-purpose) flour
¼ cup (55g) caster (superfine) sugar
1 teaspoon finely grated lemon rind
100g cold unsalted butter, chopped
2 teaspoons apple cider vinegar
¼ cup (60ml) iced water
1 teaspoon vanilla extract

To make the pastry, place the flour, sugar and lemon rind in a large bowl and mix to combine. Add the butter and, using your fingertips, rub into the flour mixture until it resembles fine breadcrumbs. Add the vinegar, water and vanilla and, using a butter knife, mix until a rough dough forms. Gently knead to bring the dough together. Shape into a disc and wrap in plastic wrap. Refrigerate for 30 minutes or until firm.

Preheat oven to 200°C (400°F). Roll out the pastry between 2 sheets of non-stick baking paper to a 4mm-thick 35cm round. Place on a large baking tray and remove the top sheet of paper. Spread the base with the almond meal, leaving a 5cm border. Place the blueberries, lemon rind, caster sugar, cornflour and thyme in a medium bowl and toss well to combine. Top the almond meal with the blueberry mixture and the butter. Fold in the edges of the pastry, pressing gently to enclose. Brush the edges with egg and sprinkle with the raw sugar. Refrigerate for 10 minutes.

Bake for 10 minutes. Reduce the heat to 180°C (350°F) and bake for a further 40 minutes or until the pastry is golden and the fruit is bubbling.

Allow the tart to cool on the tray for 10 minutes. Sprinkle with the extra thyme to serve. SERVES 6–8

plum, lemon and juniper tart

⅓ cup (40g) almond meal (ground almonds)
500g plums, cut into 2cm slices
⅓ cup (75g) caster (superfine) sugar
1 teaspoon vanilla extract
10g unsalted butter, chopped
1 egg, lightly beaten
2 tablespoons raw or Demerara sugar*
1 teaspoon juniper berries*, crushed
natural Greek-style (thick) yoghurt, to serve
pastry
1½ cups (225g) plain (all-purpose) flour
¼ cup (55g) caster (superfine) sugar
1 teaspoon finely grated lemon rind
100g cold unsalted butter, chopped
2 teaspoons apple cider vinegar
¼ cup (60ml) iced water
1 teaspoon vanilla extract

To make the pastry, place the flour, sugar and lemon rind in a large bowl and mix to combine. Add the butter and, using your fingertips, rub into the flour mixture until it resembles fine breadcrumbs. Add the vinegar, water and vanilla and, using a butter knife, mix until a rough dough forms. Gently knead to bring the dough together. Shape into a disc and wrap in plastic wrap. Refrigerate for 30 minutes or until firm.

Preheat oven to 200°C (400°F). Roll out the pastry between 2 sheets of non-stick baking paper to a 3mm-thick 30cm round. Place on a large baking tray and remove the top sheet of paper. Spread the base with the almond meal, leaving a 3cm border. Place the plum, caster sugar and vanilla in a medium bowl and toss well to combine. Top the almond meal with the plum mixture and the butter. Fold in the edges of the pastry, pressing gently to enclose. Brush the edges with egg and sprinkle with the raw sugar. Refrigerate for 10 minutes.

Bake for 15 minutes. Reduce the heat to 180°C (350°F) and bake for a further 40 minutes or until the pastry is golden and the fruit is bubbling.

Allow the tart to cool on the tray for 10 minutes. Sprinkle with the crushed juniper and serve with yoghurt. SERVES 6–8

plum, lemon and juniper tart

blackberry and banana oat cookie sandwiches
+ cheat's blackberry and vanilla jam

blackberry and banana oat cookie sandwiches

¾ cup (110g) plain (all-purpose) flour
1 cup (90g) rolled oats
⅓ cup (35g) walnuts, chopped
¼ cup (40g) sultanas
½ teaspoon ground cinnamon
75g unsalted butter
¼ cup (60ml) maple syrup
¾ cup (165g) caster (superfine) sugar
½ cup (125ml) single (pouring) cream*
½ teaspoon vanilla extract
¼ cup (65g) mashed banana
250g cream cheese, softened
2 tablespoons icing (confectioner's) sugar
1 tablespoon milk
2 teaspoons lemon juice
1 x quantity cheat's blackberry and vanilla jam (see *recipe*, below)

Preheat oven to 160°C (325°F). Line 2 large baking trays
with non-stick baking paper. Place the flour, oats, walnuts,
sultanas and cinnamon in a large bowl and mix to combine.
Place the butter, maple syrup, caster sugar, cream and
vanilla in a small saucepan over medium heat and stir until
smooth. Bring to the boil and cook for 4 minutes or until
thickened slightly. Add the butter mixture and the banana
to the oat mixture and mix until well combined. Allow to
cool for 5 minutes. Shape 1-tablespoon portions of the
mixture into balls and place on the trays, allowing room to
spread. Flatten slightly and bake for 15–18 minutes or until
golden. Allow to cool on the trays.

Place the cream cheese, icing sugar, milk and lemon juice
in a food processor and process until smooth. Spread the
cream cheese filling over half the biscuits, top with jam
and sandwich with the remaining biscuits to serve. **MAKES 9**

cheat's blackberry and vanilla jam

500g blackberries or frozen blackberries, thawed and drained
⅔ cup (150g) caster (superfine) sugar
2 tablespoons lemon juice
1 vanilla bean, split and seeds scraped

Place the blackberries, sugar, lemon juice, vanilla bean and
seeds in a large non-stick frying pan over high heat. Bring
to the boil and cook for 7–8 minutes or until thickened.
Remove the vanilla pods. Allow to cool completely. **MAKES 1 CUP**

strawberry, ricotta and rhubarb tart

¾ cup (180g) fresh firm ricotta
1 teaspoon finely grated orange rind
250g strawberries, trimmed and sliced
150g rhubarb, trimmed and cut into 2cm lengths
⅓ cup (75g) caster (superfine) sugar
1 vanilla bean, split and seeds scraped
1 egg, lightly beaten
2 tablespoons raw or Demerara sugar*
pastry
1½ cups (225g) plain (all-purpose) flour
¼ cup (55g) caster (superfine) sugar
1 teaspoon finely grated orange rind
100g cold unsalted butter, chopped
2 teaspoons apple cider vinegar
¼ cup (60ml) iced water
1 teaspoon vanilla extract

To make the pastry, place the flour, sugar and orange rind
in a large bowl and mix to combine. Add the butter and,
using your fingertips, rub into the flour mixture until it
resembles fine breadcrumbs. Add the vinegar, water and
vanilla and, using a butter knife, mix until a rough dough
forms. Gently knead to bring the dough together. Shape into
a disc and wrap in plastic wrap. Refrigerate for 30 minutes
or until firm.

Preheat oven to 200°C (400°F). Roll out the pastry
between 2 sheets of non-stick baking paper to a 4mm-thick
35cm round. Place on a large baking tray and remove the
top sheet of paper. Place the ricotta and orange rind in a
medium bowl and mix to combine. Spread over the pastry,
leaving a 5cm border. Place the strawberry, rhubarb,
caster sugar, vanilla bean and seeds in a medium bowl
and toss well to combine. Top the ricotta with the fruit
mixture. Fold in the edges of the pastry, pressing gently
to enclose. Brush the edges with egg and sprinkle with the
raw sugar. Refrigerate for 10 minutes.

Bake for 10 minutes. Reduce the heat to 180°C (350°F)
and bake for a further 40 minutes or until the pastry is
golden and the fruit is bubbling.

Allow the tart to cool on the tray for 10 minutes before
serving. **SERVES 8-10**

strawberry, ricotta and rhubarb tart

raspberry and ginger ice-cream cheesecakes

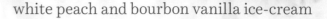

raspberry and ginger ice-cream cheesecakes

160g store-bought ginger nut (ginger snap) biscuits
2 tablespoons almond meal (ground almonds)
65g unsalted butter, melted
strawberries, blueberries and extra raspberries, to serve
cheesecake filling
125g raspberries[+]
2 tablespoons caster (superfine) sugar
250g cream cheese, softened
500ml store-bought vanilla ice-cream

Line 4 x 10cm round (1½-cup-capacity) springform tins
with non-stick baking paper. Place the biscuits and almond
meal in a food processor and process into coarse crumbs.
Add the butter and process until just combined. Divide the
mixture between the tins and gently press into the bases.
Freeze for 15 minutes or until firm.

To make the cheesecake filling, place the raspberries
and sugar in a medium non-stick frying pan over high heat.
Cook, stirring, for 2–3 minutes or until softened. Transfer
to a bowl and refrigerate until cold. Place the cream cheese
and the raspberry mixture in a food processor and process
until smooth. Add the ice-cream and process until smooth.

Working quickly, top each of the bases with the filling.
Smooth the tops and return the tins to the freezer for
1–2 hours or until firm.

Remove the cakes from the tins and place on cake stands
or plates. Top with berries and serve immediately[++]. **MAKES 4**
+ *You can also use frozen raspberries in this recipe.*
++ *We used the flowers from strawberry plants to decorate.*
Always choose pesticide-free flowers and remove before eating.

white peach and bourbon vanilla ice-cream

1 litre water
1½ cups (330g) caster (superfine) sugar
8 medium white peaches (1.2kg)
2 cups (500ml) milk
1 cup (250ml) single (pouring) cream*
1 teaspoon vanilla bean paste or vanilla extract
8 egg yolks
⅔ cup (150g) caster (superfine) sugar, extra
¼ cup (60ml) bourbon
18 store-bought amaretti biscuits* (65g), crushed to serve

Place the water and sugar in a large saucepan over high
heat, bring to the boil and stir until the sugar is dissolved.
Add the peaches, cover with a round of non-stick baking
paper and weigh down with a small plate to submerge.
Reduce the heat to medium and cook for 15–20 minutes or
until soft. Drain the peaches, reserving the syrup. Allow
to cool slightly, before peeling. Refrigerate half the peaches
for 1–2 hours or until cold. Cut the remaining peaches in
half, discarding the stones, and place in a food processor.
Process until smooth and refrigerate until cold.

Place the milk, cream and vanilla in a medium saucepan
over high heat and stir until just boiling. Remove from the
heat and set aside. Place the egg yolks and extra sugar in a
large bowl and whisk until well combined. Gradually pour
the milk mixture into the egg mixture, whisking to combine.
Return the mixture to the saucepan over low heat and cook,
stirring, for 8 minutes or until the custard is thick and coats
the back of a spoon. Transfer to a large bowl, cover with
plastic wrap and refrigerate for 1–2 hours or until cold.

Add the bourbon and the peach puree to the custard and
whisk to combine. Pour into a 20cm x 30cm slice tin or
metal container. Freeze for 8 hours or overnight until set.

Cut the ice-cream into squares. In batches, place the
squares in the cleaned food processor and process until
smooth. Return the mixture to the tin and freeze for 1 hour
or until firm.

Scoop the ice-cream into serving bowls. Drizzle with
the reserved peach syrup and sprinkle with the amaretti.
Serve with the whole poached peaches. **SERVES 4–6**

white peach and bourbon vanilla ice-cream

nectarine and honey tray pie

nectarine and honey tray pie

4 medium white nectarines (500g), sliced
4 medium yellow nectarines (500g), sliced
½ cup (110g) caster (superfine) sugar
2 tablespoons honey
2 teaspoons vanilla extract
2 tablespoons cornflour (cornstarch)
½ cup (60g) almond meal (ground almonds)
1 egg, lightly beaten
white (granulated) sugar, for sprinkling
pastry
4½ cups (675g) plain (all-purpose) flour, plus extra for dusting
375g cold unsalted butter, chopped
1½ cups (240g) icing (confectioner's) sugar
4 egg yolks
2 tablespoons iced water

To make the pastry, place the flour, butter and sugar in a food processor and process until the mixture resembles fine breadcrumbs. With the motor running, add the egg yolks and water and process until a dough just comes together. Turn out the dough onto a lightly floured surface and gently knead to bring it together. Divide the dough in half and shape into 2 discs. Wrap in plastic wrap and refrigerate for 1 hour or until firm.

Preheat oven to 160°C (325°F). Place the nectarine, caster sugar, honey, vanilla and cornflour in a large bowl. Gently mix to combine and set aside.

Roll out 1 piece of the dough between 2 sheets of non-stick baking paper to 3mm thick. Use the pastry to line the base of a 25cm x 37cm Swiss roll tin. Sprinkle the base with the almond meal and top with the nectarine mixture. Roll out the remaining dough, as above. Place it over the top of the pie. Press the edges with a fork to seal and trim any excess pastry. Using a sharp knife, cut a cross in the centre of the pie. Brush the pastry with egg and sprinkle with the white sugar. Bake for 55 minutes – 1 hour or until golden. **SERVES 8**

nectarine and semolina cake

125g unsalted butter, softened
¾ cup (165g) caster (superfine) sugar
2 teaspoons vanilla extract
2 eggs
1 cup (150g) plain (all-purpose) flour, sifted
2 teaspoons baking powder, sifted
1 cup (160g) fine semolina*
1 cup (250ml) buttermilk
4 medium nectarines (500g), thinly sliced
1 tablespoon caster (superfine) sugar, extra
2 tablespoons honey
¼ cup (60ml) orange juice

Preheat oven to 160°C (325°F). Lightly grease a 30cm round heavy-based ovenproof dish. Place the butter and sugar in the bowl of an electric mixer and beat for 6–8 minutes or until pale and creamy. Scrape down the sides of the bowl. Add the vanilla and the eggs, 1 at a time, beating well after each addition. Add the flour, baking powder, semolina and buttermilk and beat until just combined. Pour into the dish. Place the nectarine and the extra sugar in a large bowl and toss to combine. Arrange on top of the cake mixture and bake for 40–45 minutes or until golden and cooked when tested with a skewer.

Place the honey and juice in a small bowl, mix to combine and spoon over the warm cake. Allow the cake to cool slightly in the dish before serving. **SERVES 8-10**

nectarine and semolina cake

apricot and cinnamon dutch pancakes

apricot and cinnamon dutch pancakes

¼ cup (55g) caster (superfine) sugar
4 apricots (240g), halved
20g unsalted butter, melted
store-bought vanilla ice-cream, to serve
2 tablespoons ginger syrup, to serve⁺
pancake batter
4 eggs
¾ cup (180ml) milk
2 teaspoons vanilla extract
¾ cup (110g) plain (all-purpose) flour
½ teaspoon ground cinnamon
¼ cup (55g) caster (superfine) sugar

Preheat oven to 220°C (425°F). Place the sugar on a small plate. Place a medium non-stick frying pan over medium heat. Press the apricot halves, cut-side down, into the sugar. Cook, sugar-side down, for 2–3 minutes or until caramelised.

Preheat 2 x 14cm (1-litre-capacity) heavy-based ovenproof frying pans (skillets) in the oven for 5 minutes.

To make the pancake batter, place the eggs in a blender and blend for 2 minutes or until pale and frothy. Add the milk, vanilla, flour, cinnamon and sugar and blend for 1 minute or until well combined.

Carefully remove the pans from the oven and brush them generously with the butter. Divide the batter between the pans and return to the oven. Bake for 8–10 minutes or until golden and puffed.

Top the pancakes with the ice-cream, apricots and ginger syrup and serve immediately. SERVES 4
+ *Ginger syrup is available from the toppings section of some supermarkets and from specialty food stores.*

coconut and nectarine brown butter tart

2 eggs
⅓ cup (75g) caster (superfine) sugar
¼ cup (35g) plain (all-purpose) flour
½ cup (40g) desiccated coconut
75g unsalted butter, chopped
4 medium white nectarines (500g), each cut into 8 wedges
1 tablespoon caster (superfine) sugar, extra
⅓ cup (25g) freshly grated coconut
sweet shortcrust pastry
1¾ cups (255g) plain (all-purpose) flour
½ cup (80g) icing (confectioner's) sugar
125g cold unsalted butter, chopped
2 egg yolks
1 tablespoon iced water

To make the sweet shortcrust pastry, place the flour, sugar and butter in a food processor and process until the mixture resembles fine breadcrumbs. With the motor running, add the egg yolks and water and process until a dough just comes together. Turn out and bring the dough together to form a ball. Roll out the dough between 2 sheets of non-stick baking paper to 4mm thick. Refrigerate the pastry for 1 hour.

Preheat oven to 160°C (325°F). Line a 22cm loose-based fluted tart tin with the pastry. Trim the edges and prick the base with a fork. Refrigerate for 30 minutes. Line the pastry case with non-stick baking paper and fill with baking weights or uncooked rice. Bake for 10–12 minutes, remove the paper and weights and bake for a further 12–15 minutes or until the pastry is light golden. Allow to cool slightly in the tin.

Place the eggs and sugar in a food processor and process for 5 minutes or until pale. Add the flour and desiccated coconut and process to combine. Place the butter in a small non-stick frying pan over medium heat and stir until melted. Cook for a further 1–2 minutes or until golden brown with a nutty fragrance. With the processor running, add the butter to the coconut mixture in a thin, steady stream and process for 2 minutes or until well combined.

Increase the oven temperature to 180°C (350°F). Spoon the coconut mixture into the pastry case and spread evenly. Place the nectarine and extra sugar in a medium bowl and toss to combine. Arrange the nectarine over the tart filling, sprinkle with the fresh coconut and bake for 35–40 minutes or until golden and cooked through.

Allow the tart to cool completely in the tin, before placing on a cake stand or plate to serve. SERVES 6-8

coconut and nectarine brown butter tart

lemon, chia and ricotta muffins

lemon, chia and ricotta muffins

2½ cups (375g) self-raising (self-rising) flour
1 cup (220g) caster (superfine) sugar
2 tablespoons finely grated lemon rind
⅓ cup (65g) black chia seeds, plus extra for sprinkling[+]
1 cup (240g) fresh firm ricotta
2 eggs, lightly beaten
2 teaspoons vanilla extract
1 cup (280g) natural Greek-style (thick) yoghurt
½ cup (125ml) vegetable oil
lemon glaze
1 cup (160g) icing (confectioner's) sugar
1½ tablespoons lemon juice

Preheat oven to 180°C (350°F). Grease 12 x ½-cup-capacity (125ml) muffin tins. Place the flour, sugar, lemon rind and chia seeds in a large bowl and mix to combine. Add the ricotta, egg, vanilla, yoghurt and oil and, using a butter knife, mix until just combined. Spoon into the tins. Bake for 20–25 minutes or until cooked when tested with a skewer. Allow to cool in the tins for 2 minutes, before transferring to a wire rack to cool completely.

To make the lemon glaze, place the sugar and lemon juice in a small bowl and whisk to combine.

Sprinkle the muffins with extra chia seeds and, using a teaspoon, drizzle with the lemon glaze to serve. MAKES 12
+ *Find chia seeds in the health food aisle of supermarkets.*

upside-down maple and pear muffins

2 small Williams (firm green) pears (400g)
¼ cup (60ml) maple syrup, plus extra to serve
1¼ cups (185g) self-raising (self-rising) flour
¼ teaspoon ground nutmeg
¼ teaspoon ground cinnamon
¼ cup (55g) caster (superfine) sugar
1 egg, lightly beaten
1 teaspoon vanilla extract
¼ cup (60ml) milk
¼ cup (60ml) vegetable oil

Preheat oven to 180°C (350°F). Grease 6 x ¾-cup-capacity (180ml) Texas muffin tins. Slice 3 x 1cm-thick rounds from each pear to fit the base of the tins, reserving any unused pear. Place a pear round in the base of each tin. Pour the maple syrup over the pear in the tins and bake for 10 minutes or until the pear is tender.

Peel and grate the reserved pear and place it in a large bowl. Add the flour, nutmeg, cinnamon and sugar and mix to combine. Add the egg, vanilla, milk and oil, and, using a butter knife, mix until just combined. Divide the mixture between the pear-lined tins, tapping gently to settle. Bake for 15 minutes or until cooked when tested with a skewer.

Invert the tins onto a tray and allow to cool for 5 minutes. Serve muffins warm with extra maple syrup. MAKES 6

upside-down maple and pear muffins

yoghurt and passionfruit syrup cake

yoghurt and passionfruit syrup cake

¾ cup (180ml) vegetable oil
2 eggs
1 cup (280g) natural Greek-style (thick) yoghurt
1 cup (220g) caster (superfine) sugar
2 cups (300g) self-raising (self-rising) flour, sifted
passionfruit syrup
1 cup (250ml) passionfruit pulp (about 12 passionfruit)
½ cup (125ml) water
½ cup (110g) caster (superfine) sugar

Preheat oven to 160°C (325°F). Grease a 2.5-litre-capacity Bundt tin. Place the oil, eggs, yoghurt and sugar in a large bowl and whisk to combine. Add the flour and whisk until smooth. Pour into the tin and bake for 50–55 minutes or until cooked when tested with a skewer. Invert the tin onto a wire rack and allow to stand for 10 minutes before removing the tin. Allow the cake to cool completely.

To make the passionfruit syrup, place the passionfruit, water and sugar in a small saucepan over medium heat and stir until the sugar is dissolved. Bring to the boil, reduce the heat to low and cook for 10–15 minutes or until thickened slightly. Allow to cool completely.

Place the cake on a cake stand or plate and spoon the syrup over to serve. **SERVES 6-8**

passionfruit tart with rum pineapple

1½ cups (375ml) single (pouring) cream*
3 eggs
5 egg yolks, extra
¾ cup (165g) caster (superfine) sugar
¼ cup (60ml) lemon juice
¾ cup (180ml) passionfruit pulp (about 9 passionfruit)
sweet shortcrust pastry
1½ cups (225g) plain (all-purpose) flour, plus extra for dusting
½ cup (80g) icing (confectioner's) sugar
125g cold unsalted butter, chopped
2 egg yolks
1 tablespoon iced water
caramelised rum pineapple
500g pineapple, peeled, cored and sliced into 3cm pieces
½ cup (125ml) passionfruit pulp (about 6 passionfruit)
½ cup (90g) light brown sugar
¼ cup (60ml) white rum

To make the sweet shortcrust pastry, place the flour, sugar and butter in a food processor and process until the mixture resembles fine breadcrumbs. With the motor running, add the egg yolks and water, and process until a dough just comes together. Turn out onto a lightly floured surface and gently bring the dough together to form a ball. Flatten into a disc, wrap in plastic wrap and refrigerate for 30 minutes.

Preheat oven to 160°C (325°F). Roll out the dough between 2 sheets of non-stick baking paper to 3mm thick. Line a 22cm loose-based tart tin with the pastry. Trim the edges and prick the base with a fork. Refrigerate for 30 minutes. Line the pastry case with non-stick baking paper and fill with baking weights or uncooked rice. Bake for 20 minutes, remove the paper and weights and bake for a further 10–12 minutes or until the pastry is light golden. Allow to cool slightly in the tin.

Reduce the oven temperature to 140°C (275°F). Place the cream, eggs, extra yolks, sugar and lemon juice in a medium bowl and whisk to combine. Strain the mixture into a clean bowl and add the passionfruit. Pour the mixture into the pastry case and bake for 30 minutes or until just set. Allow to cool to room temperature, before refrigerating until chilled.

To make the caramelised rum pineapple, place the pineapple, passionfruit and sugar in a large non-stick frying pan over high heat. Cook for 10 minutes or until caramelised. Add the rum and cook for 3 minutes. Allow to cool slightly.

Remove the tart from the tin and place on a serving plate. Top with the caramelised rum pineapple to serve. **SERVES 6**

passionfruit tart with rum pineapple

roasted peach and blueberry ice-cream sandwiches

roasted peach and blueberry ice-cream sandwiches

6 small yellow peaches (780g), cut into wedges
1 teaspoon vanilla extract
1¾ cups (385g) white (granulated) sugar
125g blueberries
1 tablespoon finely grated orange rind
12 sheets filo (phyllo) pastry
125g unsalted butter, melted
2 litres store-bought vanilla ice-cream

Preheat oven to 200°C (400°F). Place the peach, vanilla and ¾ cup (165g) of the sugar in small roasting pan and toss to combine. Bake for 15 minutes or until just softened. Add the blueberries and bake for a further 5 minutes or until just softened. Allow to cool completely.

While the fruit is baking, line 2 large baking trays with non-stick baking paper. Place the orange rind and the remaining 1 cup (220g) sugar in a small bowl and mix to combine. Place 1 filo sheet on 1 of the trays, brush with butter and sprinkle with 1 tablespoon of the sugar mixture⁺. Repeat 5 more times, stacking the pastry, finishing with butter and sugar. Repeat to make a second pastry stack on the remaining tray, using the remaining filo, butter and sugar. Bake for 10–12 minutes or until golden and crisp.

Line a 20cm x 30cm slice tin with non-stick baking paper. While the filo stacks are still warm, trim each to fit the tin. Place 1 of the stacks in the base of the tin and freeze until ready to use.

Scoop half the ice-cream into the bowl of an electric mixer and beat for 30 seconds. Add the remaining ice-cream and beat until soft. Working quickly, add the cooled fruit and mix to combine. Spoon into the tin, smooth the surface and top with the remaining filo stack. Freeze for 5 hours or overnight until set.

Remove the slice from the tin, cut into pieces and serve immediately. MAKES 12

+ *While making the pastry stacks, cover the unused filo sheets with a clean, damp tea towel to stop them from drying out.*

rhubarb soufflés

unsalted butter, melted, for greasing
caster (superfine) sugar, for dusting
6 eggwhites, at room temperature
¼ cup (55g) caster (superfine) sugar, extra
icing (confectioner's) sugar, for dusting
rhubarb puree
300g rhubarb, trimmed and chopped into 2cm pieces
½ cup (110g) caster (superfine) sugar
2 tablespoons water
1½ tablespoons cornflour (cornstarch)
1½ tablespoons water, extra

To make the rhubarb puree, place the rhubarb, sugar and water in a medium saucepan over medium heat. Bring to the boil and cook, stirring, for 8–10 minutes or until softened. Remove from the heat, allow to cool slightly and, using a hand-held stick blender, blend until smooth. Place the puree over high heat and cook, whisking occasionally, until just boiling. Place the cornflour and extra water in a small bowl and mix until smooth. Add to the puree and cook, whisking constantly, for 30 seconds – 1 minute or until thickened. Transfer to a large bowl and refrigerate until just cold.

Preheat oven to 180°C (350°F). Brush 6 x 1-cup-capacity (250ml) ovenproof ramekins with butter and dust with caster sugar. Place the eggwhites in the bowl of an electric mixer. Whisk until soft peaks form. Add the extra caster sugar in a thin steady stream and whisk until stiff and glossy.

Mix to soften the rhubarb puree. In 2 batches, add the rhubarb to the eggwhite and gently fold to combine. Spoon the mixture into the ramekins and smooth the tops. Run your fingertip, 1cm-deep, around the inside edge of each ramekin. Place on an oven tray and bake for 12–15 minutes or until puffy and golden.

Dust the warm soufflés with icing sugar and serve immediately. MAKES 6

rhubarb soufflés

white chocolate and rhubarb jam drops

white chocolate and rhubarb jam drops

250g unsalted butter, softened
¾ cup (165g) caster (superfine) sugar
2 teaspoons vanilla extract
1 egg yolk
150g white chocolate, melted
2¼ cups (335g) plain (all-purpose) flour, sifted
quick rhubarb jam
350g rhubarb, trimmed and chopped into 2cm pieces
1 cup (220g) caster (superfine) sugar
1 teaspoon vanilla bean paste or vanilla extract
2 tablespoons water

Preheat oven to 160°C (325°F). To make the quick rhubarb jam, place the rhubarb, sugar, vanilla and water in a medium saucepan over medium heat and bring to the boil. Cook, stirring, for 10–12 minutes or until thickened. Allow to cool completely.

Place the butter and sugar in the bowl of an electric mixer and beat for 8–10 minutes or until pale and creamy. Scrape down the sides of the bowl, add the vanilla, egg yolk and chocolate and beat to combine. Add the flour and beat on low speed until a smooth dough forms. Cover the dough with plastic wrap and refrigerate for 30 minutes or until firm.

Line 2 large baking trays with non-stick baking paper. Roll 1-tablespoon portions of the dough into balls and place on the trays, allowing room to spread. Flatten slightly and, using your finger, make a deep indent in the centre of each round+. Fill each biscuit with ½ teaspoon of the jam. Bake for 15–20 minutes or until light golden in colour.

Allow the jam drops to cool on the trays for 5 minutes, before transferring to wire racks to cool completely. **MAKES 36**
+ It's best to work quickly when flattening and indenting the rounds of dough – if they dry out, the biscuits can crack. Tip: You will have some jam leftover. Keep it in an airtight container in the fridge for up to 2 weeks.

rhubarb and brown butter friands

500g rhubarb, trimmed and chopped into 8cm lengths
⅓ cup (75g) caster (superfine) sugar
2 tablespoons water
175g unsalted butter, chopped
1¼ cups (150g) almond meal (ground almonds)
2 cups (320g) icing (confectioner's) sugar, sifted
1 cup (150g) plain (all-purpose) flour, sifted
1 teaspoon baking powder, sifted
6 eggwhites
1 tablespoon finely grated lemon rind
white (granulated) sugar, for sprinkling

Preheat oven to 180°C (350°F). Place the rhubarb, caster sugar and water in a roasting pan+ and toss to combine. Arrange the rhubarb in a single layer, cover with aluminium foil and bake for 15–18 minutes or until the rhubarb is soft but still holding its shape. Allow to cool slightly. Drain the rhubarb and reserve the syrup.

Place the butter in a large non-stick frying pan over high heat and stir until melted. Cook for 2–3 minutes or until golden brown with a nutty fragrance. Transfer to a small bowl and allow to cool to room temperature.

Grease 10 x ¾-cup-capacity (180ml) rectangular tins. Place the almond meal, icing sugar, flour and baking powder in a large bowl and whisk to combine. Make a well in the centre, add the eggwhites, the browned butter and lemon rind and whisk until well combined. Divide the mixture between the tins. Top each friand with rhubarb. Sprinkle with white sugar and bake for 30–35 minutes or until golden and cooked when tested with a skewer.

Carefully run a small knife around the inside edges of the tins and place the friands on a wire rack to cool. Serve with the reserved rhubarb syrup. **MAKES 10**
+ Choose a roasting pan with sides in which the rhubarb will fit snugly in a single layer.

rhubarb and brown butter friands

smashed pavlova with mulberries and roasted raspberry jam

smashed pavlova with mulberries and roasted raspberry jam

225ml eggwhite (about 6 eggs), at room temperature[+]
1½ cups (330g) caster (superfine) sugar
1½ teaspoons white vinegar
1½ cups (375ml) single (pouring) cream*
200g mulberries[++]
micro (baby) mint leaves, to serve
icing (confectioner's) sugar, for dusting
roasted raspberry jam
500g raspberries
¾ cup (165g) caster (superfine) sugar
1 vanilla bean, split and seeds scraped

Preheat oven to 220°C (425°F). To make the raspberry jam, place the raspberries, sugar, vanilla bean and seeds in a small roasting pan and toss to combine. Bake, stirring occasionally, for 25–30 minutes or until thickened. Allow to cool completely. Remove and discard the vanilla pods.

Reduce the oven temperature to 150°C (300°F). Place the eggwhite in the bowl of an electric mixer and whisk on high speed until stiff peaks form. Add the sugar, 1 tablespoon at a time, whisking for 30 seconds before adding more. Scrape down the sides of the bowl. Whisk for a further 6 minutes or until glossy. Add the vinegar and whisk for 2 minutes.

Line a baking tray with non-stick baking paper. Place spoonfuls of the meringue onto the tray to make a rough 22cm round. Reduce the oven temperature to 120°C (250°F) and bake for 1 hour. Turn the oven off and allow the pavlova to cool completely in the oven with the door closed.

Place the cream in a clean bowl of the electric mixer and whisk until stiff peaks form. Place the pavlova on a large serving plate and gently crush with the back of a large spoon. Top with the cream and drizzle with the roasted raspberry jam. Sprinkle with the mulberries and mint and dust with icing sugar to serve. **SERVES 8-10**
+ *Making meringue is a science – be sure to measure the eggwhites carefully, remembering egg sizes do vary.*
++ *Mulberries are available from greengrocers when in season. You can also swap in blackberries or your favourite type of berries.*

salted honey and apple tarte tatin

100g unsalted butter, chopped
½ cup (180g) honey, plus extra to serve
800g Granny Smith (green) apples (about 6 apples), peeled and cut into 1cm-thick slices
2 sheets frozen butter puff pastry, thawed
½ teaspoon sea salt flakes

Preheat oven to 200°C (400°F). Place the butter and honey in a 21cm heavy-based ovenproof frying pan (skillet) over high heat. Bring to the boil and cook for 1–2 minutes or until thickened slightly. Arrange the apple slices on top and set aside.

Press the pastry sheets together to make 1 thick sheet[+]. Using a plate as a guide, cut a 24cm round from the pastry. Place the pastry over the apples and press down gently to secure. Using a sharp knife, make 3 small incisions in the centre of the pastry. Place the pan on an oven tray and bake for 35–40 minutes or until the pastry is dark golden.

Allow the tart to cool in the pan for 2 minutes before carefully turning out onto a serving plate[++]. Sprinkle with the salt to serve. **SERVES 4**
+ *By layering sheets of store-bought puff pastry twice, you'll instantly get a more buttery and flaky base that's puffed to perfection.*
++ *To turn out the tarte tatin, loosen the edges of the pastry with a palette knife, then place a serving plate over the skillet and, using a tea towel, carefully invert.*

salted honey and apple tarte tatin

chocolate, banana and malt tarte tatin

chocolate, banana and malt tarte tatin

150g unsalted butter, chopped
½ cup (125ml) malt extract, plus extra for drizzling[+]
50g dark chocolate, finely chopped
1kg bananas (about 6 bananas), peeled and halved lengthways
2 sheets frozen butter puff pastry, thawed
store-bought vanilla ice-cream, to serve
¼ cup (35g) store-bought beer nuts, roughly chopped

Preheat oven to 200°C (400°F). Place the butter and malt extract in a 21cm heavy-based ovenproof frying pan (skillet) over high heat. Bring to a simmer and cook for 30 seconds or until slightly thickened. Remove from the heat, add the chocolate and stir until smooth.

Arrange the bananas, cut-side down and overlapping, on top of the chocolate mixture. Press the pastry sheets together to make 1 thick sheet. Using a plate as a guide, cut a 24cm round from the pastry. Place the pastry over the bananas and press down gently to secure. Using a sharp knife, make 3 small incisions in the centre of the pastry. Place the pan on an oven tray and bake for 30–35 minutes or until the pastry is dark golden. Allow the tart to cool in the pan for 2 minutes before carefully turning out onto a serving plate[++]. Top with the ice-cream and nuts and drizzle with extra malt extract to serve. **SERVES 4-6**
[+] *Malt extract comes from the barley grain and is a thick, dark syrup. It's available from supermarkets.*
[++] *To turn out the tarte tatin, loosen the edges of the pastry with a palette knife, then place a serving plate over the frying pan and, using a tea towel, carefully invert.*

cranberry jam scrolls

1¼ teaspoons dry yeast
⅔ cup (160ml) lukewarm milk
2½ tablespoons caster (superfine) sugar
3¼ cups (485g) plain (all-purpose) flour, plus extra for dusting
¼ teaspoon table salt
2 eggs
125g unsalted butter, melted
1½ cups (240g) icing (confectioner's) sugar, sifted
1 tablespoon boiling water
cranberry jam
4 cups (600g) frozen cranberries
1 cup (220g) caster (superfine) sugar
2 tablespoons lemon juice
1 vanilla bean, split and seeds scraped

Place the yeast, milk and 2 teaspoons of the caster sugar in a small bowl and mix to combine. Allow to stand in a warm place for 5–10 minutes or until the surface is foamy.

Place the flour, salt, eggs, butter, the yeast mixture and the remaining 2 tablespoons of caster sugar in the bowl of an electric mixer fitted with a dough hook. Beat on low speed for 5 minutes or until the dough is smooth and elastic. Transfer to a large lightly greased bowl, cover with a clean damp tea towel and set aside in a warm place for 1 hour or until the dough has doubled in size.

While the dough is proving, make the cranberry jam. Place a large non-stick frying pan over high heat. Add the cranberries, sugar, lemon juice, vanilla bean and seeds and cook, stirring, for 9–10 minutes or until reduced and sticky. Allow to cool completely and discard the vanilla pod.

Line a 20cm x 30cm slice tin with non-stick baking paper. Roll out the dough on a lightly floured surface to form a 25cm x 60cm rectangle. Spread with the cranberry jam, leaving a 1cm border. Starting from 1 long edge, roll up the dough tightly to enclose the filling. Trim the edges and slice into 12 rounds. Arrange the scrolls in the tin. Cover with plastic wrap and set aside in a warm place for 45 minutes or until doubled in size.

Preheat oven to 180°C (350°F). Bake the scrolls for 25–30 minutes or until risen and golden brown. Allow to cool in the tin for 10 minutes before placing on a wire rack to cool completely.

Place the icing sugar and water in a small bowl, whisk to combine and drizzle over the scrolls to serve. **MAKES 12**

cranberry jam scrolls

blood orange braided brioche loaf

blood orange braided brioche loaf

1¼ teaspoons dry yeast
⅓ cup (80ml) lukewarm milk
¼ cup (55g) caster (superfine) sugar
3¼ cups (485g) plain (all-purpose) flour, plus extra for dusting
¼ teaspoon sea salt flakes
⅓ cup (80g) crème fraîche*
2 eggs
125g unsalted butter, melted
1 cup (160g) icing (confectioner's) sugar, sifted
2 teaspoons boiling water
blood orange jam
1.2kg blood oranges (about 8 oranges), peeled and chopped
¾ cup (165g) caster (superfine) sugar
1 teaspoon vanilla extract

Place the yeast, milk and 2 teaspoons of the caster sugar in a small bowl and mix to combine. Allow to stand in a warm place for 5–10 minutes or until the surface is foamy.

Place the flour, salt, crème fraîche, eggs, butter, the remaining 2½ tablespoons of caster sugar and the yeast mixture in the bowl of an electric mixer with a dough hook attached. Beat on low speed for 5 minutes or until the dough is smooth and elastic. Place in a lightly greased bowl, cover with a clean damp tea towel and set aside in a warm place for 1 hour 30 minutes – 2 hours or until the dough has doubled in size.

While the dough is proving, make the blood orange jam. Place a large deep-sided frying pan over high heat. Add the orange, sugar and vanilla and cook for 15 minutes or until thickened. Transfer to a large bowl and refrigerate until cool.

Line a 10cm x 20cm loaf tin with non-stick baking paper. Roll out the dough on a lightly floured surface to make a 30cm x 60cm rectangle. Spread with the blood orange jam, leaving a 1cm border. Starting from 1 long edge, roll up the dough tightly to enclose the filling. Cut the roll in half lengthways and twist the pieces together. Gently place the loaf in the tin. Cover with plastic wrap and set aside in a warm place for 30 minutes or until risen.

Preheat oven to 160°C (325°F). Bake the brioche for 40–45 minutes or until golden brown and cooked when tested with a skewer. Allow to cool slightly in the tin before turning out onto a wire rack to cool completely.

Place the icing sugar and water in a small bowl, whisk to combine and drizzle over the brioche to serve. **SERVES 10–12**

summer pineapple and passionfruit pavlova

1.5kg pineapple (about 1 pineapple), peeled and cored
½ cup (125ml) passionfruit pulp (about 6 passionfruit)
¼ cup (60ml) lime juice
1 vanilla bean, halved and seeds scraped
icing (confectioner's) sugar, for dusting
single (pouring) cream*, whipped to serve
meringue
300ml eggwhite (about 8 eggs)[+], at room temperature
2 cups (440g) caster (superfine) sugar
2 teaspoons white vinegar

To make the meringue, preheat oven to 150°C (300°F). Place the eggwhite in the bowl of an electric mixer and whisk on high speed until stiff peaks form. Add the sugar, 1 tablespoon at a time, whisking for 30 seconds before adding more. Scrape down the sides of the bowl and whisk for a further 6 minutes or until stiff and glossy. Add the vinegar and whisk for 2 minutes.

Cut the pineapple into thin triangles and place in a 22cm x 28cm deep-sided baking dish. Add the passionfruit, lime juice and vanilla seeds and toss to combine. Top the fruit with large spoonfuls of the meringue mixture. Bake for 1 hour or until the meringue is dry to the touch. Allow to cool for 10 minutes.

Dust with icing sugar and spoon the meringue onto serving plates. Top with the pineapple and passionfruit syrup and serve with whipped cream. **SERVES 6–8**
+ *Making meringue is a science – be sure to measure the eggwhites carefully, remembering egg sizes do vary.*

summer pineapple and passionfruit pavlova

pineapple and ginger upside-down cake

pineapple and ginger upside-down cake

190g unsalted butter, softened
1¼ cups (275g) caster (superfine) sugar
3 eggs
2 cups (300g) plain (all-purpose) flour, sifted
1 tablespoon ground ginger
1½ teaspoons baking powder, sifted
½ teaspoon bicarbonate of (baking) soda, sifted
½ cup (60g) almond meal (ground almonds)
1 cup (250ml) buttermilk
pineapple syrup
450g pineapple (about half a pineapple),
   peeled, cored and thinly sliced lengthways
½ cup (110g) caster (superfine) sugar
1½ cups (375ml) water
20g ginger, peeled and sliced

To make the pineapple syrup, place the pineapple, sugar, water and ginger in a saucepan and bring to the boil over medium heat. Cook for 10 minutes or until the pineapple is tender. Carefully remove the pineapple slices and set aside to cool slightly. Return the syrup to the heat and cook for 6–8 minutes or until thickened slightly. Remove and discard the ginger.

Preheat oven to 180°C (350°F). Line the sides of a 22cm round cake tin with non-stick baking paper. Arrange the pineapple slices, overlapping slightly, in the base of the tin and pour over half the syrup. Place the butter and sugar in an electric mixer and beat for 8–10 minutes or until pale and creamy. Scrape down the sides of the bowl and add the eggs, 1 at a time, beating well after each addition. Add the flour, ginger, baking powder, bicarbonate of soda, almond meal and buttermilk and beat on low speed until just combined. Spoon the mixture over the pineapple and bake for 1 hour. Cover loosely with aluminium foil and bake for a further 15–20 minutes or until cooked when tested with a skewer. Allow to cool in the tin for 10 minutes.

While the cake is cooling, place the remaining syrup over medium heat and bring to the boil. Cook for 3–4 minutes or until thickened.

Turn the cake out onto a serving plate. Top with the hot syrup to serve. **SERVES 8–10**

semolina, almond and blood orange syrup cakes

3 eggs
½ cup (110g) caster (superfine) sugar
1 cup (280g) natural Greek-style (thick) yoghurt
¼ cup (60ml) light-flavoured extra virgin olive oil
1 teaspoon vanilla extract
1 teaspoon finely grated blood orange rind
1 cup (160g) fine semolina*
¼ cup (35g) plain (all-purpose) flour, sifted
1 teaspoon baking powder, sifted
⅓ cup (40g) almond meal (ground almonds)
2 blood oranges, thinly sliced
2 tablespoons caster (superfine) sugar, extra
icing (confectioner's) sugar, to serve
blood orange syrup
½ cup (125ml) blood orange juice
¼ cup (60ml) water
⅓ cup (75g) caster (superfine) sugar

Preheat oven to 180°C (350°F). Grease 12 x ½-cup-capacity (125ml) muffin tins. Place the eggs and caster sugar in the bowl of an electric mixer and whisk on high speed for 3–4 minutes or until pale and thick. Add the yoghurt, oil, vanilla, orange rind, semolina, flour, baking powder and almond meal and fold to combine. Spoon the mixture into the tins. Top each cake with an orange slice and sprinkle with the extra caster sugar. Bake for 15–18 minutes or until golden and cooked when tested with a skewer. Allow the cakes to cool slightly in the tins before turning out onto wire racks to cool completely.

To make the blood orange syrup, place the juice, water and sugar in a small saucepan over high heat. Bring to the boil and cook for 4–5 minutes or until reduced and syrupy.

Spoon the blood orange syrup over the cakes and dust with icing sugar to serve. **MAKES 12**

semolina, almond and
blood orange syrup cakes

peach, honey and vanilla pie

peach, honey and vanilla pie

1.2kg small ripe peaches (about 10 peaches), thinly sliced
2 tablespoons honey
1 cup (220g) caster (superfine) sugar
¼ cup (35g) arrowroot*
1 vanilla bean, split and seeds scraped
⅓ cup (40g) almond meal (ground almonds)
1 egg, lightly beaten
2 tablespoons raw or Demerara sugar*
pastry
3 cups (450g) plain (all-purpose) flour, plus extra for dusting
⅓ cup (75g) caster (superfine) sugar
1 teaspoon sea salt flakes
200g cold unsalted butter, chopped
1 tablespoon apple cider vinegar
½ cup (125ml) iced water

To make the pastry, place the flour, sugar and salt in a large bowl. Mix to combine. Add the butter and, using your fingertips, rub into the flour mixture until it resembles fine breadcrumbs. Add the vinegar and water and, using a butter knife, mix to form a rough dough. Gently knead to bring the dough together, shape into 2 equal discs and wrap each in plastic wrap. Refrigerate for 30 minutes or until firm.

Roll out 1 of the pastry discs between 2 sheets of lightly floured non-stick baking paper to 4mm thick and use it to line an 18cm round pie tin, trimming any excess. Refrigerate for 30 minutes.

Line a large tray with non-stick baking paper. Roll out the remaining pastry disc, as above, to 3mm thick and cut into 1.5cm-wide strips. Twist the pastry strips from each end and place on the tray. Refrigerate until needed.

Preheat oven to 180°C (350°F). Place the peach, honey, caster sugar, arrowroot and vanilla seeds in a large bowl and mix to combine. Spread the almond meal in the base of the pastry case and top with the peach mixture.

Starting in the centre of the pie, arrange the twisted pastry to create a spiral pattern over the filling, pressing to join each length of pastry. Brush the pastry with egg and sprinkle with raw sugar. Place on an oven tray and bake for 45–50 minutes or until the pastry is golden brown. Allow the pie to stand for 30 minutes before serving. **SERVES 6–8**

fig and almond pies

1.2kg figs (about 16 figs), cut into wedges
¼ cup (60ml) lemon juice
1½ cups (330g) caster (superfine) sugar
1 vanilla bean, split and seeds scraped
⅓ cup (40g) almond meal (ground almonds)
½ cup (40g) flaked almonds
1 egg, lightly beaten
2 tablespoons raw or Demerara sugar*
pastry
4½ cups (675g) plain (all-purpose) flour, plus extra for dusting
½ cup (110g) caster (superfine) sugar
1½ teaspoons sea salt flakes
300g cold unsalted butter, chopped
1½ tablespoons apple cider vinegar
¾ cup (180ml) iced water

To make the pastry, place the flour, sugar and salt in a large bowl and mix to combine. Add the butter and, using your fingertips, rub into the flour mixture until it resembles fine breadcrumbs. Add the vinegar and water and, using a butter knife, mix to form a rough dough. Gently knead to bring the dough together, shape into 2 equal discs and wrap each in plastic wrap. Refrigerate for 30 minutes or until firm.

Roll out each pastry disc between 2 sheets of lightly floured non-stick baking paper to 3mm thick. Cut 2 x 16cm circles from each piece of pastry, reserving the trimmings, and use them to line 4 x 9cm round pie tins. Refrigerate for 30 minutes.

Line a large tray with non-stick baking paper. Re-roll the trimmings to 3mm thick. Using a 4cm heart-shaped cutter, cut out 56 hearts, re-rolling the pastry as necessary. Place the hearts on the tray and refrigerate until needed.

Place the fig, lemon juice, caster sugar, vanilla bean and seeds in a large saucepan over high heat. Bring to the boil and cook, stirring, for 16–18 minutes or until thickened. Strain, discard the vanilla pod, and refrigerate the syrup and fig mixture separately until cool.

Preheat oven to 180°C (350°F). Divide the almond meal between the pastry cases and top with the fig mixture. Spoon 1 tablespoon of the syrup into each pie and top with the flaked almonds. Brush the rim of each pie with egg and top with the pastry hearts, overlapping and trimming any excess. Brush all over with egg and sprinkle with raw sugar. Place on oven trays and bake for 25–30 minutes or until golden brown. Stand for 10 minutes before serving. **MAKES 4**

fig and almond pies

pear and halva crumble loaf

pear and halva crumble loaf

100g unsalted butter, chopped
¾ cup (180ml) maple syrup
¼ cup (60ml) milk
2 eggs
2 teaspoons vanilla extract
2 cups (300g) self-raising (self-rising) flour
½ teaspoon bicarbonate of (baking) soda
150g halva, finely crumbled+
2 Packham (firm green) pears (500g), peeled and chopped
½ cup (60g) pecans, finely chopped
cacao crumble
40g unsalted butter, melted
½ cup (75g) self-raising (self-rising) flour
2 tablespoons light brown sugar
2 tablespoons cacao nibs*
¼ cup (30g) pecans, chopped

Preheat oven to 160°C (325°F). Line an 11cm x 21cm loaf tin with non-stick baking paper. Place the butter in a small non-stick frying pan over high heat and stir until melted. Cook for 3–4 minutes or until golden brown with a nutty fragrance. Transfer to a large bowl and allow to cool slightly. Add the maple syrup, milk, eggs and vanilla and whisk well to combine. Add the flour, bicarbonate of soda and halva and mix to combine. Add the pear and pecans and fold to combine. Pour into the tin.

To make the cacao crumble, place the butter, flour, sugar, cacao and pecans in a small bowl and mix to combine.

Sprinkle the cacao crumble over the loaf and bake for 1 hour 15 minutes to 1 hour 20 minutes or until cooked when tested with a skewer. Allow to cool in the tin completely, before slicing to serve. **SERVES 12**
+ Halva is a dense sesame-based sweet. You can find it in Middle-Eastern stores, delicatessens and specialty grocers.

blackberry and elderflower pie

1kg blackberries
¼ cup (60ml) elderflower cordial
1 cup (220g) caster (superfine) sugar
⅓ cup (50g) arrowroot*
½ cup (70g) unsalted pistachios, finely ground
1 egg, lightly beaten
2 tablespoons raw or Demerara sugar*
store-bought vanilla ice-cream, to serve
pastry
3 cups (450g) plain (all-purpose) flour, plus extra for dusting
⅓ cup (75g) caster (superfine) sugar
1 teaspoon sea salt flakes
200g cold unsalted butter, chopped
1 tablespoon apple cider vinegar
½ cup (125ml) iced water

To make the pastry, place the flour, sugar and salt in a large bowl and mix to combine. Add the butter and, using your fingertips, rub into the flour mixture until it resembles fine breadcrumbs. Add the vinegar and water and, using a butter knife, mix to form a rough dough. Gently knead to bring the dough together, shape into 2 equal discs and wrap each in plastic wrap. Refrigerate for 30 minutes or until firm.

Line a tray with non-stick baking paper. Roll out each pastry disc between 2 sheets of lightly floured non-stick baking paper to 4mm thick. Refrigerate 1 pastry sheet and use the remaining piece to line an 18cm round pie tin. Trim and reserve any excess. Refrigerate for 30 minutes. Place the trimmings on the tray and refrigerate until needed.

Preheat oven to 180°C (350°F). Place the blackberries, cordial, caster sugar and arrowroot in a large bowl and mix to combine. Spread the ground pistachios in the base of the pastry case and top with the blackberry filling. Place the remaining pastry sheet over the filling and press the edges to seal. Trim and reserve any excess pastry. Re-roll all the trimmings into a 2mm-thick 8cm x 40cm rectangle. Slice into 6 long strips, trimming the rough edges. Plait 3 strips and repeat with the remaining strips to form 2 plaits. Brush the pie rim with egg and arrange the plaits around the rim, pinching the ends to seal. Using a small sharp knife, cut 3 incisions in the centre of the pie. Brush all over with egg and sprinkle with raw sugar. Place on an oven tray and bake for 1 hour or until the pastry is golden brown. Allow to stand for 30 minutes. Top with scoops of the ice-cream to serve. **SERVES 6–8**

blackberry and elderflower pie

upside-down chocolate, hazelnut and pear cake

upside-down chocolate, hazelnut and pear cake

⅓ cup (60g) light brown sugar
5 Corella (rosy pink) pears (550g), halved
250g unsalted butter, chopped
1 cup (250ml) unsweetened almond milk*
2 eggs
⅔ cup (160g) sour cream*
1½ cups (225g) plain (all-purpose) flour
¼ cup (25g) cocoa powder
1½ teaspoons bicarbonate of (baking) soda
1½ cups (330g) caster (superfine) sugar
1 cup (100g) hazelnut meal (ground hazelnuts)
single (pouring) cream*, to serve

Preheat oven to 160°C (325°F). Line a 22cm round springform tin with non-stick baking paper, leaving 2cm paper above the rim. Place 2 tablespoons of the brown sugar on a small plate. Dip the cut side of each pear in the brown sugar. Place a large non-stick frying pan over high heat. Add the pear, sugar-side down, and cook for 5–6 minutes or until caramelised and golden. Arrange the pear, cut-side down, in the base of the tin.

Place 25g of the butter and the remaining 2 tablespoons of brown sugar in the pan and cook for 1 minute or until thickened slightly. Pour the butter mixture over the pear.

Place the almond milk and the remaining 225g of butter in the pan and cook, stirring, until the butter is melted. Transfer to a large bowl and add the eggs, sour cream, flour, cocoa, bicarbonate of soda, caster sugar and hazelnut meal. Whisk until combined and pour into the tin. Place on an oven tray and bake for 1 hour 30 minutes or until cooked when tested with a skewer. Allow the cake to cool in the tin for 15 minutes.

Remove the cake from the tin and place on a cake stand or plate. Serve with cream. SERVES 8

spiced apple cake

⅓ cup (75g) white (granulated) sugar
3 teaspoons ground cinnamon
3 red apples, cored and chopped
1¼ cups (185g) self-raising (self-rising) flour
¾ cup (165g) caster (superfine) sugar
¼ teaspoon ground nutmeg
2 eggs
¾ cup (180ml) milk
125g unsalted butter, melted
1 teaspoon vanilla extract

Preheat oven to 180°C (350°F). Lightly grease a 20cm (2-litre-capacity) heavy-based ovenproof frying pan (skillet). Place the white sugar and 2 teaspoons of the cinnamon in a large bowl and mix to combine. Place 2 tablespoons of the cinnamon sugar in a small bowl and set aside. Add the apple to the large bowl, toss to combine and set aside.

Place the flour, caster sugar, nutmeg, eggs, milk, butter, vanilla and the remaining 1 teaspoon of cinnamon in a medium bowl and whisk to combine. Place half the apple mixture in the base of the skillet, pour over the batter and top with the remaining apple. Sprinkle with the reserved cinnamon sugar. Place on an oven tray and bake for 30–35 minutes or until cooked when tested with a skewer. Serve warm from the pan. SERVES 6-8

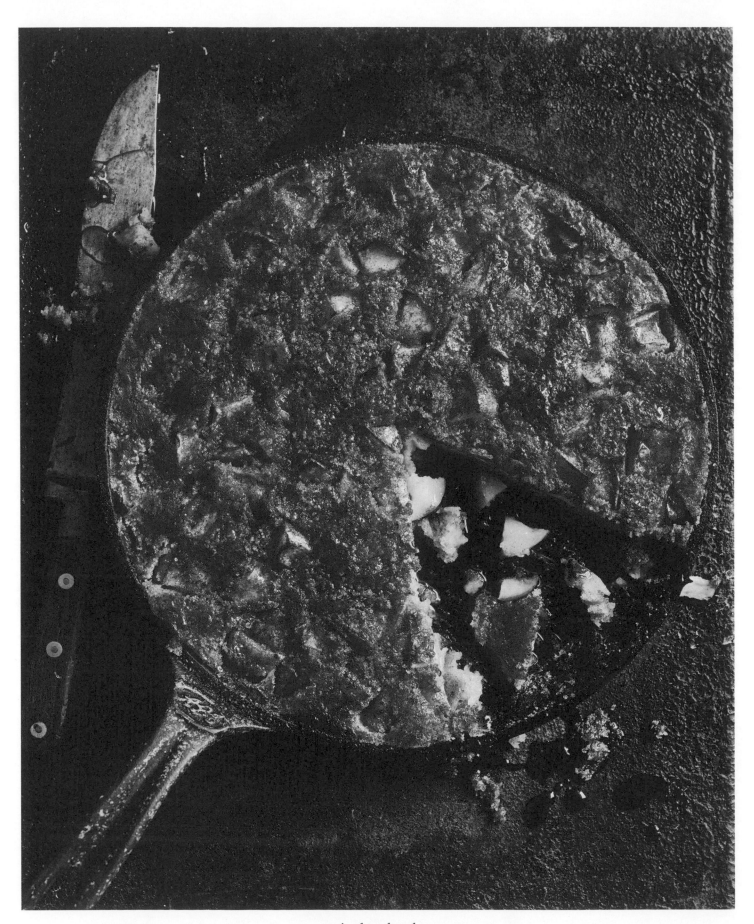

spiced apple cake

date and whiskey brioche pudding

date and whiskey brioche pudding

1½ cups (375ml) single (pouring) cream*
2 eggs
⅓ cup (100g) store-bought thick caramel or dulce de leche*
2 tablespoons light brown sugar
1 teaspoon vanilla extract
¼ cup (60ml) whiskey
250g store-bought brioche loaf, torn
7 soft fresh dates (140g), pitted and halved
2 tablespoons coffee sugar or Demerara sugar[+]

Preheat oven to 200°C (400°F). Place the cream, eggs, caramel, brown sugar, vanilla and 2 tablespoons of the whiskey in a large jug and whisk to combine.

Place the brioche and date in an 18cm (1-litre-capacity) heavy-based ovenproof frying pan (skillet). Top with the cream mixture and sprinkle with the coffee sugar. Place on an oven tray and bake for 18–20 minutes or until dark golden and the egg is set.

Drizzle with the remaining 1 tablespoon of whiskey and serve warm from the pan. **SERVES 4**
+ *Coffee sugar has a large granule and makes a crunchy sweet topping on desserts. Find it in the baking aisle of supermarkets. You could also use Demerara sugar.*

chocolate-dusted pavlovas with raspberries and pistachios

150ml eggwhite (about 4 eggs), at room temperature[+]
1 cup (220g) caster (superfine) sugar
1 teaspoon white vinegar
1 teaspoon cocoa powder
1½ cups (375ml) single (pouring) cream*
¼ cup (40g) icing (confectioner's) sugar, sifted
250g raspberries
2 tablespoons slivered pistachios, chopped

Preheat oven to 150°C (300°F). Line a large baking tray with non-stick baking paper. Place the eggwhite in the bowl of an electric mixer and whisk on high speed until stiff peaks form. Add the caster sugar, 1 tablespoon at a time, whisking for 30 seconds before adding more. Scrape down the sides of the bowl. Whisk for a further 6 minutes or until stiff and glossy. Add the vinegar and whisk for 2 minutes. Place 6 large spoonfuls of the mixture on the tray. Dust with the cocoa and bake for 50 minutes or until the meringues are dry to the touch. Turn the oven off and allow to cool completely in the oven with the door closed.

Place the cream and icing sugar in the bowl of an electric mixer and whisk until soft peaks form.

Top the meringues with the cream and sprinkle with the raspberries and pistachios to serve. **MAKES 6**
+ *Making meringue is a science – be sure to measure the eggwhites carefully, remembering egg sizes do vary.*

chocolate-dusted pavlovas
with raspberries and pistachios

QUICK

___

crushed raspberry tart
blackberry, lemon and yoghurt eton mess
pineapple and coconut sorbet sandwiches
lemon and blueberry ginger nut tarts
lemon curd impossible puddings
summer peach and passionfruit trifles
cheat's lemon cheesecake slice
lemongrass and kaffir lime fruit salad
rhubarb and almond hand pies
fig, yoghurt and honey parfaits
coconut, lime and lemon delicious pudding
apple and caramel hand pies
pina colada popsicles
pink grapefruit popsicles
pineapple, coconut and lemongrass popsicles
rockmelon and yoghurt popsicles

___

FIX

crushed raspberry tart

1 sheet frozen butter puff pastry, thawed
1 egg, lightly beaten
2 teaspoons caster (superfine) sugar
250g raspberries
2 tablespoons caster (superfine) sugar, extra
1½ cups (375ml) single (pouring) cream*
1 teaspoon vanilla extract

Preheat oven to 200°C (400°F). Line a large baking tray with non-stick baking paper. Place the pastry on the tray and, using a small sharp knife, score a 2cm border around the edge. Brush the border with egg and sprinkle with the sugar. Bake for 15 minutes or until puffed and golden. Set aside to cool a little.

Place the raspberries and extra sugar in a medium bowl and gently crush with a fork. Place the cream and vanilla in the bowl of an electric mixer and whisk until soft peaks form.

Spoon the cream onto the pastry and top with the crushed raspberries to serve. SERVES 6

blackberry, lemon and yoghurt eton mess

1 cup (150g) frozen blackberries+
1 tablespoon water
2 tablespoons icing (confectioner's) sugar, sifted,
   plus extra for dusting
1 cup (280g) natural Greek-style (thick) yoghurt
1 cup (250ml) single (pouring) cream*
½ cup (160g) store-bought lemon curd
50g store-bought mini meringues, crushed

Place the blackberries, water and 1 tablespoon of the sugar in a small saucepan over medium heat. Cook for 10 minutes or until reduced and syrupy. Transfer to a small bowl and refrigerate until cold.

Place the yoghurt, cream and remaining 1 tablespoon of sugar in the bowl of an electric mixer and whisk until soft peaks form.

Divide the yoghurt mixture, the lemon curd and the blackberry mixture between 4 x 1-cup-capacity (250ml) serving glasses to create a layered effect. Top with the meringue and dust with extra sugar to serve. SERVES 4
+ *You can also use frozen raspberries for this recipe.*

pineapple and coconut sorbet sandwiches

⅓ cup (25g) shredded coconut, toasted
2 tablespoons white (granulated) sugar
½ teaspoon vanilla bean paste or vanilla extract
1 small pineapple (750g), peeled, cored and sliced
   into 8 thin rounds
250ml store-bought coconut sorbet
2 tablespoons honey

Place the coconut in a mortar and crush with a pestle until coarse. Add the sugar and vanilla and mix to combine.

   Divide half the pineapple slices between serving plates and top each with a scoop of the sorbet. Sandwich with the remaining pineapple. Drizzle with the honey and sprinkle with the toasted coconut sugar to serve. SERVES 4

lemon and blueberry ginger nut tarts

250g store-bought ginger nut (ginger snap) biscuits
75g unsalted butter, melted
1 cup (250ml) single (pouring) cream*
1 cup (320g) store-bought lemon curd
125g blueberries, to serve

Line each of 6 x ½-cup-capacity (125ml) muffin tins with 2 strips of non-stick baking paper. Place the biscuits and butter in a food processor and process until fine. Place ¼-cup (60ml) portions of the biscuit mixture into each tin, pressing into the base and sides using the back of a spoon. Freeze for 15 minutes or until firm.

   Place the cream in a medium bowl and whisk until soft peaks form.

   Use the baking paper to help you remove the tart cases from the tins. Fill each case with the cream and top with the lemon curd and blueberries to serve. MAKES 6

lemon curd impossible puddings

1½ cups (375ml) milk
¾ cup (60g) desiccated coconut
50g unsalted butter, melted
3 eggs
⅓ cup (50g) plain (all-purpose) flour
1 cup (220g) caster (superfine) sugar
½ cup (160g) store-bought lemon curd
icing (confectioner's) sugar, for dusting

Preheat oven to 160°C (325°F). Place the milk, coconut, butter, eggs, flour, caster sugar and lemon curd in a blender and blend until smooth.

Divide the mixture between 6 x 1-cup-capacity (250ml) shallow ovenproof dishes. Place on an oven tray and bake for 18–20 minutes or until just set. Dust puddings with icing sugar to serve. MAKES 6

summer peach and passionfruit trifles

⅓ cup (80ml) passionfruit pulp (about 4 passionfruit)
¼ cup (90g) honey
⅓ cup (80ml) sweet dessert wine
12 store-bought sponge finger biscuits
1 cup (250ml) single (pouring) cream*
2 peaches, cut into wedges

Place the passionfruit and honey in a small non-stick frying pan over high heat and cook for 2–3 minutes or until reduced and thickened. Set aside to cool.

Place the wine in a small shallow bowl and add the biscuits, allowing them to soak a little. Place the cream in a medium bowl and whisk until soft peaks form.

Arrange 3 biscuits on each serving plate and top with cream and peach wedges. Spoon the passionfruit syrup over the trifles to serve. SERVES 4

cheat's lemon cheesecake slice

300g store-bought plain shortbread biscuits
100g unsalted butter, melted
1 cup (75g) shredded coconut
500g cream cheese, softened
180g white chocolate, melted
1½ cups (480g) store-bought lemon curd

Line a 20cm x 30cm slice tin with non-stick baking
paper. Place the biscuits, butter and coconut in a food
processor and process until fine. Using the back of a
spoon, firmly press the mixture into the base of the
tin. Refrigerate for 10 minutes or until firm.

Place the cream cheese, chocolate and 1 cup (320g)
of the lemon curd in the cleaned food processor and
process until smooth. Spread onto the shortbread base.
Gently spoon the remaining ½ cup (160g) lemon curd
over the slice to create a swirled effect. Refrigerate for
2 hours or until set. Remove from the tin and cut into
bars to serve. MAKES 20

lemongrass and kaffir lime fruit salad

1 stalk lemongrass, halved
6 kaffir lime leaves*
½ cup (110g) caster (superfine) sugar
½ cup (125ml) water
2 mangoes, cheeks sliced, peeled and halved
125g raspberries
natural Greek-style (thick) yoghurt, to serve

Place the lemongrass, lime leaves, sugar and water
in a small saucepan over high heat. Bring to the boil
and cook for 5 minutes or until syrupy. Allow to cool.

Place the mango and raspberries on a large serving
plate. Top with the lemongrass syrup. Serve the fruit
salad with yoghurt. SERVES 4

rhubarb and almond hand pies

200g rhubarb, trimmed and thinly sliced
¾ cup (165g) caster (superfine) sugar
2 sheets frozen butter puff pastry, thawed
¼ cup (30g) almond meal (ground almonds)
1 egg, lightly beaten
¼ cup (20g) flaked almonds

Preheat oven to 200°C (400°F). Line a large baking tray
with non-stick baking paper. Place the rhubarb and sugar
in a medium bowl and mix well to combine.

Cut each pastry sheet into 4 x 10cm squares. Place 4 of
the squares on the tray and spread with the almond meal,
leaving a 1cm border. Top with the rhubarb mixture and
the remaining pastry, pressing the edges to seal. Brush
the pies with egg, sprinkle with the almonds and bake for
15 minutes or until puffed and golden. Slice to serve. MAKES 4

fig, yoghurt and honey parfaits

1 cup (280g) natural Greek-style (thick) yoghurt
1 cup (250ml) single (pouring) cream*
2 tablespoons honey
¼ cup (90g) honey, extra
¼ teaspoon ground cinnamon
4 figs, sliced
2 tablespoons pistachios, finely chopped

Place the yoghurt, cream and honey in the bowl
of an electric mixer and whisk until soft peaks
form. Place the extra honey and the cinnamon
in a small bowl and mix to combine.

Divide the fig and the yoghurt mixture between
4 x 1½-cup-capacity (375ml) serving glasses, to
create a layered effect. Drizzle with the spiced
honey and sprinkle with the chopped pistachios
to serve. SERVES 4

coconut, lime and lemon delicious pudding

1 cup (250ml) coconut milk
¾ cup (165g) caster (superfine) sugar
½ cup (40g) desiccated coconut
2 tablespoons plain (all-purpose) flour
2 eggs, separated
⅓ cup (100g) store-bought lemon curd
40g unsalted butter, melted
1 tablespoon finely grated lime rind
125g raspberries

Preheat oven to 160°C (325°F). Lightly grease an 18cm round (1-litre-capacity) baking dish. Place the coconut milk, sugar, coconut, flour, egg yolks, lemon curd, butter and lime rind in the bowl of an electric mixer and beat until smooth. Set aside.

Place the eggwhites in a clean bowl of the electric mixer and whisk until soft peaks form.

Add the eggwhite to the coconut mixture and gently fold to combine. Spoon into the dish and top with the raspberries. Place on an oven tray and bake for 25–30 minutes or until just set. SERVES 4

apple and caramel hand pies

1 cup (180g) coarsely grated apple
2 tablespoons store-bought thick caramel or dulce de leche*
18 gow gee wrappers*
water, for brushing
¼ teaspoon ground cinnamon
2 tablespoons white (granulated) sugar
40g unsalted butter, melted

Preheat oven to 200°C (400°F). Line a large baking tray with non-stick baking paper. Place the apple in a clean tea towel and squeeze out any excess juice.

Place the drained apple in a medium bowl, add the caramel and mix to combine. Place 1-teaspoon portions of the mixture onto half of each gow gee wrapper. Brush the edges with water, fold the wrappers over to enclose the filling and press the edges to seal. Place on the tray and bake for 15 minutes or until golden.

Place the cinnamon and sugar in a small bowl and mix to combine. Brush the pies with the butter and toss in the cinnamon sugar to coat. Serve warm. MAKES 18

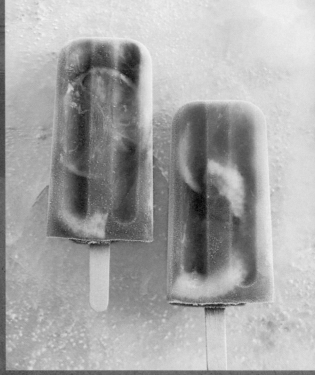

pina colada popsicles

1 cup (250ml) coconut milk
¼ cup (55g) caster (superfine) sugar
1 cup (250ml) pineapple juice

Place the coconut milk and 1½ tablespoons of the sugar in a medium jug and whisk to dissolve the sugar. Divide between 8 x ⅓-cup-capacity (80ml) popsicle moulds and freeze for 30–40 minutes or until just set.

Place the remaining 1½ tablespoons of sugar and the pineapple juice in a medium jug and whisk to dissolve the sugar. Divide between the moulds, cover with aluminium foil and insert the popsicle sticks. Freeze for a further 3–4 hours or until frozen. MAKES 8
Tip: For grown-up pina colada popsicles, replace ¼ cup (60ml) of the coconut milk with Malibu or coconut-flavoured rum.

pink grapefruit popsicles

1 lime, thinly sliced
1 pink grapefruit, halved and thinly sliced
1¾ cups (430ml) pink or ruby red grapefruit juice
2 tablespoons caster (superfine) sugar

Divide the lime and grapefruit slices between 8 x ⅓-cup-capacity (80ml) popsicle moulds.

Place the grapefruit juice and sugar in a medium jug and whisk to dissolve the sugar. Divide between the moulds, cover with aluminium foil and insert the popsicle sticks. Freeze for 3–4 hours or until frozen. MAKES 8
Tip: For grown-up pink grapefruit popsicles, replace ¼ cup (60ml) of the grapefruit juice with vodka.

pineapple, coconut and lemongrass popsicles

4 stalks lemongrass
1kg pineapple (about 1 pineapple), peeled,
 cored and chopped+
½ cup (125ml) coconut milk
1 cup (220g) caster (superfine) sugar

Cut 8 x 10cm lengths from the lemongrass stalks
to use as popsicle sticks. Chop the remaining
white parts of the lemongrass, reserving ¼ cup.
 Place the reserved lemongrass, the pineapple,
coconut milk and sugar in a blender and blend
until smooth. Strain the mixture through a sieve
into a jug, discarding the solids, and divide between
8 x ⅓-cup-capacity (80ml) popsicle moulds. Cover
with 2 layers of aluminium foil and freeze for 2 hours.
 Make a small incision in the foil in the centre of
each mould and insert the lemongrass sticks. Freeze
for a further 2–3 hours or until frozen. MAKES 8
+ *You can often buy chopped fresh pineapple in
tubs in the refrigerated section of supermarkets
and greengrocers – you'll need 500g.*

rockmelon and yoghurt popsicles

1 cup (280g) natural Greek-style (thick) yoghurt
¼ cup (55g) caster (superfine) sugar
¼ cup (60ml) water
600g rockmelon (cantaloupe) (about half a rockmelon),
 peeled, seeded and chopped+
½ cup (110g) caster (superfine) sugar, extra

Place the yoghurt, sugar and water in a medium
bowl and whisk to dissolve the sugar.
 Place the melon and the extra sugar in a blender
and blend until smooth. Starting with the melon
mixture, pour alternate layers of the melon and
yoghurt mixtures into 8 x ⅓-cup-capacity (80ml)
popsicle moulds, allowing each layer to freeze for
20–30 minutes before adding the next.
 Once all the layers have been added, cover with
aluminium foil and insert the popsicle sticks. Freeze
for a further 2–3 hours or until frozen. MAKES 8
+ *You can often buy chopped fresh rockmelon
(cantaloupe) in tubs in the refrigerated section of
supermarkets and greengrocers – you'll need 400g.*

lemon chia cake

FRESH AND LIGHT

When I'm baking afternoon treats for the office, or I want something a bit more balanced for my kids, I turn to fresh fruit – harnessing its natural sweetness and colour. From my crowd-pleaser banana bread to cute choc-cherry bars, here are my favourite fruity snacks that are low on processed sugar but big on taste.

lemon chia cake

3 eggs
1½ cups (420g) natural Greek-style (thick) yoghurt
½ cup (125ml) light-flavoured extra virgin olive oil
¾ cup (120g) rapadura sugar*
2 tablespoons finely grated lemon rind
1 teaspoon vanilla bean paste or vanilla extract
¾ cup (120g) buckwheat flour*
1½ cups (180g) almond meal (ground almonds)
3 teaspoons baking powder
2 tablespoons black chia seeds+
yoghurt topping
1 cup (280g) natural Greek-style (thick) yoghurt
2 tablespoons honey
1 tablespoon finely grated lemon rind
black chia seeds, for sprinkling+

Preheat oven to 160°C (325°F). Line an 11cm x 28cm loaf tin with non-stick baking paper. Place the eggs, yoghurt, oil, sugar, lemon rind and vanilla in a large bowl and whisk to combine. Add the flour, almond meal, baking powder and chia seeds and mix well to combine.

Pour into the tin and bake for 55 minutes – 1 hour or until cooked when tested with a skewer. Allow to cool slightly in the tin before turning out onto a wire rack to cool completely.

To make the yoghurt topping, spread the cooled loaf with the yoghurt and drizzle with the honey. Sprinkle with the lemon rind and chia seeds to serve. **SERVES 8–10**

+ These black or white seeds come from a flowering plant native to Central and South America. They're packed with protein, omega-3 fatty acids, minerals and fibre, and are sold in supermarkets.

pear, blackberry and hazelnut crumbles

2 Beurre Bosc (golden brown) pears (500g),
    peeled and thinly sliced
4 cups (600g) frozen blackberries
2 tablespoons maple syrup
½ teaspoon ground cinnamon
1 tablespoon white chia seeds*
hazelnut, date and amaranth crumble
1 cup (140g) hazelnuts, roughly chopped
6 soft fresh dates (120g), pitted and roughly chopped
½ teaspoon ground cinnamon
¼ cup (10g) puffed amaranth+
1 tablespoon maple syrup

Preheat oven to 180°C (350°F). To make the hazelnut, date and amaranth crumble, place the hazelnut, date, cinnamon, amaranth and maple syrup in a large bowl. Mix well to combine and set aside.

Place the pear, blackberries, maple syrup and cinnamon in a large saucepan over high heat. Cook, stirring, for 8 minutes or until softened. Add the chia seeds and stir to combine. Spoon the mixture into 4 x 1-cup-capacity (250ml) ovenproof ramekins and top with the crumble mixture. Place on an oven tray and bake for 8 minutes or until golden. **MAKES 4**

+ Similar to quinoa, amaranth is not a grain but a seed. It's gluten free and high in protein and minerals. When it's popped, or puffed, it becomes light and aerated, making it the perfect addition to crumbles, muesli bars or slices.

pear, blackberry and
hazelnut crumbles

strawberry chia jam and coconut slice

strawberry chia jam and coconut slice

1 egg yolk
¾ cup (120g) almonds
6 soft fresh dates (120g), pitted
40g unsalted butter, chopped
⅓ cup (60g) white rice flour⁺
2 tablespoons raw caster (superfine) sugar
2 eggwhites
2 cups (150g) shredded coconut
strawberry chia jam
400g strawberries, hulled and roughly chopped
1 tablespoon lemon juice
2 tablespoons water
¼ cup (60ml) maple syrup
1 vanilla bean, split and seeds scraped
2 tablespoons white chia seeds*

Preheat oven to 160°C (325°F). Line a 20cm square slice tin with non-stick baking paper, leaving 4cm paper above 2 of the edges. Place the egg yolk, almonds, dates, butter and flour in a food processor and process for 1 minute or until finely chopped. Press the mixture firmly into the base of the tin, using the back of a spoon. Bake for 25 minutes or until firm and golden.

While the base is baking, make the strawberry chia jam. Place the strawberry, lemon juice, water, maple syrup and vanilla bean and seeds in a medium saucepan over high heat and cook, stirring, for 12–15 minutes. Remove and discard the vanilla pod. Add the chia seeds, mix to combine and allow to cool for 15 minutes or until thickened.

Place the sugar and eggwhites in a medium bowl and gently whisk to combine. Add the coconut and whisk to combine. Pour the jam over the almond base and spread evenly to coat. Top with the coconut mixture and bake for 20–25 minutes or until golden. Allow to cool slightly before refrigerating for 30 minutes or until cold.

Use the baking paper to help you lift the slice from the tin. Cut into pieces to serve. **SERVES 10–12**
+ *Rice flour, made from finely ground rice, is gluten free and available from the baking aisle of supermarkets.*
Tip: Keep this slice refrigerated in an airtight container for up to 5 days.

blueberry crumble slice

2 cups (240g) oat bran
¾ cup (75g) LSA⁺
12 soft fresh dates (240g), pitted
½ cup (125ml) melted coconut oil*
2 teaspoons vanilla bean paste or vanilla extract,
  plus extra to serve
500g blueberries
2 tablespoons raw or Demerara sugar*
2 tablespoons white chia seeds*
natural Greek-style (thick) yoghurt, to serve

Preheat oven to 160°C (325°F). Line a 20cm x 30cm slice tin with non-stick baking paper. Place the oat bran, LSA, dates, oil and vanilla in a food processor and process for 3–4 minutes or until the mixture comes together. Reserve and set aside 1 cup (250ml) of the mixture. Using the back of a spoon, press the remaining mixture firmly into the base of the tin. Bake for 18–20 minutes or until light golden.

While the base is baking, place the blueberries and sugar in a medium saucepan over medium heat. Cook, stirring, for 4 minutes or until the blueberries soften. Add the chia seeds and cook, stirring, for 10 minutes or until thickened.

Spread the blueberry jam over the base and top with the reserved oat bran mixture. Bake for 20 minutes or until the top is golden. Allow to cool slightly before refrigerating for 30 minutes or until cold.

Swirl some extra vanilla into the yoghurt. Remove the slice from the tin and cut into pieces. Serve with the vanilla yoghurt. **MAKES 15**
+ *LSA is a mixture of ground linseeds, sunflower seeds and almonds. Find it in the health food aisle of supermarkets.*

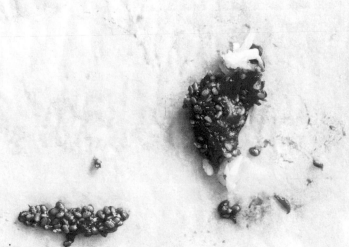

blueberry crumble slice

puffed quinoa blueberry bars with yoghurt

puffed quinoa blueberry bars with yoghurt

250g blueberries
1 cup (30g) puffed quinoa*
1½ cups (135g) rolled oats
½ cup (40g) shredded coconut
2 tablespoons white chia seeds*
½ cup (140g) natural cashew butter*
½ cup (125ml) maple syrup
2 teaspoons vanilla extract
yoghurt drizzle
½ cup (140g) natural Greek-style (thick) yoghurt
2 tablespoons icing (confectioner's) sugar, sifted
1½ tablespoons melted coconut oil*

Preheat oven to 180°C (350°F). Line a baking tray with non-stick baking paper. Place the blueberries on the tray and bake for 35–40 minutes or until softened and dried.

Line a 20cm square slice tin with non-stick baking paper. Place the puffed quinoa, oats, coconut and chia seeds in a medium bowl. Place the cashew butter, maple syrup and vanilla in a medium saucepan over high heat. Cook, whisking, for 5–6 minutes or until thickened slightly. Add the quinoa mixture and mix well to combine. Add the blueberries and gently stir to combine. Using the back of a spoon, press the mixture into the base of the tin. Freeze for 30 minutes or until firm.

To make the yoghurt drizzle, place the yoghurt and sugar in a medium jug and, using a hand-held stick blender, blend until smooth. Add the coconut oil and blend to combine.

Line a tray with non-stick baking paper. Remove the slice from the tin and cut into bars. Place on the tray, top with the yoghurt drizzle and freeze for 30 minutes or until set, before serving. MAKES 10–12
Tip: Keep these bars in the fridge or freezer in an airtight container for up to 1 week.

raw chocolate, cherry and coconut bars

6 soft fresh dates (120g), pitted
1 cup (80g) desiccated coconut
⅓ cup (80ml) melted coconut oil*
1 teaspoon vanilla bean paste or vanilla extract
1½ cups (225g) cherries, pitted[+]
100g raw organic 70% dark chocolate[++]
2 teaspoons vegetable oil
coconut base
1 cup (150g) cashews
1 cup (80g) desiccated coconut
¼ cup (90g) rice malt syrup*

To make the coconut base, line a 20cm square slice tin with non-stick baking paper. Place the cashews, coconut and rice malt syrup in a food processor and process for 1–2 minutes, scraping down the sides of the bowl, until the mixture comes together. Press the mixture into the base of the tin, using the back of a spoon. Refrigerate for 30 minutes or until set.

Place the dates, coconut, coconut oil and vanilla in the cleaned food processor and process for 1 minute or until the mixture comes together. Add the cherries and process for a further 30 seconds or until just combined. Pour the cherry mixture over the base and spread evenly. Refrigerate for a further 30 minutes or until firm.

Place the chocolate in a heatproof bowl over a saucepan of simmering water (the bowl shouldn't touch the water) and stir until melted. Add the vegetable oil and stir to combine. Pour the chocolate mixture over the slice and smooth the top. Refrigerate for 1 hour or until set.

Remove the slice from the tin and, using a hot knife, slice into bars. Refrigerate until ready to serve. MAKES 20
+ You can use frozen pitted cherries in place of the fresh cherries – thaw and drain well on absorbent kitchen paper.
++ Raw organic chocolate is available at health food stores and specialty grocers. If you can't find it, you can use 70% dark chocolate. To keep the chocolate raw while melting, use a sugar (candy) thermometer to ensure it stays under 42°C (107°F).

raw chocolate, cherry
and coconut bars

mixed berry and granola ice-cream bars

mixed berry and granola ice-cream bars

1 cup (150g) frozen raspberries
1 cup (150g) frozen blueberries
⅓ cup (80ml) maple syrup
2 medium bananas, peeled and sliced
2½ cups (625ml) coconut cream
2 teaspoons vanilla bean paste or vanilla extract
1 cup (130g) store-bought granola

Preheat oven to 180°C (350°F). Line a roasting pan with non-stick baking paper. Add the berries and 1 tablespoon of the maple syrup to the tray, toss gently to combine and bake for 15 minutes or until soft. Allow to cool completely.

Place the banana, coconut cream, vanilla and the remaining ¼ cup (60ml) of maple syrup in a large jug. Using a hand-held stick blender, blend until smooth.

Line a 20cm square tin with non-stick baking paper. Place alternate spoonfuls of the berry mixture and the banana mixture into the tin. Gently mix to create a swirled effect. Sprinkle with the granola and freeze for 4 hours or overnight until firm.

Remove the slice from the tin. Allow to stand at room temperature for 10 minutes. Use a hot knife to cut the slice into bars to serve. MAKES 8

strawberries and cream ice-cream bars

50g 70% dark chocolate, melted
10g freeze-dried strawberries*, finely chopped
strawberry layer
400g strawberries, hulled and chopped
¼ cup (60ml) maple syrup
1 teaspoon vanilla bean paste or vanilla extract
cream layer
2 medium bananas (360g), peeled and sliced
2½ cups (625ml) coconut cream
½ cup (125ml) maple syrup
1 teaspoon vanilla bean paste or vanilla extract

To make the strawberry layer, place the strawberry, maple syrup and vanilla in a medium saucepan over medium heat. Cook, stirring, for 15 minutes or until the strawberry is soft and the liquid has thickened. Allow to cool slightly. Roughly mash with a fork and set aside.

To make the cream layer, place the banana, coconut cream, maple syrup and vanilla in a large jug. Using a hand-held stick blender, blend until smooth.

Add 1 cup (250ml) of the cream mixture to the strawberry mixture. Stir to combine and refrigerate until needed.

Line a 20cm square slice tin with non-stick baking paper. Pour the remaining cream mixture into the tin and freeze for 2 hours or until firm. Spread evenly with the strawberry mixture and freeze for 4 hours or overnight until firm.

Allow to stand at room temperature for 10 minutes. Use a hot knife to cut the slice into bars. Drizzle with the chocolate and sprinkle with the chopped freeze-dried strawberries to serve. MAKES 8

strawberries and cream ice-cream bars

banana and raspberry ice-cream

banana and raspberry ice-cream

500g bananas (about 3 medium bananas), peeled
1 cup (150g) frozen raspberries
⅓ cup (80ml) maple syrup
1 teaspoon vanilla bean paste or vanilla extract

Slice the bananas into even rounds. Layer in a freeze-proof container between sheets of non-stick baking paper. Freeze for 4 hours or overnight.

Place the banana slices, raspberries, maple syrup and vanilla in a food processor and process for 2–3 minutes or until smooth. Spoon into a 1.5-litre-capacity metal container and freeze for 3–4 hours or until firm. **SERVES 4-6**
Tip: When you have an abundance of bananas in the fruit bowl, why not slice and freeze a few, as in step one. Then you'll be ready to whip-up this ice-cream whenever you like.

banana bread

1½ cups (240g) buckwheat flour*
1 cup (160g) rapadura or coconut sugar⁺
1 teaspoon baking powder
½ teaspoon bicarbonate of (baking) soda
2 teaspoons ground cinnamon
1 cup (260g) mashed ripe banana (about 3 bananas)
1 egg
½ cup (140g) natural Greek-style (thick) yoghurt
¼ cup (60ml) grapeseed oil
⅓ cup (80ml) maple syrup, plus extra for brushing
2 teaspoons vanilla bean paste or vanilla extract
1 banana, extra, peeled and halved lengthways

Preheat oven to 160°C (325°F). Line a 10cm x 21cm loaf tin with non-stick baking paper. Place the flour, sugar, baking powder, bicarbonate of soda and cinnamon in a large bowl and mix to combine. Add the mashed banana, egg, yoghurt, oil, maple syrup and vanilla and mix to combine. Pour into the tin and top with the extra banana. Bake for 1 hour – 1 hour 10 minutes or until cooked when tested with a skewer.

Allow to cool in the tin for 5 minutes before placing onto a wire rack to cool completely. Brush with extra maple syrup to serve. **SERVES 6-8**
⁺ Rapadura sugar, or panela, is extracted from the pure juice of cane sugar. It's evaporated over low heat, so it retains more of the minerals and vitamins from the cane. Coconut sugar, or coconut palm sugar, comes from the flowers of the coconut palm. Its rich flavour gives a caramelly depth to baked goods. Both these sugars can be found in the health food aisle of major supermarkets or in health food stores and specialty grocers.

banana bread

milk and cream

Whipped and spun into dreamy delights, these recipes call for mild milks, fresh curds and puffy creams. They're my go-to when elegance is required, for their delicate pillowy textures. With gentle vanilla or a hint of lemon folded through, it's dessert as it should be – pure and simple.

meringues poached in vanilla milk

meringues poached in vanilla milk

1.5 litres milk
1 tablespoon vanilla extract
¾ cup (120g) icing (confectioner's) sugar
2 tablespoons cornflour (cornstarch)
poached meringues
110ml eggwhite (about 3 eggs), at room temperature+
⅓ cup (75g) caster (superfine) sugar
¾ cup (120g) icing (confectioner's) sugar mixture, sifted
½ tablespoon cornflour (cornstarch), sifted

To make the poached meringues, place the eggwhite in the bowl of an electric mixer and whisk on high speed until stiff peaks form. Add the caster sugar, 1 tablespoon at a time, whisking for 30 seconds before adding more. Scrape down the sides of the bowl. Gradually add the icing sugar mixture and cornflour and whisk until stiff and glossy.

Place the milk, vanilla, icing sugar and cornflour in a deep-sided frying pan over medium heat. Cook, whisking occasionally, for 6 minutes or until almost simmering. Reduce the heat to low and, working in batches and using a large metal spoon, carefully drop in spoonfuls of the meringue mixture. Cover with a tight-fitting lid and cook for 3 minutes or until the meringue is firm to the touch. Remove the meringues from the pan and keep warm.

Strain the poaching milk into a heatproof jug, discarding any solids, and divide between serving bowls. Top with the meringues to serve. **SERVES 6**
+ *Making meringue is a science – be sure to measure the eggwhites carefully, remembering egg sizes do vary.*

buttermilk panna cottas

⅓ cup (80ml) warm water
3 teaspoons gelatine powder*
1 cup (250ml) single (pouring) cream*
1 cup (220g) caster (superfine) sugar
2 teaspoons vanilla bean paste or vanilla extract
1½ cups (375ml) milk
1½ cups (375ml) buttermilk

Place the water in a small bowl and sprinkle with the gelatine. Set aside for 5 minutes or until the gelatine is absorbed. Place the cream, sugar and vanilla in a medium saucepan over medium heat and stir to dissolve the sugar. Bring to the boil, add the gelatine mixture and stir to combine. Remove from the heat and strain into a large bowl.

Add the milk and buttermilk, stir to combine and divide the mixture between 6 x 10cm round (¾-cup-capacity) deep-fluted tart tins. Refrigerate for 3–4 hours or until set+.

Turn the panna cottas out onto plates to serve. **MAKES 6**
+ *For best results, make these panna cottas ahead of time so you can refrigerate them overnight.*
Tip: To turn the panna cottas out onto serving plates, invert the tin onto the plate and shake lightly to release.

buttermilk panna cottas

coconut layer meringue cake

coconut layer meringue cake

600ml eggwhite (about 16 eggs), at room temperature[+]
3 cups (660g) caster (superfine) sugar
2 tablespoons cornflour (cornstarch), plus extra for dusting
2 tablespoons white vinegar
2 cups (100g) coconut flakes
vanilla coconut cream
1 cup (250ml) double (thick) cream*
1 cup (250ml) coconut cream, chilled
1 teaspoon vanilla extract

Preheat oven to 160°C (325°F). Grease a 24cm x 34cm slice tin. Place half the eggwhite in the bowl of an electric mixer and whisk on high speed until soft peaks form. Add half the sugar, 1 tablespoon at a time, whisking for 30 seconds before adding more. Scrape down the sides of the bowl and whisk for 8 minutes or until thick. Place half the cornflour and half the vinegar in a small bowl and mix to combine. Add to the meringue mixture and whisk for 2 minutes or until thick and glossy. Spoon into the tin and smooth the top. Bake for 16 minutes or until the top is just dry to the touch. Allow to cool in the tin for 5 minutes before turning out onto a tray lightly dusted with cornflour to cool completely. Trim the meringue to make 2 equal rectangles, discarding the uneven edges[++] and set aside.

Repeat with the remaining eggwhite, sugar, cornflour and vinegar to create 2 more meringue rectangles.

To make the vanilla coconut cream, place the cream, coconut cream and vanilla in a clean bowl of the electric mixer and whisk until stiff peaks form.

To assemble, place 1 meringue rectangle on a cake stand or plate. Spoon ⅓ cup (80ml) of the vanilla coconut cream over the meringue. Continue layering with meringue and vanilla coconut cream, finishing with the cream. Lightly spread the remaining cream over the sides and sprinkle all over with the coconut flakes, pressing gently to secure. Serve immediately[+++]. **SERVES 6**
+ *Making meringue is a science – be sure to measure the eggwhites carefully, remembering egg sizes do vary.*
++ *The meringue will shrink by about 3–5cm as it cools. We've trimmed the edges to create a straight, clean edge. You can leave the edges intact if you prefer a larger cake.*
+++ *This cake will keep refrigerated for 2 hours before serving.*

raspberry and cream angel food cake

12 eggwhites, at room temperature
1 teaspoon cream of tartar
¾ cup (165g) caster (superfine) sugar
2 teaspoons vanilla extract
1 cup (150g) plain (all-purpose) flour
½ cup (110g) caster (superfine) sugar, extra
2 cups (500g) mascarpone
1½ cups (375ml) single (pouring) cream*
1 cup (320g) store-bought raspberry jam
italian meringue
⅓ cup (80ml) water
½ teaspoon cream of tartar
2 cups (440g) caster (superfine) sugar
150ml eggwhite (about 4 eggs), at room temperature

Preheat oven to 180°C (350°F). Place the eggwhites and cream of tartar in the bowl of an electric mixer and whisk on high speed until soft peaks form. Gradually add the sugar and half the vanilla, whisking until thick and glossy.

Sift the flour and the extra sugar into a bowl. Sift for a second time, then sift for the third time over the eggwhite mixture. Gently fold to combine. Spoon into an ungreased 21cm round angel food cake tin and smooth the top. Bake for 30 minutes or until the cake comes away from the sides of the tin. Invert the tin and allow to cool for 1 hour.

Place the mascarpone, cream and remaining vanilla in the bowl of an electric mixer and whisk until stiff peaks form.

Using a butter knife, gently loosen the edges of the cake and twist the middle funnel to remove it from the tin. Using a large serrated knife, slice the cake horizontally into 3 even layers. Place 1 layer on a cake stand or plate and top with half the jam. Top with half the cream mixture. Repeat using the remaining cake, jam and cream, finishing with cake.

To make the Italian meringue, place the water, cream of tartar and half the sugar in a small saucepan over high heat. Cook, stirring, until the sugar has dissolved. Bring to the boil, reduce the heat to medium and cook for 4 minutes. Place the eggwhite in a clean bowl of the electric mixer and whisk on high speed until stiff peaks form. Add the remaining sugar, 1 tablespoon at a time, whisking for 30 seconds before adding more. Gradually add the hot sugar syrup in a thin steady stream and whisk for 4 minutes or until thick and glossy.

Using a palette knife, spread the cake with the Italian meringue and serve immediately[+]. **SERVES 10**
+ *This cake will keep refrigerated for 2 hours before serving.*

raspberry and cream angel food cake

limoncello and coconut ice-cream cake

limoncello and coconut ice-cream cake

2 cups (160g) desiccated coconut
½ cup (110g) caster (superfine) sugar
2 eggwhites
2 litres store-bought vanilla ice-cream
½ cup (125ml) limoncello or lemon liqueur

Preheat oven to 120°C (250°F). Line a 20cm round springform tin with non-stick baking paper. Place the coconut, sugar and eggwhites in a bowl and mix until well combined. Press the mixture into the base of the tin, using the back of a spoon. Cover with aluminium foil and bake for 25 minutes. Remove the foil. Bake for a further 10–15 minutes or until crisp but not golden. Allow to cool and refrigerate until cold.

Scoop the ice-cream into the bowl of an electric mixer and beat on low speed for 1–2 minutes or until softened. Add the limoncello and beat until just combined. Pour onto the coconut base and freeze for 3–4 hours or overnight.

Allow the cake to stand at room temperature for 5 minutes before releasing it from the tin⁺. Place on a cake stand or plate and serve immediately. SERVES 8–10
+ A warm tea towel around the tin helps release the cake.

fairy floss marshmallow ice-creams

750ml (525g) store-bought vanilla ice-cream, chopped⁺
1 cup (90g) white marshmallows, finely chopped
360g white chocolate, melted
2 tablespoons vegetable oil
white Persian fairy (candy) floss*, to serve

Place the ice-cream in the bowl of an electric mixer and beat on low speed until softened. Add the marshmallow and mix to combine. Spoon into 8 x ⅓-cup-capacity (80ml) popsicle moulds and insert the popsicle sticks. Freeze for 8 hours or overnight.

Line a large tray with non-stick baking paper. Run the popsicle moulds under hot water for 10 seconds. Remove and place the popsicles on the tray. Freeze until needed.

Place the chocolate and oil in a small bowl and mix until smooth. Allow to cool to room temperature. Working quickly, dip the popsicles, at an angle, into the chocolate mixture. Wrap with fairy floss to serve. MAKES 8
+ Because all store-bought ice-creams vary, for this recipe we've given a volume and weight suggestion. Use the volume measurement to help you purchase enough ice-cream at the supermarket. At home, weigh the ice-cream before you begin and you'll end up with 8 perfectly sized popsicles.
Tip: Keep these ice-creams in the freezer for up to 2 days.

fairy floss marshmallow ice-creams

passionfruit three-milk ice-cream cake

passionfruit three-milk ice-cream cake

90g unsalted butter, softened

½ cup (110g) caster (superfine) sugar

1 teaspoon vanilla extract

3 eggs

¾ cup (110g) self-raising (self-rising) flour, sifted

2 litres store-bought vanilla ice-cream

½ cup (125ml) sweetened condensed milk

1 cup (250ml) milk

½ cup (125ml) buttermilk

½ cup (125ml) single (pouring) cream*

½ cup (120g) sour cream*

1 tablespoon icing (confectioner's) sugar

¼ cup (60ml) passionfruit pulp (about 3 passionfruit)

Line a 20cm round deep-sided loose-based cake tin with non-stick baking paper. Preheat oven to 160°C (325°C). Place the butter, caster sugar and vanilla in the bowl of an electric mixer and beat for 8–10 minutes or until pale and creamy. Scrape down the sides of the bowl and add the eggs, 1 at a time, beating well after each addition. Add the flour and beat on low speed until just combined. Spoon the mixture into the tin and bake for 30–35 minutes or until cooked when tested with a skewer. Allow to cool in the tin for 5 minutes before placing on a wire rack to cool completely.

Re-line the cleaned tin with non-stick baking paper, place on a tray and freeze until ready to use. Place the ice-cream in the bowl of an electric mixer and beat on low speed for 1–2 minutes or until softened. Spoon into the tin and spread evenly. Freeze for 3–4 hours or until frozen.

Use a skewer to make multiple holes in the cooled cake and place on top of the frozen base. Place the condensed milk, milk and buttermilk in a medium bowl and whisk to combine. Place the tin on a tray to catch any spills and pour the milk mixture, ½ cup (125ml) at a time, over the cake. Freeze for 30 minutes or until chilled.

Place the cream, sour cream and icing sugar in the bowl of an electric mixer and whisk until stiff peaks form. Turn the cake out onto a cake stand or plate. Top with the cream and passionfruit and serve immediately. SERVES 8-10

orange ricotta soufflés

unsalted butter, melted for greasing

¼ cup (55g) caster (superfine) sugar

30g unsalted butter, extra

¼ cup (35g) plain (all-purpose) flour

½ cup (125ml) milk

½ cup (80g) icing (confectioner's) sugar,
    plus extra for dusting

3 egg yolks

2 teaspoons finely grated orange rind

1 teaspoon vanilla extract

1 cup (240g) fresh firm ricotta

4 eggwhites, at room temperature

Preheat oven to 180°C (350°F). Brush the base and sides of 4 x 1-cup-capacity (250ml) ovenproof ramekins with melted butter and dust with 1 tablespoon of the caster sugar.

Place the extra butter in a small saucepan over low heat and stir until melted. Add the flour and cook, stirring, for 2 minutes. Increase the heat to medium, gradually add the milk and whisk until smooth. Cook, stirring, for 2 minutes or until very thick. Place in a large bowl and refrigerate for 10 minutes or until firm. Add the icing sugar, egg yolks, orange rind, vanilla and ricotta to the flour mixture and mix until well combined.

Place the eggwhites in the bowl of an electric mixer and whisk until soft peaks form. Gradually add the remaining 2 tablespoons of caster sugar and whisk until thick. Add the eggwhite mixture, in 3 batches, to the ricotta mixture and gently fold to combine. Divide between the ramekins and, using a knife, smooth the tops. Run your fingertip 5mm deep around the inside edge of each ramekin. Place on an oven tray and bake for 22–25 minutes or until the soufflés have risen and are light golden.

Dust with icing sugar and serve immediately. MAKES 4

orange ricotta soufflés

ricotta and buttermilk ice-cream

ricotta and buttermilk ice-cream

4 cups (960g) fresh firm ricotta
1 teaspoon vanilla extract
1¼ cups (200g) icing (confectioner's) sugar, sifted
½ cup (125ml) buttermilk
1 tablespoon finely grated lemon rind
¼ cup (60ml) lemon juice

Place the ricotta, vanilla, sugar, buttermilk, lemon rind
and juice in a food processor and process until smooth.
Pour into a 20cm x 30cm slice tin or metal container and
freeze for 4–6 hours or until frozen.

Allow to soften at room temperature for 5–10 minutes.
Cut into squares and, in batches, place in the food processor
and process until smooth. Return the mixture to the tin
and freeze for 1 hour or until firm.

Allow to stand at room temperature for 5 minutes before
scooping into bowls to serve. MAKES 1 LITRE

lemon, ricotta and almond cakes

120g unsalted butter, softened
1¼ cups (275g) caster (superfine) sugar
1 vanilla bean, split and seeds scraped
¼ cup finely grated lemon rind
4 eggs, separated and at room temperature
2 cups (240g) almond meal (ground almonds)
1¼ cups (300g) fresh firm ricotta
¾ cup (60g) flaked almonds
icing (confectioner's) sugar, for dusting

Preheat oven to 160°C (325°F). Line 6 x 10cm round
springform tins with non-stick baking paper. Place the
butter, ¾ cup (165g) of the caster sugar, the vanilla seeds
and lemon rind in the bowl of an electric mixer and beat
on high speed for 8–10 minutes or until pale and creamy.
Scrape down the sides of the bowl, add the egg yolks and
beat for 1–2 minutes or until well combined. Add the
almond meal and beat to combine.

Place the eggwhites in a clean bowl of the electric
mixer and whisk until stiff peaks form. Gradually add the
remaining ½ cup (110g) of caster sugar and whisk until thick.
In 2 batches, add the eggwhite mixture and the ricotta to
the almond mixture and gently fold to combine. Divide
between the tins and smooth the tops. Arrange the flaked
almonds on the cakes and bake for 40–45 minutes or until
cooked when tested with a skewer. Allow the cakes to cool
completely in the tins.

Carefully remove the cakes from the tins and dust with
icing sugar to serve. MAKES 6

lemon, ricotta and almond cakes

vanilla yoghurt pastries with lavender sugar

vanilla yoghurt pastries with lavender sugar

2 sheets frozen butter puff pastry, thawed
⅓ cup (55g) icing (confectioner's) sugar, sifted
1 tablespoon thick vanilla yoghurt
1 teaspoon edible dried lavender+
1 teaspoon white (granulated) sugar
vanilla yoghurt cream
¾ cup (180ml) single (pouring) cream*
¾ cup (210g) thick vanilla yoghurt
¼ cup (40g) icing (confectioner's) sugar, sifted

Preheat oven to 180°C (350°F). Line 2 large baking trays with non-stick baking paper. Cut each pastry sheet into 12 x 4cm x 12cm rectangles. Place 12 rectangles on each tray. Top each tray with a sheet of non-stick baking paper and a second baking tray for weight. Bake for 10 minutes. Remove the top trays and sheets of paper and bake for a further 5 minutes or until golden. Set aside to cool.

Place the icing sugar and yoghurt in a small bowl and whisk until smooth. Spread 1 teaspoon onto each of half the pastry rectangles. Allow the icing to set for 10 minutes.

To make the vanilla yoghurt cream, place the cream, yoghurt and sugar in the bowl of an electric mixer. Whisk for 1–2 minutes or until very thick.

Place the vanilla yoghurt cream in a piping bag fitted with a 1.7cm round nozzle. Pipe the cream mixture onto the remaining 12 pastry rectangles and sandwich with the iced halves. Refrigerate until ready to serve.

Place the lavender and white sugar in a small bowl and mix to combine. Place the pastries onto serving plates and sprinkle with the lavender sugar to serve. MAKES 12
+ *You can find edible (pesticide-free) dried lavender at health food stores and tea shops.*

lemon and vanilla ricotta cheesecake

2½ cups (600g) fresh firm ricotta
250g cream cheese, softened
¾ cup (165g) caster (superfine) sugar
1 tablespoon finely grated lemon rind
3 eggs
1½ tablespoons cornflour (cornstarch)
¼ cup (60ml) lemon juice
¼ cup (60ml) single (pouring) cream*
1 teaspoon vanilla extract
icing (confectioner's) sugar and ground cinnamon, for dusting
vanilla pastry
150g unsalted butter, softened
¾ cup (165g) caster (superfine) sugar
1 egg, plus 1 egg yolk, extra
⅓ cup (80ml) single (pouring) cream*
1 teaspoon vanilla extract
3 cups (450g) plain (all-purpose) flour, sifted
1½ tablespoons baking powder, sifted

Preheat oven to 160°C (325°F). Line the base of a 22cm round springform tin with non-stick baking paper. To make the vanilla pastry, place the butter and sugar in the bowl of an electric mixer and beat for 6–8 minutes. Add the egg and extra yolk and beat until well combined. Add the cream, vanilla, flour and baking powder and beat to combine. Turn out onto a lightly floured surface, shape into a ball and divide in half. Roll 1 half between 2 sheets of non-stick baking paper to a 25cm x 45cm rectangle and refrigerate. Divide the remaining pastry in half again and roll each piece between sheets of baking paper to make 2 x 22cm rounds. Refrigerate 1 pastry round and place the other in the base of the tin. Refrigerate the tin for 5 minutes. Prick the base all over with a fork and bake for 8–10 minutes or until dry to touch.

Place the ricotta, cream cheese, sugar and lemon rind in a clean bowl of the electric mixer and beat on medium speed for 3 minutes or until smooth. Add the eggs and beat until just combined. Mix the cornflour and juice in a small bowl. Add the cream, vanilla and cornflour mixture to the ricotta mixture and beat until just combined. Lightly grease the sides of the tin. Cut the pastry rectangle in half lengthways and use it to line the sides, pressing to join the base. Pour in the filling and fold the pastry over. Press the remaining pastry round on top and bake for 45 minutes. Cover with aluminium foil. Bake for 30 minutes or until golden. Refrigerate until cold.

Dust with icing sugar and cinnamon to serve. SERVES 8–10

lemon and vanilla ricotta cheesecake

baked ricotta and lime filo cheesecake with lemon balm

baked ricotta and lime filo cheesecake with lemon balm

2½ cups (600g) fresh firm ricotta
250g cream cheese, softened
¾ cup (165g) caster (superfine) sugar
1 tablespoon cornflour (cornstarch)
3 eggs
1 tablespoon vanilla extract
¼ cup (60ml) lime juice
2 teaspoons finely grated lime rind
8 sheets filo (phyllo) pastry
50g unsalted butter, melted
icing (confectioner's) sugar, for dusting
micro (baby) lemon balm leaves, to serve

Preheat oven to 180°C (350°F). Line a 22cm round springform tin with non-stick baking paper. Place the ricotta, cream cheese, caster sugar, cornflour, eggs, vanilla, lime juice and lime rind in a food processor and process for 1–2 minutes or until smooth. Set aside.

Brush 4 of the pastry sheets with butter and stack them on top of one another[+]. Repeat with the remaining pastry to create a second stack. Line the tin with 1 stack of the pastry. Place the second stack crossways on top, gently pressing to cover the base and sides and leaving the excess hanging over the edges. Pour the ricotta filling into the tin and smooth the top. Fold in the excess pastry to enclose the filling and brush with butter. Place on an oven tray and bake for 35–40 minutes or until the filling is set and the pastry is crisp. Allow to cool in the tin completely.

Remove the cake from the tin and place on a cake stand or plate. Dust with icing sugar and sprinkle with lemon balm to serve. SERVES 6-8
+ *When working with filo pastry, have a clean damp tea towel on-hand to place on the sheets still to be used, to stop them from drying out.*

yoghurt, mascarpone and cherry tarts

1½ cups (375g) mascarpone
1 vanilla bean, split and seeds scraped
½ cup (80g) icing (confectioner's) sugar, sifted
1½ cups (420g) natural Greek-style (thick) yoghurt
2 cups (300g) white (Rainier) or red cherries, halved and pitted, plus extra, whole with stems intact, to serve[+]
1 tablespoon icing (confectioner's) sugar, extra
yoghurt pastry
1½ cups (225g) plain (all-purpose) flour
125g cold unsalted butter, chopped
½ cup (80g) icing (confectioner's) sugar
1 egg yolk
2 tablespoons natural Greek-style (thick) yoghurt

To make the yoghurt pastry, place the flour, butter and sugar in a food processor and process until the mixture resembles fine breadcrumbs. Add the egg yolk and yoghurt and process until a dough just comes together. Turn out the dough and gently knead to bring it together. Flatten into a disc shape, cover in plastic wrap and refrigerate for 1 hour.

Divide the pastry into 8 pieces. Roll out each piece between 2 sheets of non-stick baking paper to 3mm thick. Use the pastry to line 4 x 8cm and 4 x 11cm round loose-based fluted tart tins. Trim the edges of the tarts and prick the bases with a fork. Place on a baking tray and refrigerate for 30 minutes.

Preheat oven to 160°C (325°F). Line each pastry case with non-stick baking paper and fill with baking weights or uncooked rice. Bake for 18–20 minutes, remove the paper and weights and bake for a further 8–10 minutes or until the pastry is light golden. Allow to cool completely in the tins. Remove from the tins and set aside.

Place the mascarpone, vanilla seeds and sugar in the bowl of an electric mixer and whisk until thickened. Add the yoghurt and whisk to combine. Refrigerate for 30 minutes or until slightly firm. Place the cherries and extra sugar in a bowl and toss to combine. Allow to macerate for 10 minutes.

Divide the yoghurt cream between the tart shells and top with the cherries, any juices and extra whole cherries to serve. MAKES 8
+ *White, or Rainier, cherries have pale flesh and a lovely honey-like flavour. Their blush tones and heart shape make them a pretty alternative to regular cherries, if available.*

yoghurt, mascarpone and cherry tarts

coconut yoghurt and passionfruit brûlée tarts

coconut yoghurt and passionfruit brûlée tarts

¼ cup (60ml) passionfruit pulp (about 3 passionfruit)
2 cups (500g) coconut yoghurt⁺
⅔ cup (150g) white (granulated) sugar
1 teaspoon passionfruit pulp, extra
shortcrust pastry
1½ cups (225g) plain (all-purpose) flour
½ cup (40g) desiccated coconut
1 tablespoon finely grated lemon rind
½ cup (80g) icing (confectioner's) sugar
125g cold unsalted butter, chopped
2 egg yolks
1 tablespoon iced water

To make the shortcrust pastry, place the flour, coconut, lemon rind, sugar and butter in a food processor and process until the mixture resembles fine breadcrumbs. With the motor running, add the egg yolks and water and process until a dough just comes together. Turn out the dough and gently knead to bring together into a ball. Roll the dough out between 2 sheets of non-stick baking paper to 3mm thick. Refrigerate for 1 hour.

Use a 12cm cookie cutter to cut 6 rounds from the pastry, re-rolling if necessary. Use the rounds to line 6 x 8cm round tart tins. Trim the edges and prick the bases with a fork. Place on a baking tray and refrigerate for 20 minutes.

Preheat oven to 160°C (325°F). Line each pastry case with non-stick baking paper and fill with baking weights or uncooked rice. Bake for 10–12 minutes, remove the paper and weights and bake for a further 12–15 minutes or until the pastry is light golden. Allow to cool completely in the tins.

Remove the pastry cases from the tins. Divide the passionfruit between the cases and fill each with yoghurt. Refrigerate for 1 hour or until firm.

Place the sugar and extra passionfruit in a bowl and use your fingers to combine. Sprinkle over the tarts in a thin layer. Using a small kitchen blowtorch, caramelise the tops. Allow to stand for 5 minutes before serving. MAKES 6
+ *You can buy yoghurt made with coconut milk at some supermarkets and at grocers and specialty food stores.*

yoghurt panna cotta tart

¼ cup (60ml) warm water
2 teaspoons gelatine powder*
½ cup (125ml) single (pouring) cream*
1 cup (220g) caster (superfine) sugar
¾ cup (180ml) milk
1½ cups (420g) natural Greek-style (thick) yoghurt
½ cup (125ml) passionfruit pulp (about 6 passionfruit)
yoghurt pastry
1½ cups (225g) plain (all-purpose) flour
125g cold unsalted butter, chopped
½ cup (80g) icing (confectioner's) sugar
1 egg yolk
2 tablespoons natural Greek-style (thick) yoghurt

To make the yoghurt pastry, place the flour, butter and sugar in a food processor and process until the mixture resembles fine breadcrumbs. Add the egg yolk and yoghurt and process until a dough just comes together. Turn out the dough and gently knead to bring it together. Flatten into a disc shape, cover in plastic wrap and refrigerate for 1 hour.

Line a large baking tray with non-stick baking paper. Place a 22cm round pastry ring (3.5cm-deep) on the tray. Roll the pastry out between 2 sheets of non-stick baking paper to 3mm thick. Use it to line the base and sides of the pastry ring. Refrigerate for 30 minutes.

Preheat oven to 160°C (325°F). Trim the edges of the tart and prick the base with a fork. Line the pastry case with non-stick baking paper and fill with uncooked rice⁺. Bake for 20 minutes, remove the paper and rice and bake for a further 10–12 minutes or until the pastry is golden. Allow to cool completely in the ring.

Place the water in a small bowl and sprinkle with the gelatine. Set aside for 5 minutes or until the gelatine is absorbed. Place the cream and ¾ cup (165g) of the sugar in a small saucepan over medium heat and stir to dissolve the sugar. Bring to the boil, add the gelatine mixture and stir to combine. Remove from the heat and strain into a large bowl. Add the milk and yoghurt and whisk to combine. Carefully pour the filling into the tart case and refrigerate for 4 hours.

Place the passionfruit and the remaining ¼ cup (55g) of the sugar in a small saucepan over medium heat. Bring to the boil. Cook for 4 minutes or until syrupy. Allow to cool.

Remove the pastry ring and place the tart on a serving plate. Drizzle with passionfruit syrup to serve. SERVES 8–10
+ *Use uncooked rice instead of baking weights for this tart.*

yoghurt panna cotta tart

yoghurt crème with blood oranges

yoghurt crème with blood oranges

½ cup (125g) mascarpone
½ cup (125g) coconut yoghurt+
¾ cup (165g) caster (superfine) sugar
½ cup (125ml) double (thick) cream*
1½ cups (420g) natural Greek-style (thick) yoghurt
blood oranges with syrup
6 blood oranges
½ cup (110g) caster (superfine) sugar

Place the mascarpone, coconut yoghurt and sugar in a food processor and process until the sugar has dissolved. Add the cream and natural yoghurt and process to combine. Cut 4 x 25cm squares from a piece of damp muslin. Divide the mixture between the muslin squares, carefully gather up the edges and tie with string. Place on a small wire rack over a deep baking tray, allowing the excess moisture to drain. Cover loosely with plastic wrap and refrigerate for 6 hours or until firm.

To make the blood oranges with syrup, peel and thinly slice 3 of the oranges and set aside. Juice the remaining oranges and pour into a small saucepan over high heat. Add the sugar and bring to the boil. Reduce the heat to medium and cook for 6–8 minutes or syrupy. Allow to cool.

Cut open the muslin and transfer the crèmes to serving plates. Serve with the orange slices and syrup. **SERVES 4**
+ You can find yoghurt made with coconut milk at some supermarkets and at grocers and specialty food stores.

banana and coconut three-milk cake

180g unsalted butter, softened
1 cup (220g) caster (superfine) sugar
2 teaspoons vanilla extract
5 eggs
1 cup (260g) mashed ripe banana (about 3 bananas)
1½ cups (225g) self-raising (self-rising) flour
1 cup (250ml) coconut milk
1 cup (250ml) milk
395g can sweetened condensed milk
2 cups (500ml) single (pouring) cream*, whipped
½ cup (25g) coconut flakes, toasted

Preheat oven to 160°C (325°F). Lightly grease a 22cm round springform tin. Place the butter, sugar and vanilla in the bowl of an electric mixer and beat for 6–8 minutes or until pale and creamy. Scrape down the sides of the bowl and add the eggs, 1 at a time, beating well after each addition. Add the banana and flour and beat on low speed until just combined. Spoon the mixture into the tin. Bake for 45–50 minutes or until cooked when tested with a skewer. Allow the cake to cool completely in the tin.

Use the skewer to make holes all over the cake, pushing it three-quarters of the way to the base. Place the coconut milk, milk and sweetened condensed milk in a large jug and whisk well to combine. Place the cake tin on a tray to catch any spills and gradually pour the milk mixture over the cake. Refrigerate for 2–3 hours or until the milk mixture has been absorbed.

Top the cake with the cream and sprinkle with the coconut flakes. Slice to serve. **SERVES 8**

banana and coconut three-milk cake

hazelnut, orange and ricotta cake

hazelnut, orange and ricotta cake

1 cup (140g) hazelnuts, toasted and skins rubbed off
⅓ cup (50g) plain (all-purpose) flour
3 eggs
½ cup (110g) caster (superfine) sugar
40g unsalted butter, melted
4 cups (960g) fresh firm ricotta
1 cup (220g) caster (superfine) sugar, extra
2 tablespoons finely grated orange rind
1 teaspoon vanilla extract
1 cup (250ml) single (pouring) cream*, whipped
icing (confectioner's) sugar, for dusting
1 cup (150g) cherries, to serve

Preheat oven to 180°C (350°F). Line 2 x 22cm round springform tins with non-stick baking paper. Place the hazelnuts and flour in a food processor and process until fine. Place the eggs and sugar in the bowl of an electric mixer and beat for 6 minutes or until tripled in size. In 3 batches, using a large metal spoon, fold the hazelnut mixture into the egg mixture. Add the butter and gently fold to combine. Divide between the tins and bake for 15 minutes or until dry to the touch. Allow to cool in the tins for 15 minutes. Place onto wire racks to cool completely.

Place the ricotta, extra sugar, orange rind and vanilla in the bowl of an electric mixer and beat on high speed for 4 minutes or until smooth. Add the whipped cream and gently fold to combine.

Re-line 1 of the cleaned tins with non-stick baking paper. Place 1 of the cakes in the base of the tin. Spoon the ricotta mixture over the cake and smooth with a palette knife. Top with the remaining cake and press gently to secure. Freeze for 1 hour or until set.

Remove the cake from the tin and place it on a cake stand or plate. Dust with the icing sugar and top with the cherries to serve. SERVES 8–10
Tip: Keep this cake refrigerated in an airtight container for up to 2 days.

crème brûlée custard doughnuts

½ cup (125ml) sparkling clear lemonade
1 teaspoon vanilla bean paste or vanilla extract
2¼ cups (335g) plain (all-purpose) flour,
    plus extra for dusting
⅓ cup (75g) caster (superfine) sugar
2 teaspoons dry yeast
4 egg yolks
50g unsalted butter, softened
¼ cup (60ml) double (thick) cream*
1 cup (280g) store-bought thick vanilla-bean custard
¾ cup (165g) white (granulated) sugar
2 tablespoons water

Place the lemonade and vanilla in a small saucepan over medium heat until just warm. Place the flour, sugar and yeast in the bowl of an electric mixer fitted with a dough hook and beat on medium speed until combined. Add the warm lemonade mixture and egg yolks and beat until just combined. Add the butter and cream and beat for 6–8 minutes or until a smooth sticky dough forms.

Place the dough in a lightly greased bowl, cover with a clean damp tea towel and set aside in a warm place for 1 hour – 1 hour 30 minutes or until doubled in size.

Line a baking tray with non-stick baking paper. Roll out the dough on a lightly floured surface to 1.5cm thick. Using an 8.5cm round cookie cutter, lightly dusted in flour, cut out 6 rounds from the dough. Place the rounds on the tray, allowing room to spread. Set aside for 30 minutes or until risen.

Preheat oven to 180°C (350°F). Bake the doughnuts for 8–10 minutes or until golden and puffed. Allow to cool completely.

Place the custard in a piping bag fitted with a 5mm nozzle. Carefully press the nozzle through the base of each cooled doughnut and fill with custard.

To glaze the doughnuts, place them on a wire rack set over a tray. Place the sugar and water in a small bowl and mix to combine. Spoon the sugar mixture over each doughnut and allow to set for 5 minutes. Using a small kitchen blowtorch, caramelise until golden to serve. MAKES 6

crème brûlée custard doughnuts

chai portuguese custard tarts

chai portuguese custard tarts

¾ cup (165g) caster (superfine) sugar
¾ cup (180ml) water
6 whole cloves
2 sticks cinnamon
8 green cardamom pods, bruised
2 star anise
rind of 1 lemon
1 vanilla bean, split and seeds scraped
¼ cup (35g) cornflour (cornstarch)
1½ cups (375ml) milk
3 egg yolks
½ teaspoon loose-leaf chai tea
1 teaspoon light brown sugar
¼ teaspoon ground cinnamon
2 sheets frozen butter puff pastry, thawed
1 tablespoon water, for brushing

Preheat oven to 200°C (400°F). Place the caster sugar, water, cloves, cinnamon sticks, cardamom, star anise, lemon rind and vanilla bean and seeds in a medium saucepan over low heat and stir until the sugar has dissolved. Increase the heat to high and bring to the boil for 4 minutes or until thickened slightly. Strain the syrup into a heatproof bowl, discarding the solids. Place the cornflour and ½ cup (125ml) of the milk in a medium saucepan and mix until smooth. Add the egg yolks and whisk to combine. Add the remaining milk and the sugar syrup and whisk to combine. Place over medium heat and bring to the boil. Reduce the heat to low and cook, whisking continuously, for 6 minutes or until thickened. Transfer to a large bowl, cover with plastic wrap and set aside to cool completely.

Lightly grease 12 x ½-cup-capacity (125ml) muffin tins. Place the chai, brown sugar and ground cinnamon in a small bowl and mix to combine. Brush 1 sheet of the pastry lightly with water and sprinkle with the tea mixture. Sandwich with the remaining sheet, pressing well to seal. Tightly roll the pastry into a log and cut into 12 x 1cm-thick rounds. Roll out the rounds between 2 sheets of non-stick baking paper to make 12 x 12cm rounds and use them to line the tins. Divide the cooled custard between the pastry cases and smooth the tops. Bake for 28–30 minutes or until the custard is just blistered and golden. Allow to cool in the tins for 5 minutes before serving or place onto a wire rack to cool completely. MAKES 12

ricotta and dulce de leche doughnuts with smoked salt sugar

¾ cup (180ml) lukewarm milk
3 teaspoons dry yeast
¼ cup (55g) caster (superfine) sugar
2 cups (300g) plain (all-purpose) flour, plus extra for dusting
2 egg yolks
25g unsalted butter, softened
½ cup (110g) white (granulated) sugar
2 teaspoons smoked sea salt flakes+
vegetable oil, for deep-frying
ricotta filling
1½ cups (360g) fresh firm ricotta
⅓ cup (100g) store-bought dulce de leche* or thick caramel
¼ cup (40g) icing (confectioner's) sugar, sifted
½ teaspoon smoked sea salt flakes+

Place the milk, yeast and 1 tablespoon of the caster sugar in a small bowl and mix to combine. Set aside in a warm place for 5–10 minutes or until foamy. Place the flour, egg yolks, butter, the yeast mixture and the remaining 2 tablespoons of caster sugar in the bowl of an electric mixer with a dough hook attached. Beat on low speed for 4–5 minutes or until the dough is smooth and elastic. Place in a lightly greased bowl, cover with plastic wrap and set aside in a warm place for 45 minutes or until the dough has doubled in size.

Line a large baking tray with non-stick baking paper. Turn out the dough onto a lightly floured surface and knead for 2 minutes or until smooth and elastic. Roll out to 1cm thick. Using a 5.5cm round cutter, lightly dusted in flour, cut 14 rounds from the dough. Place the rounds on the tray and cover loosely with plastic wrap. Set aside in a warm place for 25–30 minutes or until the dough has doubled in size.

While the dough is proving, make the ricotta filling. Place the ricotta, dulce de leche, icing sugar and salt in a medium bowl and whisk until smooth. Place in a piping bag fitted with a 5mm round nozzle and refrigerate until needed.

Place the white sugar and salt in a small shallow tray and set aside. Half-fill a large, deep saucepan with oil and place over medium heat until the temperature reaches 180°C (350°F) on a deep-frying thermometer. In batches, cook the dough rounds, turning halfway, for 1–2 minutes or until golden. Immediately toss in the smoked salt sugar.

Using a small sharp knife, cut a hole in the side of each doughnut and pipe in the filling to serve. MAKES 14
+ *Find smoked sea salt flakes at delicatessens.*

ricotta and dulce de leche doughnuts with smoked salt sugar

vanilla slice with vanilla bean praline

vanilla slice with vanilla bean praline

2¼ cups (560ml) milk
2¼ cups (560ml) single (pouring) cream*
90g unsalted butter, chopped
1½ cups (330g) caster (superfine) sugar
2 vanilla beans, split and seeds scraped
⅔ cup (100g) cornflour (cornstarch)
¾ cup (180ml) water
9 egg yolks
1 x quantity vanilla bean praline (see *recipe*, right), to serve
rough puff pastry
3 cups (450g) plain (all-purpose) flour, plus extra for dusting
450g chilled unsalted butter, chopped into 2cm pieces
1 cup (250ml) iced water

To make the rough puff pastry, place the flour and butter in a large bowl. Using your fingertips, rub the butter into the flour until roughly combined (the butter should still be lumpy, about 1cm pieces). Make a well in the centre, add the water and mix, using a butter knife, into a dough. Turn out onto a lightly floured surface. Roll the dough out to a 20cm x 50cm rectangle (there will still be lumps of butter in the pastry).

Starting at the top short edge, fold the pastry down to the middle, and fold the bottom up to overlap the top. Turn the pastry a quarter turn, and roll out again to a 20cm x 50cm rectangle. Repeat the folding process 5 more times. Wrap in plastic wrap and refrigerate for 1 hour to firm.

Preheat oven to 200°C (400°F). Line 2 baking trays with non-stick baking paper. Halve the pastry and roll out, on a lightly floured surface, to make 2 x 30cm x 40cm rectangles. Place on the trays and bake for 30–35 minutes or until golden brown and puffed. Allow to cool completely.

Line a 20cm x 30cm slice tin with non-stick baking paper, leaving 4cm paper over the rim. Trim each pastry sheet into a 20cm x 30cm rectangle and use 1 to line the base of the tin.

Place the milk, cream, butter, sugar and vanilla bean and seeds in a medium saucepan over medium heat. Bring to just below the boil. Remove from the heat and discard the vanilla pods. Place the cornflour and water in a small bowl and mix to combine. Add the cornflour mixture and egg yolks to the milk mixture, return to the heat and whisk for 30 seconds or until thickened. Pour the mixture into the tin, smooth into an even layer and top with the second sheet of pastry. Refrigerate for 4 hours or until completely cold and set.

Cut the slice into lengths, place onto serving plates and sprinkle with the vanilla bean praline to serve. SERVES 8-10

vanilla bean praline

½ cup (110g) caster (superfine) sugar
¼ cup (60ml) water
1 vanilla bean, split and seeds scraped

Line a small tray with non-stick baking paper. Place the sugar and water in a small saucepan over low heat and cook for 4–5 minutes or until the sugar is dissolved. Increase the heat to high and cook, without stirring, for 8–9 minutes or until dark golden brown. Remove from the heat, add the vanilla seeds and stir to combine. Carefully pour onto the tray and allow to cool completely.

Once the praline is set, break it into pieces and place in a mortar. Pound with a pestle until fine. MAKES ½ CUP

tiramisu swirl ice-cream waffle cones

¾ cup (135g) light brown sugar
½ cup (125ml) espresso coffee
8 store-bought sponge finger biscuits, roughly chopped
2 tablespoons coffee liqueur
2 litres store-bought vanilla ice-cream, softened
50g 70% dark chocolate, finely grated
1 tablespoon finely crushed coffee beans
8 store-bought waffle cones

Place the sugar and coffee in a small saucepan over high heat. Bring to the boil and cook for 5–6 minutes or until reduced and syrupy. Set aside to cool completely.

Place the chopped biscuits in a large bowl, drizzle with the coffee liqueur. Mix to combine. Add the ice-cream and mix to combine. Add the coffee syrup and gently fold to combine to create a swirled effect. Spoon into a 1-litre-capacity metal container and freeze for 3–4 hours or until firm.

Place the chocolate and crushed coffee beans on a small plate. Scoop the ice-cream into the cones and dip in the chocolate mixture to serve. MAKES 8

tiramisu swirl ice-cream waffle cones

tiramisu cheat's soft-serve sandwiches

tiramisu cheat's soft-serve sandwiches

100g dark chocolate, melted
12 store-bought stroopwafel (syrup wafer) biscuits[+]
2 tablespoons store-bought chocolate-coated
    coffee beans, crushed
¾ cup (180g) mascarpone
¾ cup (180ml) single (pouring) cream*
2 litres store-bought vanilla ice-cream, softened

Line a large tray with non-stick baking paper. Place the chocolate in a small bowl. Dip 1 edge of each biscuit into the chocolate and place on the tray. Sprinkle the chocolate with the crushed coffee beans and refrigerate until set.

Place the mascarpone and cream in the bowl of an electric mixer and beat on low speed for 1 minute or until well combined. Add the ice-cream and beat for 1 minute or until smooth. Spoon the mixture into a piping bag fitted with a 1.5cm star-shaped nozzle and freeze for 30 minutes or until just firm.

Pipe a swirl of ice-cream onto 1 of the biscuits and top with another biscuit. Repeat to make 6 ice-cream sandwiches. Serve immediately. **MAKES 6**

+ *Stroopwafels, or syrup wafers, are Dutch biscuits with 2 thin waffle layers and a caramel filling. Find them in the international aisle of supermarkets or at specialty grocers. Tip: These soft-serve sandwiches can be made up to 1 day in advance. Keep them in an airtight container in the freezer until 5 minutes before you're ready to serve, giving them just enough time to soften.*

vanilla soft-serve ice-cream with maple and bourbon syrup

3 cups (750ml) single (pouring) cream*
1 cup (250ml) milk
1 cup (160g) icing (confectioner's) sugar, sifted
1 tablespoon vanilla extract
maple and bourbon syrup
3 teaspoons vanilla bean paste or vanilla extract
¼ cup (60ml) maple syrup
¼ cup (60ml) water
1 tablespoon bourbon

Place the cream, milk, sugar and vanilla in a large jug and whisk to dissolve the sugar. Divide the mixture between 2 large zip-lock plastic bags, pressing out as much air as possible, and seal. Lay each bag flat on a tray and freeze for 2 hours 30 minutes or until firm and just frozen.

While the ice-cream is freezing, make the maple and bourbon syrup. Place the vanilla, maple syrup and water in a small saucepan over medium heat. Bring to the boil, reduce the heat to low and cook for 4 minutes or until reduced and syrupy. Add the bourbon and stir to combine. Pour into a small jug and refrigerate until cold.

Remove the ice-cream from the freezer and bend the bags to break up the mixture into small pieces. Empty the mixture into a food processor and process for 2–3 minutes or until just smooth, breaking up any large pieces with a spoon. Spoon the ice-cream into a large piping bag fitted with a 1.5cm star-shaped nozzle[+]. Pipe the ice-cream into cups and drizzle with the syrup to serve. **SERVES 8**

+ *You can place the filled piping bag in the freezer for 10–15 minutes if the ice-cream needs firming.*

vanilla soft-serve ice-cream with maple and bourbon syrup

lemon and yoghurt cake

coconut crumbed deep-fried ice-cream bars

2 litres store-bought vanilla ice-cream
1 egg
1 cup (150g) plain (all-purpose) flour
¾ cup (180ml) iced water
2 cups (150g) shredded coconut
2 cups (150g) panko (Japanese) breadcrumbs*
150g dark chocolate, chopped
½ cup (125ml) single (pouring) cream*
vegetable oil, for deep-frying
½ cup (70g) beer nuts, chopped

Line a 20cm square cake tin with non-stick baking paper and freeze until ready to use. Scoop the ice-cream into the bowl of an electric mixer and beat on low speed for 30 seconds or until softened. Working quickly, spoon the ice-cream into the tin and smooth the top with a palette knife. Freeze for 3–4 hours or until firm.

Line a tray with non-stick baking paper and freeze until ready to use. Remove the ice-cream from the tin and, working quickly, cut into 12 x 3cm x 10cm bars. Place on the tray and freeze until needed.

Place the egg, flour and water in a medium bowl and whisk to combine. Place the coconut and breadcrumbs in a shallow bowl and mix to combine. Working quickly, remove 2–3 ice-cream bars at a time from the tray in the freezer. Dip each bar in the egg mixture, shaking off any excess, and roll in the coconut mixture to coat. Return to the freezer and repeat with the remaining bars and the egg and coconut mixtures. Freeze for 1–2 hours or until very firm.

Place the chocolate and cream in a small saucepan over low heat and cook, stirring, for 3–4 minutes or until melted and smooth. Set aside and keep warm.

Fill a large, deep saucepan half-full with oil. Place over medium heat until the temperature reaches 190°C (375°F) on a deep-frying thermometer. Deep-fry the ice-cream bars, in batches, for 30 seconds – 1 minute or until golden brown and crisp. Drain on absorbent kitchen paper.

Place onto serving plates and drizzle with the chocolate. Sprinkle with the nuts and serve immediately. MAKES 12

lemon and yoghurt cake

¾ cup (180ml) vegetable oil
2 eggs
1 tablespoon finely grated lemon rind
¼ cup (60ml) lemon juice
1 cup (280g) natural Greek-style (thick) yoghurt
1¾ cups (385g) caster (superfine) sugar
2 cups (300g) self-raising (self-rising) flour
2 tablespoons thyme leaves
lemon icing
1 cup (160g) icing (confectioner's) sugar
1 tablespoon lemon juice
½ tablespoon boiling water

Preheat oven to 160°C (325°F). Grease a 2.5-litre-capacity Bundt tin. Place the oil, eggs, lemon rind, lemon juice, yoghurt and sugar in a large bowl and whisk to combine. Sift in the flour and whisk until smooth. Pour into the tin and bake for 50–55 minutes or until cooked when tested with a skewer. Allow to cool in the tin for 5 minutes.

To make the lemon icing, sift the sugar into a medium bowl. Add the lemon juice and water and mix to combine.

Carefully turn the cake out onto a cake stand or plate. While the cake is still hot, spoon over the lemon icing and sprinkle with the thyme leaves. Allow to set for 10 minutes before slicing to serve. SERVES 10–12

coconut crumbed deep-fried ice-cream bars

chocolate and vanilla brûlée cheesecake

chocolate and vanilla brûlée cheesecake

340g store-bought plain chocolate biscuits
⅓ cup (40g) almond meal (ground almonds)
100g unsalted butter, melted
¼ cup (55g) white (granulated) sugar
filling
500g cream cheese, chopped and softened
1½ cups (360g) fresh firm ricotta
1 cup (220g) caster (superfine) sugar
4 eggs
2 teaspoons vanilla extract
200g dark chocolate, melted
2 teaspoons cornflour (cornstarch)

Line a 20cm round springform tin with non-stick baking paper. Place the biscuits and almond meal in a food processor and process into coarse crumbs. Add the butter and process until combined. Press into the base and sides of the tin, using the back of a spoon. Refrigerate for 30 minutes or until cold.

Preheat oven to 150°C (300°F). To make the filling, place the cream cheese, ricotta and sugar in the cleaned food processor and process for 2 minutes or until smooth. Scrape down the sides of the bowl, add the eggs and half the vanilla and process for 1 minute. Transfer two-thirds of the filling to a large bowl and set aside.

Add the chocolate to the remaining filling in the food processor and process until well combined. Pour onto the chilled base and smooth the top.

Place the cornflour and the remaining vanilla in a small bowl and mix to combine. Add the cornflour mixture to the remaining filling in the bowl and mix well. Gently spread into the tin and smooth the top.

Bake for 55 minutes – 1 hour or until the edges are just set and the centre still has a slight wobble. Turn the oven off and allow the cake to set in the oven with the door closed for 20 minutes. Allow to stand at room temperature for 30 minutes, before refrigerating for 2–3 hours or until cold. Carefully remove the tin.

Place the cheesecake on a cake stand or plate. Sprinkle with the sugar and caramelise the top, using a small kitchen blowtorch, to serve. **SERVES 10**

lemon and raspberry three-milk cake

270g unsalted butter, chopped and softened
1½ cups (330g) caster (superfine) sugar
2 tablespoons vanilla extract
2 tablespoons finely grated lemon rind
7 eggs
2¼ cups (335g) self-raising (self-rising) flour
3 cups (750ml) milk
395g can sweetened condensed milk
1 cup (250ml) buttermilk
375g raspberries
¼ cup (55g) caster (superfine) sugar, extra
2½ cups (625ml) single (pouring) cream*, whipped
freeze-dried raspberries*, crushed to serve

Preheat oven to 160°C (325°F). Lightly grease a 30cm round cake tin. Place the butter and sugar in the bowl of an electric mixer and beat for 8–10 minutes or until pale and creamy. Add 1 tablespoon of the vanilla and the lemon rind and beat to combine. Add the eggs, 1 at a time, beating well after each addition. Gradually add the flour and beat until just combined. Spoon the mixture into the tin and bake for 45 minutes or until cooked when tested with a skewer. Use the skewer to make holes all over the cake, pushing it three-quarters of the way to the base. Refrigerate to cool completely in the tin.

Place the milk, condensed milk, buttermilk and the remaining 1 tablespoon of vanilla in a large jug and whisk well to combine. With the cake still in the tin, pour the milk mixture over the cake and refrigerate for 2 hours or until the milk mixture is absorbed.

Place the fresh raspberries and extra sugar in a large non-stick frying pan over high heat. Cook, stirring, for 6–8 minutes or until thickened. Set aside to cool completely.

Top the cake with the raspberry jam, the cream and crushed freeze-dried raspberries. Slice to serve. **SERVES 8–10**

lemon and raspberry three-milk cake

QUICK

———

quick lychee and coconut sorbet
caramel and biscotti tiramisu
cookies and cream ice-cream sandwiches
milk and honey jellies
hazelnut and cream layered slice
baked sweet ricotta with honeycomb
cheat's yoghurt and white chocolate crèmes brûlées
blistered bananas with quick caramelised coconut yoghurt
rose and strawberry chilled rice puddings
ricotta and orange crostoli
crème fraîche and jam sweet buns
cheat's raspberry pavlova ice-cream
lemon and ginger possets
mascarpone and passionfruit shortbread sandwiches
sheep's milk yoghurt with pistachio and mint sugar
frozen yoghurt and white chocolate bark

———

FIX

quick lychee and coconut sorbet

560g canned pitted lychees in syrup, drained
½ cup (125ml) light agave syrup*
1 tablespoon lime juice
1⅔ cups (400ml) coconut cream

Place the lychees, agave and lime juice in a food processor and process until smooth. Add the coconut cream and pulse to combine. Pour into a 20cm x 30cm slice tin or shallow metal container and freeze for 3 hours or until frozen.

Remove the sorbet from the tin and chop into squares. Place in a food processor and process, scraping down the sides of the bowl, until just smooth.

Scoop the sorbet into cups. Serve immediately. SERVES 6–8

caramel and biscotti tiramisu

1 cup (250g) mascarpone
2½ cups (625ml) single (pouring) cream*
¼ cup (40g) icing (confectioner's) sugar, sifted
¼ cup (60ml) hazelnut liqueur
16 store-bought thin almond biscotti
2 tablespoons store-bought thick caramel or dulce de leche*
1 teaspoon cocoa powder, for dusting

Place the mascarpone, cream and sugar in a large bowl and whisk until soft peaks form. Spread ⅓ cup (80ml) of the cream mixture into the base of each of 4 x 1⅓-cup-capacity (330ml) serving dishes.

Place the liqueur in a small shallow bowl. Dipping the biscotti in the liqueur first, place 2 biscotti in each dish and top with 1 teaspoon of the caramel. Spread each tiramisu with ⅓ cup (80ml) of the cream mixture. Repeat this layering 1 more time with the remaining biscotti, liqueur, caramel and cream mixture. Refrigerate for 30 minutes.

Dust each tiramisu with cocoa to serve. MAKES 4

cookies and cream ice-cream sandwiches

30 store-bought plain chocolate biscuits
1 litre store-bought vanilla ice-cream, softened
1 teaspoon vanilla bean paste or vanilla extract

Roughly crumble 6 of the biscuits. Place the ice-cream
in a large bowl. Add the crushed biscuit and vanilla and
gently fold to combine. Spoon into a 1-litre-capacity metal
container and freeze for 2–3 hours or until firm.

Line a tray with non-stick baking paper. Place 12 of the
biscuits, base-side up, on the tray. Top each with 1 scoop
of the ice-cream. Sandwich with the remaining biscuits.
Return to the freezer until ready to serve. MAKES 12

milk and honey jellies

2 tablespoons water
1 teaspoon gelatine powder*
1 cup (250ml) milk
⅓ cup (120g) honey
2 cups (500ml) single (pouring) cream*
¼ cup (40g) icing (confectioner's) sugar,
    plus extra for dusting
125g blueberries, to serve

Place the water in a small bowl, sprinkle with the
gelatine and stir to combine. Set aside for 5 minutes
or until the gelatine is absorbed. Place the milk and
honey in a medium saucepan over medium heat
and stir until the honey is melted. Add the gelatine
mixture and stir until smooth. Remove from the
heat, add half the cream and stir to combine. Divide
between 4 x 1-cup-capacity (250ml) shallow serving
bowls and refrigerate for 4–6 hours or until set.

Place the sugar and remaining cream in the bowl
of an electric mixer and whisk until soft peaks form.

Top the jellies with the cream mixture and the
blueberries. Dust with extra icing sugar to serve. MAKES 4

hazelnut and cream layered slice

1½ cups (375ml) single (pouring) cream*
1½ cups (360g) sour cream*
⅓ cup (55g) icing (confectioner's) sugar, sifted
½ cup (125ml) hazelnut liqueur
20 store-bought plain sweet rectangular biscuits
store-bought hazelnut brittle, chopped to serve⁺

Line an 8cm x 22cm deep loaf tin with non-stick baking paper. Place the cream, sour cream and sugar in the bowl of an electric mixer and whisk until stiff peaks form. Spoon one-third of the mixture into the tin and spread to evenly coat the base and sides.

Place the liqueur in a small shallow bowl. Dip 4 of the biscuits in the liqueur and place on the cream base. Top with one-fifth of the remaining cream mixture and spread evenly. Repeat this layering 4 more times, using the remaining biscuits, liqueur and cream. Cover with plastic wrap and refrigerate for 2 hours or until set.

Turn the slice out onto a serving plate and sprinkle with the hazelnut brittle to serve. SERVES 6-8
+ *Find hazelnut brittle at confectionery stores. You could also use peanut brittle.*

baked sweet ricotta with honeycomb

2 cups (480g) fresh firm ricotta
2 eggs
1 teaspoon vanilla extract
2 teaspoons finely grated lemon rind
1 tablespoon plain (all-purpose) flour
fresh honeycomb, to serve⁺
store-bought biscotti, to serve

Preheat oven to 180°C (350°F). Grease 4 x ¾-cup-capacity (180ml) Texas muffin tins. Place the ricotta, eggs, vanilla, lemon rind and flour in a large bowl and whisk to combine. Spoon into the tins and bake for 25–30 minutes or until just set. Allow to cool in the tins for 10 minutes.

Place onto serving plates and top with honeycomb. Serve with biscotti. MAKES 4
+ *Buy fresh honeycomb from most grocers and health food stores. Use regular honey if unavailable.*

cheat's yoghurt and white chocolate crèmes brûlées

180g white chocolate, finely chopped
1½ cups (420g) natural Greek-style (thick) yoghurt
1 teaspoon vanilla extract
white (granulated) sugar, for sprinkling

Place the chocolate and ½ cup (140g) of the yoghurt in a small saucepan over low heat and stir until the chocolate has melted. Allow to cool for 2 minutes.

Place the remaining yoghurt and the vanilla in a medium bowl. Add the chocolate mixture and fold until smooth and combined. Divide the mixture between 4 x ½-cup-capacity (125ml) serving dishes. Refrigerate for 1 hour or until cold.

Sprinkle each dish with sugar and, using a small kitchen blowtorch, caramelise the tops until golden to serve. MAKES 4

blistered bananas with quick caramelised coconut yoghurt

⅓ cup (60g) dark brown sugar
4 ladyfinger bananas, skin on and halved lengthways
2 cups (500g) coconut yoghurt⁺
1½ tablespoons dark brown sugar, extra

Heat a large non-stick frying pan over medium heat. Spread the sugar on a small tray. Press the bananas, cut-side down, into the sugar to coat. In 2 batches, cook the bananas, sugar-side down, for 2 minutes or until golden and caramelised.

Divide the yoghurt between 4 serving glasses and sprinkle with the extra sugar. Allow to stand for 5 minutes or until the sugar has dissolved.

Serve bananas with the caramelised yoghurt. SERVES 4
+ *You can find yoghurt made with coconut milk at some supermarkets and at grocers and specialty food stores.*

rose and strawberry chilled rice puddings

1½ cups (280g) cooked white rice, cold
1 cup (250ml) single (pouring) cream*
½ cup (125ml) milk
⅓ cup (120g) honey
1 teaspoon vanilla extract
250g strawberries, hulled and halved
½ teaspoon rosewater
edible dried rose petals, to serve+
pistachios, chopped to serve

Place the rice, cream, milk, ¼ cup (90g) of the honey
and the vanilla in a medium saucepan over medium heat.
Cook, stirring occasionally, for 6–8 minutes or until hot
and thickened. Divide between 4 x ¾-cup-capacity (180ml)
serving glasses and refrigerate for 1 hour or until cold.

Place the strawberry, the remaining 1 tablespoon of
honey and the rosewater in a medium bowl and gently
toss to combine.

Top each pudding with the strawberry mixture.
Sprinkle with rose petals and pistachios to serve. MAKES 4
+ *Find edible dried rose petals (pesticide-free) at specialty
food stores, grocers and delicatessens.*

ricotta and orange crostoli

vegetable oil, for deep-frying
1 cup (240g) fresh firm ricotta
1 teaspoon finely grated orange rind
½ cup (80g) icing (confectioner's) sugar, sifted,
    plus extra for dusting
28 square wonton wrappers*
water, for brushing

Half-fill a large saucepan with oil and place over medium
heat until the temperature reaches 180°C (350°F) on a
deep-frying thermometer.

While the oil is heating, place the ricotta, orange rind
and sugar in a medium bowl and mix to combine. Place
2-teaspoon portions of the mixture in the centre of each
of half the wonton wrappers. Brush the edges with water
and sandwich with the remaining wrappers, pressing
the edges to seal.

In batches, deep-fry the crostoli, turning halfway, for
2 minutes or until golden. Drain on absorbent kitchen paper.
Dust with extra sugar and serve immediately. MAKES 14

crème fraîche and jam sweet buns

1 cup (250ml) single (pouring) cream*
½ cup (120g) crème fraîche
¼ cup (40g) icing (confectioner's) sugar, sifted,
   plus extra for dusting
1 teaspoon vanilla extract
4 mini brioche slider buns*, halved
⅓ cup (110g) raspberry jam

Place the cream, crème fraîche, sugar and vanilla
in the bowl of an electric mixer and whisk until
stiff peaks form. Place in a piping bag fitted with
a 1cm star-shaped nozzle.

Pipe the cream mixture onto the bases of the
buns. Top with the jam and sandwich with the bun
tops. Dust with extra icing sugar to serve. MAKES 4

cheat's raspberry pavlova ice-cream

125g raspberries, plus extra to serve
2 tablespoons icing (confectioner's) sugar
1 teaspoon vanilla bean paste or vanilla extract
40g store-bought meringues, crushed,
   plus extra for sprinkling
1 litre store-bought vanilla ice-cream, softened
1 passionfruit, to serve

Place the raspberries, sugar and vanilla in a large
bowl. Using a fork, gently crush the raspberries.
Add the meringue and ice-cream and gently fold to
combine. Spoon the mixture into a 1.5-litre capacity
metal container and freeze for 3 hours or until firm.

Top the ice-cream with extra raspberries, meringue
and the passionfruit pulp to serve. SERVES 4–6

lemon and ginger possets

2 cups (500ml) single (pouring) cream*
½ cup (110g) caster (superfine) sugar
½ teaspoon finely grated ginger
⅓ cup (80ml) lemon juice

Place the cream, sugar and ginger in a small saucepan over medium heat and cook, stirring occasionally, for 6 minutes. Add the lemon juice and cook for a further 2 minutes or until the mixture is hot and thickened.

Pour into 4 x 1-cup-capacity (250ml) serving glasses and refrigerate for 2–3 hours or until set. MAKES 4

mascarpone and passionfruit shortbread sandwiches

1½ cups (375ml) single (pouring) cream*
1 cup (250g) mascarpone
¼ cup (40g) icing (confectioner's) sugar, sifted,
    plus extra for dusting
1 teaspoon vanilla extract
16 store-bought plain shortbread biscuits
4 passionfruit, to serve

Place the cream, mascarpone, sugar and vanilla in a medium bowl and whisk until soft peaks form. Spoon the mascarpone mixture onto half the biscuits. Sandwich with the remaining biscuits.

Place onto serving plates, dust with extra icing sugar and top with passionfruit pulp to serve. MAKES 8

sheep's milk yoghurt with pistachio and mint sugar

⅓ cup mint leaves
2 tablespoons white (granulated) sugar
¼ cup (45g) pistachios, finely chopped
3 cups (760g) sheep's milk yoghurt
2 oranges, peeled and sliced

Place the mint in a small food processor and pulse until finely chopped. Add the sugar and pulse until just combined. Transfer to a small bowl, add the chopped pistachios and mix to combine.

Spoon the yoghurt onto serving plates and top with the orange slices. Sprinkle with the pistachio and mint sugar to serve. **SERVES 4**

frozen yoghurt and white chocolate bark

360g white chocolate, melted
1½ cups (420g) natural Greek-style (thick) yoghurt
2 tablespoons melted coconut oil*
½ cup (65g) store-bought granola
¼ cup (35g) dried cranberries, chopped
¼ cup (35g) slivered pistachios

Line a large tray with non-stick baking paper. Place the chocolate, yoghurt and coconut oil in a medium bowl and mix until smooth. Spread onto the tray and sprinkle with the granola, chopped cranberries and pistachios. Freeze for 1 hour or until firm.

Slice or break the bark into pieces to serve. **SERVES 6**
Tip: Keep this bark frozen in an airtight container for up to 1 week.

FRESH

AND

LIGHT

———

In deluxe creamy desserts and milky iced treats, I'm forever adding the goodness of natural yoghurt where I can. But there's also a world of delicate flavour to be found beyond pure dairy. Smooth and sweet almond milks, churned cashew creams and lush coconut milks are my latest loves.

coconut and roasted plum frozen cheesecakes

coconut and roasted plum frozen cheesecakes

4 blood plums (400g), halved
2 tablespoons water
2 tablespoons honey
1 cup (130g) store-bought granola
¼ cup (20g) shredded coconut
2 tablespoons melted coconut oil*
125g raspberries, to serve
cheesecake filling
2 cups (500g) coconut yoghurt⁺
1 cup (240g) fresh firm ricotta
1 teaspoon vanilla extract
⅓ cup (120g) honey

Preheat oven to 200°C (400°F). Place the plums and water in a small baking dish. Drizzle with the honey and bake for 15–18 minutes or until soft. Allow to cool slightly. Roughly chop the plums, reserving the syrup.

Line 4 x 10cm round (1½-cup-capacity) springform cake tins with non-stick baking paper. Place the granola, coconut and coconut oil in a small food processor and pulse until finely chopped. Press into the base of the tins, using the back of a spoon, and freeze for 10 minutes.

While the bases are freezing, make the cheesecake filling. Place the yoghurt, ricotta, vanilla and honey in a large bowl and whisk until smooth.

Add the chopped plums to the cheesecake filling and gently fold to combine. Spoon into the tins and smooth the tops. Freeze for 3–4 hours or until firm.

Remove the cheesecakes from the tins and place onto serving plates. Drizzle with the reserved plum syrup and top with the raspberries. Serve immediately. **MAKES 4**
+ You can buy yoghurt made with coconut milk at some supermarkets and at grocers and specialty food stores.
Tip: This recipe can also make 1 large cheesecake using a 20cm round springform cake tin.

rhubarb and yoghurt loaf cake

260g rhubarb, trimmed and cut into 10cm lengths
2 tablespoons honey
1 cup (160g) rapadura sugar*
1 cup (80g) desiccated coconut
1 cup (160g) buckwheat flour*, sifted
2 teaspoons baking powder
2 eggs
1 cup (280g) natural Greek-style (thick) yoghurt,
    plus extra to serve
½ cup (125ml) light-flavoured extra virgin olive oil
2 teaspoons vanilla extract
1 tablespoon finely grated orange rind

Preheat oven to 160°C (325°F). Line a 10cm x 20cm loaf tin with non-stick baking paper. Place the rhubarb, honey and ¼ cup (40g) of the sugar in a large bowl. Toss to combine and set aside.

Place the coconut, flour, baking powder, eggs, yoghurt, oil, vanilla, orange rind and the remaining ¾ cup (120g) of sugar in a separate large bowl and mix to combine. Pour into the tin and arrange the rhubarb on top. Bake for 1 hour 10 minutes or until cooked when tested with a skewer. Allow to cool in the tin for 5 minutes before placing on a wire rack to cool completely.

Slice and serve with extra yoghurt. **SERVES 8-10**

rhubarb and yoghurt loaf cake

steamed almond milk pudding with almond and maple sauce

steamed almond milk pudding with almond and maple sauce

½ cup (140g) natural almond butter*
70g unsalted butter, softened
½ cup (110g) raw caster (superfine) sugar
1 teaspoon vanilla extract
3 eggs
1 cup (160g) wholemeal (whole-wheat) self-raising
    (self-rising) flour*
⅔ cup (80g) almond meal (ground almonds)
½ cup (125ml) unsweetened almond milk*
almond and maple sauce
1½ cups (375ml) unsweetened almond milk*
⅓ cup (80ml) maple syrup
2 teaspoons cornflour (cornstarch)
1 teaspoon vanilla extract

Line a 2-litre-capacity pudding bowl with non-stick baking paper. Place the almond butter, butter, sugar and vanilla in the bowl of an electric mixer and beat on high speed for 6 minutes or until pale and creamy. Scrape down the sides of the bowl and add the eggs, 1 at a time, beating well after each addition. Add the flour, almond meal and almond milk and beat on low speed to combine. Spoon into the pudding bowl and spread evenly. Top with a round of non-stick baking paper and cover the top of the bowl tightly with foil. Secure with kitchen string.

Place the pudding in a large saucepan over medium heat and pour in enough boiling water to come two-thirds of the way up the side of the bowl. Bring to the boil, reduce the heat to low and cover the saucepan with a tight-fitting lid. Cook, adding more boiling water if needed, for 1 hour 30 minutes or until the pudding is springy to the touch. Remove the bowl from the saucepan carefully and allow to stand for 10 minutes, before inverting onto a serving plate.

While the pudding is standing, make the almond and maple sauce. Place the almond milk, maple syrup, cornflour and vanilla in a small saucepan over medium heat and whisk to combine. Bring to the boil and cook, stirring occasionally, for 6–8 minutes or until thickened.

Pour the hot sauce over the pudding to serve. SERVES 8

coconut chia puddings with passionfruit and lime granita

½ cup (90g) white chia seeds*
1½ cups (375ml) coconut milk
1 cup (250ml) milk
2 tablespoons honey
passionfruit and lime granita
1 cup (250ml) passionfruit pulp (about 12 passionfruit)
2 tablespoons honey
3 cups (750ml) coconut water
2 teaspoons finely grated lime rind
1 tablespoon lime juice

To make the passionfruit and lime granita, place the passionfruit and honey in a small saucepan over medium heat. Bring to a simmer and cook for 6 minutes or until thickened slightly. Remove from the heat, add the coconut water, lime rind and juice and mix to combine. Pour into a 20cm x 30cm slice tin or shallow metal container and freeze for 4 hours or until frozen.

Place the chia seeds, coconut milk, milk and honey in a large bowl and mix to combine. Refrigerate for 30 minutes or until thickened.

Rake the granita into crystals using a fork. Divide the chia pudding between 4 x 1¾-cup-capacity (430ml) serving glasses and top with the granita. Serve immediately. MAKES 4

coconut chia puddings with passionfruit and lime granita

lemon and yoghurt panna cottas with passionfruit

lemon and yoghurt panna cottas with passionfruit

1 tablespoon cold water
¾ teaspoon gelatine powder*
1 cup (250ml) milk
¼ cup (55g) caster (superfine) sugar
2 teaspoons finely grated lemon rind
1¼ cups (350g) vanilla-bean yoghurt
passionfruit pulp, to serve

Place the water in a small bowl and sprinkle with the gelatine. Allow to stand for 5 minutes or until the gelatine is absorbed.

Place the milk and sugar in a medium saucepan over medium heat and whisk until hot, but not boiling. Add the gelatine mixture and whisk continuously for 1 minute. Remove from the heat and allow to cool slightly. Add the lemon rind and yoghurt and whisk to combine. Divide between 4 x 1-cup-capacity (250ml) serving glasses. Refrigerate for 4 hours or until set.

Top panna cottas with passionfruit to serve. MAKES 4

fig, coconut and almond slice

½ cup (45g) rolled oats
½ cup (40g) desiccated coconut
½ cup (60g) almond meal (ground almonds)
40g unsalted butter, melted
½ cup (150g) dried figs
4 small figs (240g), sliced
coconut filling
1¾ cups (140g) desiccated coconut
1¼ cups (310ml) coconut milk
1½ tablespoons coconut oil*

Preheat oven to 160°C (325°F). Line a 20cm square slice tin with non-stick baking paper. Place the oats, coconut, almond meal, butter and dried figs in a food processor and process for 2–3 minutes or until chopped and well combined. Press into the base of the tin, using the back of a spoon, and smooth the top. Bake for 10 minutes or until golden brown. Set aside to cool completely.

To make the coconut filling, place the coconut, coconut milk and coconut oil in a blender and blend, scraping down the sides if necessary, for 1 minute or until well combined and fluffy. Spread the filling evenly onto the base. Arrange the fresh fig slices on top and refrigerate for 1 hour or until set.

Remove the slice from the tin and cut into pieces to serve. MAKES 8

fig, coconut and almond slice

banana and honey sesame crunch ice-cream cake

banana and honey sesame crunch ice-cream cake

450g chopped peeled frozen banana (about 4 large bananas)[+]
1½ cups (420g) natural Greek-style (thick) yoghurt
1 teaspoon vanilla bean paste or vanilla extract
¼ cup (90g) honey, plus extra to serve
3 bananas, peeled and halved lengthways, to serve
freshly grated nutmeg, to serve
sesame crunch
¾ cup (20g) puffed brown rice*
2 tablespoons rolled oats
2 tablespoons white sesame seeds
2 tablespoons honey

To make the sesame crunch, preheat oven to 180°C (350°F).
Line a 20cm round springform tin with non-stick baking
paper. Place the puffed rice, oats, sesame seeds and honey
in a medium bowl and mix to combine. Press into the base
of the tin, using the back of a spoon. Place on an oven tray
and bake for 12–15 minutes or until golden brown. Allow to
cool completely.

Place the frozen banana, yoghurt, vanilla and honey in
a blender and blend until smooth. Pour the mixture over
the sesame crunch and freeze for 6 hours or until firm.

Remove the cake from the tin and place on a cake stand
or plate. Top with the banana and sprinkle with nutmeg.
Drizzle with extra honey and serve immediately. SERVES 8–10
+ *To freeze the banana, layer slices in an airtight*
container between sheets of non-stick baking paper
and place in the freezer until solid.

yoghurt granola popsicles

1⅓ cups (160g) store-bought granola[+]
1½ tablespoons date syrup[++]
2 cups (560g) natural Greek-style (thick) yoghurt

Place the granola and date syrup in a small bowl and mix
to combine. Divide between 8 x ⅓-cup-capacity (80ml)
popsicle moulds and pack down firmly with the end of a
wooden spoon.

Fill each mould with the yoghurt, cover with aluminium
foil and insert the popsicle sticks. Freeze for 3–4 hours or
until frozen. Remove from the moulds and serve. MAKES 8
+ *Look for low-sugar granola in the health food aisle*
of your supermarket.
++ *Date syrup is a natural sweetener with richness*
and a treacly depth. Find it in health food stores.
You could also use dark agave syrup or coconut
blossom syrup.

yoghurt granola popsicles

coconut caramel with coconut ice-cream

almond milk and date cake with creamy cashew icing

8 soft fresh dates (160g), pitted and chopped
¼ cup (60ml) boiling water
1 teaspoon bicarbonate of (baking) soda
¾ cup (180ml) unsweetened almond milk*
2 eggs
⅓ cup (75g) raw caster (superfine) sugar
1¼ cups (160g) white spelt flour*
¾ cup (90g) almond meal (ground almonds)
1 teaspoon vanilla extract
2 tablespoons light-flavoured extra virgin olive oil
¼ cup (40g) cashews
1 tablespoon maple syrup
creamy cashew icing
1 cup (150g) cashews
1 cup (250ml) boiling water
¼ cup (60ml) unsweetened almond milk*
2 tablespoons natural almond butter*
2 tablespoons raw caster (superfine) sugar
1 teaspoon vanilla extract

Preheat oven to 160°C (325°F). Line a 20cm round cake tin with non-stick baking paper. Place the date, water and bicarbonate of soda in a medium heatproof bowl. Stir to combine and allow to soak for 5 minutes. Place in a food processor, add the almond milk and process until smooth.

Place the eggs and sugar in the bowl of an electric mixer and whisk on high speed for 6–8 minutes or until thick and tripled in volume. Add the date mixture, flour, almond meal, vanilla and oil and gently fold to combine. Pour into the tin and bake for 40–45 minutes or until cooked when tested with a skewer. Allow to cool in the tin for 10 minutes, before turning out onto a wire rack to cool completely.

To make the creamy cashew icing, place the cashews and boiling water in a medium heatproof bowl and allow to soak for 20–30 minutes or until softened. Drain and place in a food processor with the almond milk, almond butter, sugar and vanilla and process, scraping down the sides of the bowl, for 2 minutes or until smooth and creamy. Set aside.

Increase the oven temperature to 200°C (400°F). Place the cashews in a small roasting pan and drizzle with the maple syrup. Roast for 10 minutes or until golden. Allow to cool for 5 minutes before roughly chopping.

Place the cake on a cake stand or plate. Spread with the icing and top with the maple cashews to serve. **SERVES 10-12**

coconut caramel with coconut ice-cream

⅓ cup (80ml) coconut milk
1 cup (140g) coconut sugar*
1 teaspoon vanilla bean paste or vanilla extract
store-bought coconut ice-cream, to serve
shredded coconut, to serve

Place the coconut milk, sugar and vanilla in a small saucepan over high heat and bring to the boil. Reduce the heat to medium and cook for 1–2 minutes, or until thickened. Allow to cool to room temperature.

Scoop the ice-cream into serving cups, drizzle with the caramel and sprinkle with coconut to serve. **SERVES 4**
+ *Keep the caramel at room temperature in an airtight container for up to 3 days.*

almond milk and date cake with creamy cashew icing

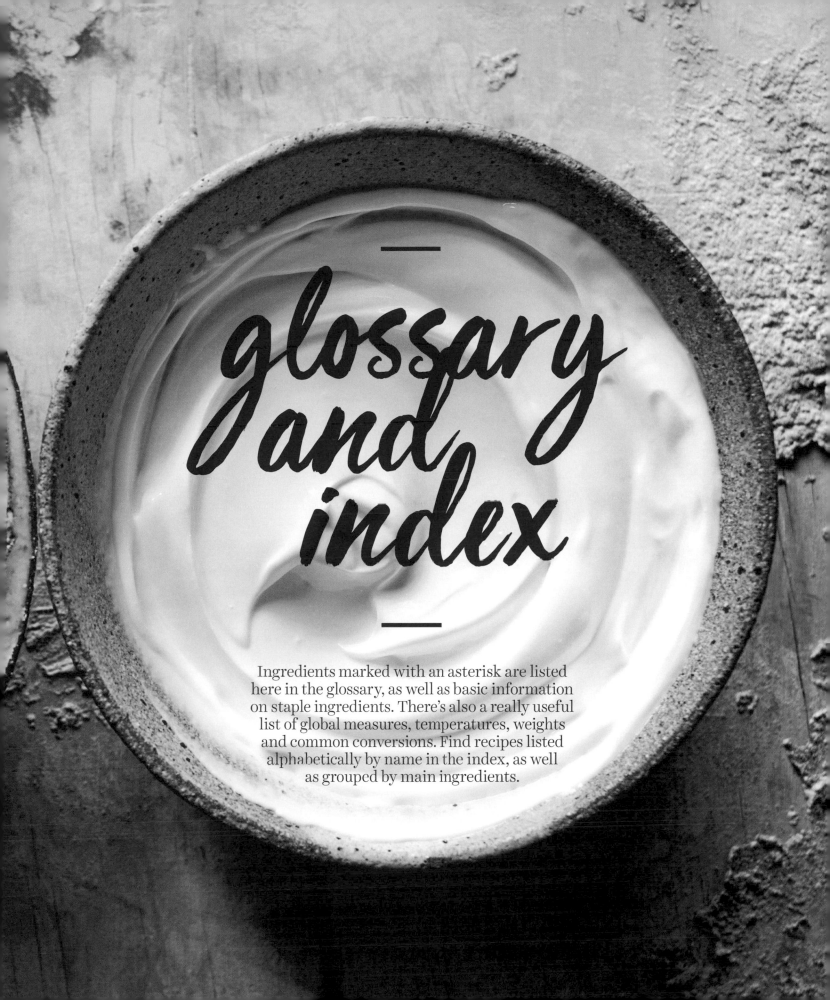

glossary and index

Ingredients marked with an asterisk are listed here in the glossary, as well as basic information on staple ingredients. There's also a really useful list of global measures, temperatures, weights and common conversions. Find recipes listed alphabetically by name in the index, as well as grouped by main ingredients.

marked ingredients

agave syrup
Agave syrup is the nectar of the agave succulent and has a mild, neutral sweetness. It's often used in place of sugar, maple syrup or honey. It's available from the health food aisle of supermarkets.

almond

butter
Sometimes called almond spread, this paste is made from crushed almonds and is available at most supermarkets and health food stores (choose jars labelled with 100% almonds to avoid additives). It's a popular alternative to peanut butter for those with allergies (always read the label).

milk
Buy natural fresh, unsweetened almond milk from the chilled section of supermarkets and grocers. With its velvety texture and mild nutty flavour, it's a popular dairy-free alternative to cow's milk, and is becoming more readily available. You can also make your own almond milk using this recipe:

1½ cups (240g) almonds
1 litre water

Place the almonds in a large bowl and cover with cold water. Cover with plastic wrap and allow to soak for 6 hours or overnight. Drain and rinse the almonds under cold running water. Place in a blender, add the water and blend for 2 minutes or until well combined. Line a fine sieve with muslin and strain the mixture into a large bowl, in batches, squeezing to remove the milk. Keep the almond milk refrigerated for up to 4 days. MAKES 1.25 LITRES

natural flaked
Natural flaked almonds, sometimes sold as natural sliced almonds, are simply thin slices of almonds with the skin left on. Find them in the health food aisle of the supermarket or substitute with regular (skinless) flaked almonds.

amaranth
Similar to quinoa, amaranth is not a grain but a seed harvested from an annual plant. Gluten free and high in protein and minerals, it's available in health food stores and specialty grocers.

flakes
Amaranth seeds that have been rolled into flakes make for a nourishing porridge or crispy addition to baked treats. Find amaranth flakes at health food stores.

puffed
Puffed amaranth, similar to puffed rice, is amaranth seeds that have been heated and popped, or puffed, to become light and aerated. Perfect in cereals, bars or slices, find puffed amaranth at health food stores.

amaretti biscuits
Amaretti biscuits, or macarons, are traditional Italian almond-flavoured biscuits. Made with sugar, eggwhites and almonds, they're light, crisp and often have a slightly chewy centre. Find them in supermarkets, Italian grocers and delicatessens.

arrowroot
Also known as tapioca flour, arrowroot flour (or powder) is used in baked goods, puddings, pies and sauces as a thickener and glazing agent. It's gluten free (always check the label) and is sold in the baking section of supermarkets.

black sea salt flakes
Naturally coloured with carbon or charcoal, black sea salt flakes taste similar to, and are interchangeable with, regular sea salt flakes. Their inky tone adds drama to whatever they're sprinkled on. Find them at gourmet food stores, specialty grocers and at most supermarkets.

brioche slider buns
Soft and light with a glossy exterior, these small French-style brioche rolls are mostly used to make mini burgers, but they're great for filling with sweet things, too. Find brioche buns at good bakeries, specialty and Italian grocers, plus most supermarkets.

buckwheat
Buckwheat is the seed of a plant related to rhubarb. Once cooked, it can be used like rice or pasta. Buy raw buckwheat at health food stores and some supermarkets.

candied clementines
You can buy these glossy preserved citrus fruits in packs or jars at gourmet food stores and delicatessens.

cashew butter
Sometimes called cashew spread, this paste is made from crushed cashews. It's available from the health food aisle of most supermarkets and at health food stores (choose jars labelled with 100% cashews to avoid additives).

chia seeds
These tiny seeds come from an ancient flowering plant and are full of protein, omega-3 fatty acids, minerals and fibre. You can use the black or white seeds interchangeably. They're available in supermarkets and health food stores and are great for smoothies and baking.

chipotle chillies

Chipotle chillies are smoke-dried jalapeño peppers commonly used in Mexican cooking. Find them at spice shops and specialty grocers.

coconut oil

Extracted from mature coconuts, coconut oil is sold in jars as a solid, so you may need to melt it before using. It adds a touch of tropical flavour to baked treats and slices and is sometimes used as a dairy-free alternative to butter. Look for virgin coconut oil in supermarkets and health food stores.

coconut yoghurt

Yoghurt made from coconut milk and probiotic cultures. Find this dairy alternative in grocers, health food stores and some supermarkets.

cream

The fat content of these different varieties of creams determines their names and uses.

crème fraîche

A rich, tangy, fermented cream, traditionally from France, with a minimum fat content of 35 per cent. Available at grocers, delicatessens and most supermarkets.

double (thick)

Often called heavy cream, this has a butter fat content of 40–50 per cent. It's usually served as a side with warm puddings, pies and rich cakes.

single (pouring)

With a butter fat content of 20–30 per cent, this thin cream is most commonly used for making ice-cream, panna cotta and custard. It can be whipped to a light and airy consistency. Often called pure or whipping cream.

sour

A fermented cream with a minimum fat content of 35 per cent, sour cream is readily available in supermarkets and used for its creamy-yet-tangy flavour.

thickened

Thickened cream is a single (pouring) cream that has had a vegetable gum added to stabilise it. The gum makes the cream a little thicker and easier to whip.

date syrup

A dark, treacle-like sweetener made from dates. Buy it from health food stores, online or from the health food aisle of supermarkets.

dried lavender

Edible dried lavender, or lavender tea, infuses an aromatic flavour into sweets and adds its pastel colour. Buy it, pesticide-free, from health food stores, specialty grocers and tea shops.

dried rose petals

Pesticide-free organic rose petals are sold dried in packs at cake decorating stores, specialty food shops and online. Ensure the packaging states they're edible. They can be used in and on treats for their delicate flavour and colour.

dulce de leche

This thick milk caramel, common in Latin American desserts, is made by slowly heating and thickening sweetened milk. You can buy it ready-made in jars from supermarkets and grocers. Make your own by gently boiling an unopened can (not a ring-pull can) of sweetened condensed milk for 2–3 hours. The longer it's cooked, the thicker, darker and more intense the caramel flavour becomes. Dulce de leche can be used as a filling for tarts, as a topping on cakes or drizzled over ice-cream.

edible gold leaf

Edible gold leaf is available from gourmet food shops, cake-decorating stores and online. It's best to follow the instructions for application on the packet, as products can vary.

flour

buckwheat

Despite its name, buckwheat flour isn't from a grain but milled from the seed of a plant related to rhubarb and sorrel. Often used in pancakes and noodles for its rich, nutty flavour and wholesome benefits, it's also gluten free.

rice

Rice flour is a fine flour made from ground rice. Available in white and brown varieties, it's often used as a thickening agent in baking, in cookies and shortbreads, and to coat foods when cooking Asian dishes – particularly those needing a crispy finish, such as tofu. It's gluten free and available in supermarkets and health food shops.

spelt

Milled from the ancient cereal grain, spelt flour boasts more nutrients and is better tolerated by some than regular flour. White spelt flour is easier to bake with, while wholemeal has more of the grain's goodness. It lends a warm, nutty flavour to breads and cakes. Find spelt flour in the health aisle of supermarkets.

wholemeal (whole-wheat)

Ground from the whole grain of wheat and thus keeping more of its nutrients and fibre, this flour is available in plain (all-purpose) and self-raising (self-rising) varieties from most supermarkets and health food stores. Aside from its nutritional value, it gives cakes, breads and other baked goods a unique body and flavour.

freeze-dried berries

Freeze-dried raspberries and strawberries, intense in both colour and flavour, are available from gourmet food stores and specialty grocers.

gelatine powder

Available as a powder or in leaf form, gelatine is a thickening agent made from collagen. It must be dissolved in warm water before being added to recipes. Agar-agar is a vegetarian alternative.

ginger syrup

Sweet with a warming ginger flavour, find ginger syrup in the health food aisle of supermarkets and gourmet food shops. Use in a similar way to maple syrup.

goji berries

Goji berries, with origins in Chinese medicine, are still thought of by many today as a superfood. Sweet-yet-tart in flavour and pink in colour, they're available dried from the health food aisle of supermarkets.

gow gee wrappers

Chinese in origin, these round, thin sheets of dough are available fresh or frozen from supermarkets and Asian grocers. Usually used for dumplings, they can double as a cheat's pastry.

hazelnut butter

Sometimes called hazelnut spread, this paste is made from crushed hazelnuts and is available at health food stores. Choose jars labelled with 100% hazelnuts to avoid any unwanted additives.

juniper berries

The aromatic and bitter dried berries of a hardy evergreen bush, juniper is used for pickling vegetables, flavouring sauces and, most famously, for infusing gin.

kaffir lime leaves

These fragrant leaves from the kaffir lime tree have a distinctive double-leaf structure. Usually crushed or shredded and stirred into Thai dishes, they can also infuse Asian-style desserts with their flavour. They're available fresh or dried from Asian food stores. The fresh leaves tend to have more intensity – buy them and store any extras in the freezer.

liquid glucose

Liquid glucose is used in the making of confectionery such as hard candy, marshmallow and jellies. Find it in the baking aisle of supermarkets.

LSA

A mix of ground linseeds, sunflower seeds and almonds, find LSA in the health food aisles of supermarkets.

malt extract

From the barley grain, malt extract is a thick, dark, sweet syrup. It's available from the baking aisle of supermarkets.

miso paste

A traditional Japanese ingredient produced by fermenting rice, barley or soy beans to a paste. It's used for sauces and spreads, pickling vegetables, and is often mixed with dashi stock to serve as miso soup. Sometimes labelled simply 'miso', white, yellow and red varieties are available – their flavour increasing in intensity with their colour. Find it in supermarkets and Asian grocers.

molasses

A by-product of sugar cane in the production of refined sugar, this syrup varies in colour and sweetness. Usually, darker molasses is more nutrient-dense, with a complex, slightly bitter flavour. Find molasses in supermarkets and health food stores.

natural peanut butter

Regular peanut butter can contain extra sodium, oils and sugar, so it's a good idea to use a natural variety where possible. Find it in the health food section of supermarkets or have it made fresh at health food stores.

panko (japanese) breadcrumbs

Made from crustless white bread, these breadcrumbs are light, airy and delicate, making them extra crisp and flaky when fried. Find them at Asian grocery stores and most supermarkets.

pepitas (pumpkin seeds)

Pumpkin seeds are hulled to reveal these olive green kernels that, once dried, are nutty in flavour and easy to use in smoothies, baking and salads. Find them in supermarkets.

persian fairy (candy) floss

Also known as pashmak or Persian cotton candy, this traditional sugar confection is hand-spun into fine, wool-like strands and is often used in cake decorating for its delicate colours and fluffy texture. Buy it in packs at gourmet food stores, cake decorating shops and delicatessens.

pretzels

The pretzels called for in this book are the salted, glossy hard-baked crackers that can be found in the snack food section of supermarkets and grocers. Mini pretzels are mostly sold in individual snack-sized portions.

psyllium husks

The husks of the psyllium seed are super-rich in fibre and are often used in gluten-free baking as a binding agent. They're available in health food shops and supermarkets.

puffed brown rice

Whole grains of rice are heated and pressured to puff into a light, aerated cereal. Great as part of a muesli blend or baked into treats. Find them in the health food aisle of the supermarket and at health food shops.

quinoa

Not a grain but actually a seed, from South America. Packed with protein, it has a nutty flavour and is fluffy when cooked.

flakes

Simply quinoa seeds that have been steamrolled into flakes. Quinoa flakes can be used in breakfast cereals or baked goods. Available from health food stores and some supermarkets.

puffed

Quinoa seeds that have been heated and puffed into light cereal, perfect for muesli mixes or baking. Find it in the health food section of the supermarket or at health food stores.

raw cacao

nibs

Raw cacao nibs come from tropical cacao beans that have been cold pressed. Thought of by many as a superfood, these natural chocolate chips are available in the health food aisle of supermarkets and at grocers.

powder

Also derived from the cold pressing of the cacao bean, raw cacao powder is similar to cocoa powder – though thanks to lower processing temperatures, it holds onto more of the cacao beans' naturally occurring nutrients. Rich, dark and pleasantly bitter, find raw cacao powder in the health food aisle of supermarkets and grocers.

rice malt syrup

Made by culturing cooked brown rice with enzymes to break down the starches, this honey-like syrup is a great sweetener. It contains no fructose (unlike honey or maple syrup). Find it in some supermarkets and health food stores.

rolled spelt oats

From the ancient cereal grain that's part of the wider wheat family, spelt oats have a warm, slightly nutty flavour. Similar to regular rolled oats, use spelt oats to make porridge or in baking. Find them at health food shops.

semolina

A flour made from ground durum wheat, semolina is the base ingredient for pasta, sweet puddings and many Middle-Eastern cakes. Choose fine semolina for the recipes in this book.

sugar

coconut

With an earthy, butterscotch taste, coconut sugar, or coconut palm sugar, comes from the flowers of the coconut palm. It gives a lovely depth to baked goods. Find it in specialty food shops, Asian grocers and health food stores.

coffee

Coffee sugar has large granules, making it a lovely crunchy topping for baked treats. Find it in most supermarkets, or you can use Demerara sugar in its place.

Demerara

With its large crystals, rich golden colour and mild caramel flavour, this is the sugar to use if you want a pronounced crust on baked goods or a distinctive flavour in coffee. If unavailable, substitute with a mixture of 3 parts white sugar to 1 part brown sugar.

palm

Produced by tapping the sap of palm trees, palm sugar is allowed to crystallise and is sold in cubes or round blocks, which you can shave and add to curries, dressings and Asian desserts. Available from supermarkets, Asian food stores and specialty grocers.

rapadura

Extracted from the pure juice of cane sugar, rapadura (or panela) is evaporated over low heat, which means some minerals and vitamins in the cane are retained. Find it at specialty food shops and health food stores.

sugar (candy) thermometers

A handy tool to have in the kitchen, these are available in cookware shops and some supermarkets. They take the guesswork out of heating creams and syrups for treats like caramel and toffee.

tahini

Tahini is a thick paste made from ground sesame seeds, used in Middle-Eastern cooking. It's available in jars from supermarkets and health food shops.

treacle

The syrup produced from the refining process applied to sugar, treacle can come as a pale syrup known as golden syrup or a darker, more molasses-like version with a bitter flavour. It's mostly used in puddings and baking, like the famous English dessert treacle tart.

wonton wrappers

Chinese in origin, these square thin sheets of dough are available fresh or frozen from supermarkets and Asian grocers. Usually filled with meat and vegetables to make dumplings, they're versatile enough to use as a crunchy base for nibbles and sweet little tarts.

basic ingredients

almond
flaked
These skinned almonds that have been cut into delicate, paper-thin slices are used in baking and to decorate cakes.

meal (ground almonds)
Buy almond meal from the baking section of supermarkets and grocers. Make your own by processing whole skinned almonds to a fine meal in a food processor (125g almonds will give 1 cup almond meal). To blanch (remove the skins from) almonds, soak them in boiling water, allow to cool, then, using your fingers, slide the skins off. Drain well and dry before processing as above.

slivered
Used as a topping in baking, slivered almonds are skinned almonds that have been cut lengthways into small pieces.

baking powder
A raising agent used in baking, consisting of bicarbonate of soda and/or cream of tartar. Most are gluten free (check the labels). Baking powder that's kept beyond its use-by date can lose effectiveness. For a makeshift self-raising (self-rising) flour, add 2 teaspoons of baking powder to each 1 cup (150g) plain (all-purpose) flour and sift repeatedly to combine.

bicarbonate of (baking) soda
Also known as baking soda, bicarbonate of soda (sodium bicarbonate) is a pantry staple. It's an alkaline powder primarily used to help leaven baked goods and neutralise acids. In addition, it's hailed as having multiple uses around the home, notably as an effective cleaner.

blood orange
An almost seedless citrus with streaky red rind and flesh, blood oranges have a sweet raspberry-coloured juice.

brioche
A sweet, buttery French yeast bread made in loaf or bun form, brioche is traditionally dunked into coffee and eaten for breakfast. Available from good French bakeries and most supermarkets, it makes great bread and butter pudding.

butter
Unless stated otherwise in a recipe, butter should be at room temperature for cooking. It should not be half-melted or too soft to handle. We use unsalted butter in sweet recipes.

buttermilk
Once a by-product of the butter churning process, commercial buttermilk is created by adding a bacteria to skimmed milk. Its acidity and tangy creaminess is often harnessed to make fluffy pancakes, moist cakes, light scones and rich dressings. It's sold in cartons at supermarkets.

chocolate
dark
Rich and semi-sweet, regular dark chocolate usually contains 45–55% cocoa solids. It's sold in blocks and is ideal for use in baking. Dark chocolate that has 70% cocoa solids is labelled as such, and has a more bitter, intense flavour with a slightly powdery texture.

melted
To melt chocolate, place the required amount of chopped chocolate in a heatproof bowl over a saucepan of simmering water (the bowl shouldn't touch the water). Stir until smooth.

milk
Sweet, creamy and smooth, with a lighter colour than dark chocolate, milk chocolate is the most popular for eating. Sold in blocks, it usually contains around 25% cocoa solids.

coconut
cream
The cream that rises to the top after the first pressing of coconut milk, coconut cream is a rich, sweet liquid that is higher in both energy and fat than coconut milk. A common ingredient in curries and Asian sweets.

desiccated
Coconut flesh which has been shredded and dried, desiccated coconut is unsweetened and quite powdery.

flakes
Coconut flakes are large and thin and have been shaved from coconut flesh and dried. Sweet with a chewy texture, they're used for decorating cakes and in baking or muesli. You can toast them in the oven until golden.

milk
Coconut milk is a sweet liquid made by soaking grated fresh coconut flesh in water, then extracting its milk. Sold in cans at the supermarket, coconut milk shouldn't be confused with clear coconut water.

shredded
Coarser than desiccated coconut, shredded coconut is perfect for adding texture to slices and cookies.

water
The clear liquid that's found inside a young coconut, coconut water is popular for drinking due to its refreshing flavour. It's available in cartons at supermarkets.

dry yeast
Sometimes called active dry yeast, this granular raising agent is primarily used to make dough for breads, pizzas and sweet baked treats. Buy it in sachets from the supermarket.

eggs
The standard egg size used in this book is 60g. It is important to use the right sized eggs for baking recipes, as it will affect the outcome of some cakes and desserts. The correct volume is especially important when using eggwhites to make meringue. The recipes for meringue in this book suggest measuring the quantity of eggwhite carefully. Eggs at room temperature are best for baking, so try to remember to remove them from the fridge about 30 minutes before you begin a recipe.

flour
cornflour (cornstarch)
When made from ground corn or maize, cornflour is gluten free (always check the label). It's often used, blended with water or stock, as a thickening agent. Take care not to confuse it with American cornflour which is more like ground cornmeal or polenta.

plain (all-purpose)
Ground from the endosperm (centre) of wheat, plain white flour contains no raising agent. Keep this useful flour on-hand in your pantry for both sweet and savoury cooking.

self-raising (self-rising)
Ground from the endosperm of wheat, self-raising flour contains raising agents including sodium carbonates and calcium phosphates. Keep this flour on-hand in your pantry. To make it using plain flour, add 2 teaspoons baking powder to every 1 cup (150g) plain (all-purpose) flour.

fresh dates
One of the oldest cultivated fruits in the world, dates have a toffee-like sweetness which makes them a good flavoursome substitute for refined sugar. Their rich caramelly texture when processed makes them perfect for slices and bliss balls. They're a high source of soluble dietary fibre, so they're good for digestion, plus they contain bone-strengthening vitamins. Soft and plump, fresh dates are sold loose, with their seeds intact, in supermarkets and greengrocers.

ginger
crystallised
Crystallised ginger gives cookies and slices a warm spicy flavour with a sweet finish. The firm, dried ginger pieces, coated in sugar, are available in supermarkets and health food stores.

glacé
Glacé ginger is ginger pieces that have been preserved or candied, sometimes in syrup. Similar to but slightly softer than crystallised ginger, without the granular sugar coating.

ginger nut (ginger snap) biscuits
A popular, commercially-made sweet biscuit flavoured with ground ginger and spices. Sometimes used crushed or ground in baking to make biscuit bases for slices and cheesecakes. Similar but different to ginger snap biscuits – ginger nuts are very hard in texture. Sold in packs at supermarkets.

golden syrup
Sometimes known as light treacle, golden syrup is a staple ingredient for any baker. A by-product of the sugar refining process, it has a warm sweet flavour and a honey-like consistency.

granola
Buy this golden toasted muesli from the cereal aisle of supermarkets or the health food section of grocers. Choose your favourite blend of nuts, grains, oats and fruit, keeping watch for unwanted added sugars.

lemongrass
A tall lemon-scented grass used in Asian cooking, particularly in Thai dishes. Peel away the outer leaves and chop the tender white root-end finely, or add it in large pieces during cooking and remove before serving. If adding in bigger pieces, bruise them with the back of a large knife.

maple syrup
A syrup made from the sap of the Canadian maple tree with a distinct warm, sweet flavour. Retaining some natural minerals, it is often used as an alternative sweetener to regular refined sugar. Be sure to use pure maple syrup rather than imitation or pancake syrup, which is made from corn syrup flavoured with maple.

mascarpone
A fresh Italian triple-cream curd-style cheese, mascarpone has a smooth consistency, similar to thick (double) cream. Available in tubs from specialty food stores, delicatessens and some supermarkets, it's used in sauces and desserts such as tiramisu, as well as in icings and frostings for its luscious creaminess and subtle tang.

micro (baby) herbs
The baby version of fresh herbs, these tiny edible leaves have a great intensity of flavour despite their size. They make a beautiful garnish and addition to salads. Available in small pots and in a loose mix at farmers' markets and greengrocers.

oil

grapeseed
Pressed from the seeds of grapes and thus a by-product of wine-making, this oil has a particularly light, clean flavour, meaning it's useful when oil is called for in baking.

olive
Olive oil is graded according to its flavour, aroma and acidity. Extra virgin is the highest quality olive oil – it contains no more than 1% acid. Virgin is the next best – it contains 1.5% or less acid. Bottles labelled simply 'olive oil' contain a blend of refined and unrefined virgin olive oil. 'Light' olive oil is the least pure in quality and shouldn't be confused with light-flavoured extra virgin olive oil. Choose extra virgin olive oil and light-flavoured extra virgin olive oil for baking, where possible.

vegetable
Oils sourced from plants or seeds, such as sunflower or grapeseed oil, with very mild, unobtrusive flavours. Often called for in baking recipes, like muffins or loaf cakes. Keep an oil labelled simply 'vegetable oil' on-hand in your pantry.

pastry
Make your own or use one of the many store-bought varieties, including shortcrust and puff, which are sold frozen in blocks or ready-rolled into sheets. Defrost in the fridge before use.

filo (phyllo)
Extremely thin sheets of pastry, popular in Greek, Turkish and Middle-Eastern baking. Each sheet of pastry usually needs to be brushed with oil or melted butter and then layered, before encasing a filling. While working with this pastry, keep it from drying out by covering with a clean damp tea towel.

puff and butter puff
This pastry is quite difficult to make, so many cooks opt to use store-bought puff pastry. It can be bought in blocks from patisseries, or is sold in both block and sheet forms in supermarkets. Butter puff pastry is light and flaky, perfect for sweet pies and tarts. Often labelled 'all butter puff', good-quality sheets are usually thicker. If you can only buy thin sheets of butter puff, don't be afraid to stack 2 thawed sheets together.

shortcrust
A savoury or sweet pastry that is available ready-made in blocks and frozen sheets. Keep a supply in the freezer for last-minute pies, or make your own pastry:

1½ cups (225g) plain (all-purpose) flour
125g cold unsalted butter, chopped
3 egg yolks
1 tablespoon iced water

Place the flour and butter in a food processor and process in short bursts until the mixture resembles fine breadcrumbs. While the motor is running, add the egg yolks and water. Process until a dough just comes together. Turn out the dough onto a lightly floured surface and gently bring together to form a ball. Flatten the dough into a disk, wrap in plastic wrap and refrigerate for 30 minutes or until firm. When ready to use, roll out on a lightly floured surface to 3mm thick. To make sweet shortcrust pastry, add ½ cup (80g) icing (confectioner's) sugar.

peppermint extract
A flavouring containing refined natural peppermint oil that can be added to sweets, chocolate and ice-cream for an aromatic peppermint taste. Available from the baking aisle of supermarkets.

pistachios
A delicately flavoured green nut inside a hard outer shell, pistachios are available salted or unsalted. They're commonly used in Middle-Eastern cuisine as well as in salads and sweets, such as baklava.

polenta (cornmeal)
Used extensively in northern Italy, cornmeal is cooked in simmering water until it has a porridge-like consistency. In this form it is enriched with butter or cheese and served as a side dish. It can also be used as an ingredient in gluten-free cakes. Instant polenta is made from precooked cornmeal.

ricotta
A creamy, fine-grained white cheese, ricotta means 'recooked' in Italian, a reference to the way the cheese is produced – which is by heating the whey leftover from making other cheeses. Fresh full-cream ricotta is available at the deli counter of supermarkets. It's firmer in texture than the smooth ricotta that's sold pre-packaged in tubs. The fresh firm variety is best for making the recipes in this book, especially cheesecakes and pancakes. It should not be substituted for the smooth, pre-packaged variety.

rosewater
An essence distilled from rose petals, rosewater is a cornerstone flavour of Indian, Middle-Eastern and Turkish tables. Used in sweets, it's the distinctive flavour in Turkish delight (lokum).

sesame seeds
Small glossy seeds with a creamy, nutty flavour, sesame seeds can be used in savoury and sweet cooking. White seeds are the most common variety, but black, or unhulled, seeds are popular for coatings in Asian cooking and desserts.

sponge finger biscuits

Sweet and light Italian finger-shaped biscuits, also known as savoiardi. Great for desserts such as tiramisu because they absorb other flavours and soften well, yet at the same time maintain their shape. These biscuits are available in both large and small versions at supermarkets and delicatessens.

star anise

A small brown seed cluster that is shaped like a star. It has a strong aniseed flavour and can be used whole or ground in sweet and savoury dishes. In this book it's tossed with fruits and roasted.

sugar

Extracted as crystals from the juice of the sugar cane plant, sugar is a sweetener, flavour enhancer and food preservative.

brown

Light and dark brown sugars are made from refined sugar with natural molasses added. The amount, or percentage, of molasses in relation to the sugar determines its classification as dark or light. The molasses gives the sugar a smooth caramel flavour and also a soft, slightly moist texture. An important ingredient in cookies, puddings, dense cakes and brownies, you can find both varieties of brown sugar in supermarkets. Light and dark varieties are interchangeable if either is unavailable.

caster (superfine)

The fine granule of this sugar gives baked products a light texture and crumb, which is important for many cakes and delicate desserts. Caster sugar is essential for making meringue, as the fine crystals dissolve more easily in the whipped eggwhite.

icing (confectioner's)

Regular granulated sugar ground to a very fine powder. It often clumps together and needs to be sifted before using. Unless specified in a recipe, use pure icing sugar not icing sugar mixture, which contains cornflour (cornstarch).

raw

Light brown in colour and honey-like in flavour, raw sugar is slightly less refined than white sugar with a larger granule. It lends a more pronounced flavour and colour to baked goods. You can use Demerara sugar in its place.

white (granulated)

Regular granulated sugar is used in baking when a light texture is not crucial. The crystals are larger, so you need to beat, add liquids or heat this sugar if you want to dissolve it.

sunflower seeds

Small grey kernels from inside the black and white seeds of sunflowers. Mostly processed for their oil, the kernels are also found in snack mixes and muesli, and can be baked into breads and slices. Buy sunflower seeds in supermarkets and health food stores.

tarragon

Called the king of herbs by the French and used in many of their classic sauces such as bearnaise and tartare. It has a slight aniseed flavour.

vanilla

bean paste

This store-bought paste is a convenient way to replace whole vanilla beans and is great in desserts. One teaspoon of paste substitutes for one vanilla bean. You can also use it in place of vanilla extract, for a stronger vanilla flavour and the appealing appearance of vanilla seeds.

beans

These fragrant cured pods from the vanilla orchid are used whole or split, with the tiny seeds inside scraped into mixtures, infusing flavour into custard and cream-based recipes. They offer rich and rounded notes of vanilla.

extract

For a purer vanilla taste, choose a good-quality vanilla extract, not an essence or imitation flavouring. Vanilla bean paste, with a more intense flavour and the fleck of vanilla bean, can be used in place of vanilla extract – simply swap in the same quantity.

vinegar

apple cider

Made from apple must, cider vinegar has a golden-amber hue and a sour appley flavour. Use it in dressings, marinades, fruit chutneys and fillings.

white

A strong, everyday vinegar made from distilled grain alcohol. Often used in baking to stabilise whipped eggwhites.

yoghurt

natural Greek-style (thick)

Nearly all the recipes in this book call for natural, unsweetened, full-fat Greek-style (thick) yoghurt. Buy it from the chilled section of the supermarket, checking the label for any unwanted added sweeteners or artificial flavours.

vanilla-bean

On occasion, a slightly sweetened full-fat vanilla-bean flavoured yoghurt is called for. Buy it from the chilled section of supermarkets, checking the label for any unwanted artificial flavours. You could also swirl a little vanilla bean paste through natural Greek-style (thick) yoghurt, if you prefer.

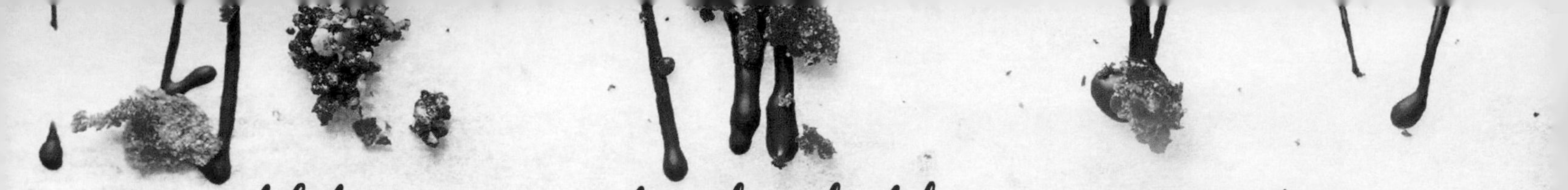

global measures

Measures vary from Europe to the US and even from Australia to New Zealand.

metric and imperial

Measuring cups and spoons may vary slightly from one country to another, but the difference is generally not sufficient to affect a recipe. The recipes in this book use Australian measures. All cup and spoon measures are level. An Australian measuring cup holds 250ml (8 fl oz).

One Australian metric teaspoon holds 5ml, one Australian tablespoon holds 20ml (4 teaspoons). However, in North America, New Zealand and the UK, 15ml (3-teaspoon) tablespoons are used.

When measuring liquid ingredients, remember that 1 American pint contains 500ml (16 fl oz) but 1 Imperial pint contains 600ml (20 fl oz).

When measuring dry ingredients, add the ingredient loosely to the cup and level with a knife. Don't tap or shake to compact the ingredient unless the recipe requests 'firmly packed'.

liquids and solids

Measuring cups, spoons and a set of scales are great assets in the kitchen.

liquids

cup	metric	imperial
⅛ cup	30ml	1 fl oz
¼ cup	60ml	2 fl oz
⅓ cup	80ml	2½ fl oz
½ cup	125ml	4 fl oz
⅔ cup	160ml	5 fl oz
¾ cup	180ml	6 fl oz
1 cup	250ml	8 fl oz
2 cups	500ml	16 fl oz
2¼ cups	560ml	20 fl oz
4 cups	1 litre	32 fl oz

solids

metric	imperial
20g	½ oz
60g	2 oz
125g	4 oz
180g	6 oz
250g	8 oz
500g	16 oz (1lb)
1kg	32 oz (2lb)

more equivalents

Here are some equivalents for metric and imperial measures, plus ingredient names.

millimetres to inches

metric	imperial
3mm	⅛ inch
6mm	¼ inch
1cm	½ inch
2.5cm	1 inch
5cm	2 inches
18cm	7 inches
20cm	8 inches
23cm	9 inches
25cm	10 inches
30cm	12 inches

ingredient equivalents

almond meal	ground almonds
bicarbonate of soda	baking soda
capsicum	bell pepper
caster sugar	superfine sugar
celeriac	celery root
chickpeas	garbanzo beans
coriander	cilantro
cornflour	cornstarch
cos lettuce	romaine lettuce
eggplant	aubergine
gai lan	chinese broccoli
green onion	scallion
icing sugar	confectioner's sugar
plain flour	all-purpose flour
rocket	arugula
self-raising flour	self-rising flour
snow pea	mange tout
white sugar	granulated sugar
zucchini	courgette

oven temperatures

Setting the oven to the right temperature can be crucial when baking sweet things.

celsius to fahrenheit

celsius	fahrenheit
100°C	200°F
120°C	250°F
140°C	275°F
150°C	300°F
160°C	325°F
180°C	350°F
190°C	375°F
200°C	400°F
220°C	425°F

electric to gas

celsius	gas
110°C	¼
130°C	½
140°C	1
150°C	2
170°C	3
180°C	4
190°C	5
200°C	6
220°C	7
230°C	8
240°C	9
250°C	10

butter and eggs

Let 'fresh is best' be your mantra when it comes to selecting eggs and dairy goods.

butter

We generally use unsalted butter as it allows for a little more control over a recipe's flavour. Either way, the impact is minimal. Salted butter has a longer shelf life and is preferred by some people. One American stick of butter is 125g (4 oz). One Australian block of butter is 250g (8 oz).

eggs

Unless otherwise indicated, we use large (60g) chicken eggs. To preserve freshness, store eggs in the refrigerator in the carton they are sold in. Use only the freshest eggs in recipes such as mayonnaise or dressings that use raw or barely cooked eggs. Be extra cautious if there is a salmonella problem in your community, particularly in food that is to be served to children, the elderly or pregnant women.

useful weights

Here are a few simple weight conversions for cupfuls of commonly used ingredients.

common ingredients

almond meal (ground almonds)
1 cup | 120g
brown sugar
1 cup | 175g
white (granulated) sugar
1 cup | 220g
caster (superfine) sugar
1 cup | 220g
icing (confectioner's) sugar
1 cup | 160g
plain (all-purpose)
or self-raising (self-rising) flour
1 cup | 150g
fresh breadcrumbs
1 cup | 70g
finely grated parmesan
1 cup | 80g
uncooked white rice
1 cup | 200g
cooked white rice
1 cup | 165g
uncooked couscous
1 cup | 200g
cooked shredded chicken, pork or beef
1 cup | 160g
olives
1 cup | 150g

a

affogatos
caramel, with cinnamon churros 95
irish coffee 138
almond
amaretto syrup 169
butter, spiced 172
candied, ice-creams 116
caramel coffee bliss balls 133
and date scones with whipped butter 166
doughnut cookies 175
fig and coconut slice 370
and fig pies 267
lemon and ricotta cakes 320
and maple sauce 367
meal, how to make your own 384
milk – *see* almond milk
and nutmeg layer cake 210
pancakes with spiced almond butter
and maple syrup 172
and rhubarb hand pies 284
syrup cake 169
almond milk
crepes with whipped ricotta 219
and date cake with creamy cashew
icing 376
how to make your own 380
steamed pudding with almond and
maple sauce 367
amaretto syrup 169
angel food cake
raspberry and cream 311
with white chocolate ganache 175
apple
berry, coconut and quinoa crumble 210
cake, spiced 273
and caramel hand pies 285
and ginger crumble muffins 222
and honey tarte tatin, salted 255
spiced layered cake 169
apricot and cinnamon dutch pancakes 240

b

baked ricotta
and cinnamon cheesecakes 178
and lime filo cheesecake with lemon
balm 326
sweet, with honeycomb 356
banana
banoffee cheesecake 145
banoffee wafer sandwiches 136

and blackberry oat cookie sandwiches 231
blistered, with (quick) caramelised
coconut yoghurt 357
bread 302
chocolate and coconut muffins 42
chocolate and malt tarte tatin 258
chocolate and maple cake 12
and coconut three-milk cake 332
and honey sesame crunch ice-cream
cake 373
maple toffee cookies 104
and raspberry ice-cream 302
banoffee
cheesecake 145
wafer sandwiches 136
bark
choc-toffee pretzel 133
frozen yoghurt and white chocolate 361
bars and slices
blueberry crumble slice 293
chocolate mousse slice 80
chocolate and raspberry marshmallow
slice 39
chocolate shortbread slice 58
crispy chocolate coconut bars 61
fig, coconut and almond slice 370
ginger nut crunch bars 213
hazelnut and cream layered slice 356
lemon cheesecake slice (cheat's) 283
mixed berry and granola ice-cream
bars 299
mixed spice and raspberry slice 196
no-bake chocolate and walnut brownies 65
pistachio, rosewater and sour cherry
squares 213
puffed quinoa blueberry bars with
yoghurt 296
raw caramel peanut crunch bars 148
raw caramel slice 151
raw chocolate, cherry and coconut bars 296
raw peppermint slice 80
s'more caramel slice 98
strawberry chia jam and coconut slice 293
strawberries and cream ice-cream bars 299
vanilla slice 341
berries – *see* blackberry; blueberry;
cranberry; mixed berry; mulberries;
raspberry; strawberry
berry, apple, coconut and quinoa crumble 210
biscuits, spiced vanilla 166
bites, cacao caramel 154
blackberry
and banana oat cookie sandwiches 231

chia jam 71
and elderflower pie 270
lemon and yoghurt eton mess 280
pear and hazelnut crumbles 290
and vanilla jam 231
bliss balls, carrot cake 216
blistered bananas with quick caramelised
coconut yoghurt 357
blood orange
braided brioche loaf 261
jam 261
semolina and almond cakes 264
syrup 264
with syrup 332
with yoghurt crème 332
blueberry
crumble slice 293
and lemon ginger nut tarts 281
and roasted peach ice-cream
sandwiches 249
and thyme tart 228
bourbon sugar and pretzel truffles 190
bread and butter puddings,
fruit and nut 204
brioche
bake, peach and raspberry 202
blood orange braided loaf 261
caramelised, with ice-cream and
honeycomb 134
cinnamon churros with caramel 206
crème fraîche and jam sweet buns 359
pillows, chocolate and pear sugared 200
pudding, date and whiskey 276
trifles, spiced cream and maple 205
brown butter glaze 178
brownie(s)
caramel pecan brownies 110
no-bake chocolate and walnut
brownies 65
peanut butter brownies 30
peanut butter brownie ice-cream bars 64
raspberry and chocolate brownie
trifles 63
salted caramel brownie squares 86
brûlée
black rice pudding with coconut gelato 190
coconut yoghurt and passionfruit tarts 329
buckwheat cacao crackles 77
burnt butter and salted maple sticky buns 193
butter, spiced almond 172
buttermilk
panna cottas 308
and ricotta pikelets 181

butterscotch
    chocolate swirls 61
    toffee icing 122

cacao
    buckwheat crackles 77
    caramel bites 154
    coconut and walnut cake 74
    crumble (topping) 270
    cupcakes with ricotta maple frosting 68
    flourless cake 68
cake(s)
    almond and nutmeg layer cake 210
    almond milk and date cake with
        creamy cashew icing 376
    almond syrup cake 169
    angel food cake with white chocolate
        ganache 175
    banana and coconut three-milk cake 332
    banana and honey sesame crunch
        ice-cream cake 373
    banana bread 302
    cacao cupcakes with ricotta maple
        frosting 68
    caramel and cardamom kisses 104
    caramel gingerbread cakes 95
    caramel swirl meringue cake 113
    carrot cake with cream cheese icing 172
    chocolate canelés 51
    chocolate custard poke cake 15
    chocolate and maple banana cake 12
    chocolate meringue cake 54
    chocolate mousse cake 48
    chocolate and pecan cake 48
    chocolate swirl loaf cake 18
    coconut and meringue layer cake 311
    coffee and brown sugar tray cake 101
    crunchy chocolate caramel layer cake 51
    dark chocolate pretzel cake 12
    date and walnut cake with
        butterscotch toffee icing 122
    flourless cacao cake 68
    glazed chocolate bundt cake 33
    hazelnut, orange and ricotta cake 335
    lavender and honey madeleines 160
    lemon chia cake 290
    lemon and raspberry three-milk cake 350
    lemon, ricotta and almond cake 320
    lemon and yoghurt cake 347
    limoncello and coconut ice-cream cake 314
    mocha meringue cake 119
    molten dulce de leche lava cakes 98

nectarine and semolina cake 237
orange and cinnamon syrup cake 222
passionfruit three-milk ice-cream
    cake 317
pear and halva crumble loaf 270
pineapple and ginger upside-down
    cake 264
raspberry and cream angel food cake 311
raw cacao, coconut and walnut cake 74
raw lamingtons with blackberry jam 71
rhubarb and brown butter friands 252
rhubarb and yoghurt loaf cake 364
salted dark chocolate layer cake with
    milk chocolate ganache 15
semolina, almond and blood orange
    syrup cakes 264
soft vanilla sponge cake 163
spiced apple cake 273
spiced chai bundt cake 193
spiced layered apple cake 169
sticky date meringue cake 125
syrupy coffee and date cake 142
tiramisu sponge cake 119
upside-down chocolate, hazelnut
    and pear cake 273
vanilla almond cake with tarragon
    and mint 160
whiskey-frosted brownie cake 27
white chocolate and amaretti bundt
    cake 18
yoghurt and passionfruit syrup cake 246
see also brioche; cheesecake;
    doughnuts; muffins
candied almond ice-creams 116
candied clementine and chocolate
    pudding 21
canelés, chocolate 51
cannoli, whipped ricotta, orange and
    nutmeg 201
caramel
    affogatos with cinnamon churros 95
    and apple hand pies 285
    and biscotti tiramisu 354
    brownie squares 86
    and cardamom kisses 104
    cacao bites 154
    cheesecake 142
    chia pecan pies, raw 151
    chocolate layer cake, crunchy 51
    coconut, with coconut ice-cream 376
    coffee bliss balls 133
    coffee sauce (quick) 139
    date 148, 151

filled peanut cookies (cheat's) 138
and ginger pecan pies (cheat's) 205
gingerbread cakes 95
and peanut butter fudge 135
peanut crunch bars, raw 148
pecan brownies 110
popcorn, salted almond and malt
    cookies 89
salted – *see* salted caramel
sauce 134, 142
slice, raw 151
slice, s'more 98
swirl meringue cake 113
swirl meringues 128
see also caramels
caramelised brioche with ice-cream
    and honeycomb 134
caramelised fig meringues 137
caramelised rum pineapple 246
caramels
    cardamom and pistachio 110
    chocolate peppermint 107
    salted peanut 107
cardamom and caramel kisses 104
cardamom and pistachio caramels 110
carrot
    cake bliss balls 216
    cake with cream cheese icing 172
    cake muffins with spiced honey glaze 187
chai
    bundt cake, spiced 193
    coconut granita 204
    portuguese custard tarts 338
cheat's blackberry and vanilla jam 231
cheat's caramel-filled peanut cookies 138
cheat's chocolate and pear crumbles 62
cheat's custard tarts 207
cheat's ginger and caramel pecan pies 205
cheat's hazelnut chocolate fudge 60
cheat's lemon cheesecake slice 283
cheat's raspberry pavlova ice-cream 359
cheat's sugar cookies with jam and cream 203
cheat's yoghurt and white chocolate
    crèmes brûlées 357
cheesecake(s)
    banoffee cheesecake 145
    caramel cheesecake 142
    chocolate and vanilla brûlée
        cheesecake 350
    coconut and roasted plum frozen
        cheesecakes 364
    coffee cheesecake with coffee syrup 92
    lemon cheesecake slice (cheat's) 283

lemon and vanilla ricotta cheesecake 323
raspberry and ginger ice-cream
    cheesecakes 234
ricotta and cinnamon cheesecakes,
    baked 178
ricotta and lime filo cheesecake with
    lemon balm, baked 326
tiramisu cheesecakes 125

cherry
coconut and raw chocolate bars 296
yoghurt and mascarpone tarts 326
chewy cinnamon and date cookies 219

chia
caramel 151
caramel pecan pies, raw 151
coconut puddings with passionfruit
    and lime granita 367
chipotle stout praline 45

chocolate
and amaretti bundt cake 18
banana and coconut muffins 42
banana and malt tarte tatin 258
bars, crispy coconut 61
brownie cookies, salted 27
bundt cake, glazed 33
butterscotch swirls 61
cacao caramel bites 154
and candied clementine pudding 21
canelés 51
caramel filling 51
caramel layer cake, crunchy 51
cheesecake filling 145
cherry and coconut bars 296
coated raw cookies with raspberry
    and coconut filling 77
coating 24
coconut cups 58
and coconut muffins, one-bowl 65
curls 15
custard icing 15
custard poke cake 15
dipped dried orange slices 59
dusted pavlovas with raspberries
    and pistachios 276
and fig teardrop truffles 24
and frozen yoghurt bark 361
ganache (quick) 15
ganache, white 175
and ginger truffles 207
glaze 33, 48
hazelnut fudge (cheat's) 60
hazelnut and pear upside-down cake 273
ice-cream pie 60

icing 71
malt and pecan cookies 21
and maple banana cake 12
meringue cake 54
mousse cake 48
mousse slice 80
panna cottas, cocoa 30
peanut butter cups, salted 59
and peanut butter date fudge 154
and pear crumbles (cheat's) 62
and pear sugared brioche pillows 200
and pecan cake 48
peppermint caramels 107
puddings, magic molten 64
and raspberry brownie trifles 63
raspberry and coconut buttons 62
and raspberry marshmallow slice 39
and rhubarb jam drops 252
s'more cookie sandwiches 33
s'more ice-cream 36
s'more meringue pie 36
salted – see salted chocolate
salted caramel cookies 101
shortbread slice 58
stout doughnuts with chipotle stout
    praline 45
swirl loaf cake 18
tiramisu mousse 136
tiramisu pie 122
toffee pretzel bark 133
and vanilla brûlée cheesecake 350
and walnut brownies, no-bake 65
and yoghurt crèmes brûlées 357
see also mocha; salted chocolate
choc-toffee pretzel bark 133

churros
cinnamon 95
cinnamon brioche with caramel 206

cinnamon
brioche churros with caramel 206
churros 95
and date cookies, chewy 219
scrolls, crème fraîche-glazed 163
sugar crostini with ricotta 202
clementine and chocolate pudding 21

cocoa
coffee and hazelnut crisps 54
dusted coffee cookies 89
panna cottas 30

coconut
and banana three-milk cake 332
bars, crispy chocolate 61
caramel with coconut ice-cream 376

caramel sauce 145
chai granita 204
chia puddings with passionfruit
    and lime granita 367
chocolate cups 58
and chocolate muffins, one-bowl 65
cherry and raw chocolate bars 296
chocolate and banana muffins 42
crumbed deep-fried ice-cream bars 347
fig and almond slice 370
gelato with brûlée black rice pudding 190
goji bliss balls 71
layer meringue cake 311
lime and lemon delicious pudding 285
and limoncello ice-cream cake 314
and lychee sorbet (quick) 354
and nectarine brown butter tart 240
pina colada popsicles 286
pineapple and lemongrass popsicles 287
and pineapple sorbet sandwiches 281
and raspberry chocolate buttons 62
and roasted plum frozen cheesecakes 364
and strawberry chia jam slice 293
and strawberry filo tarts 203
tahini and date fudge, crunchy 216
walnut and cacao cake 74
yoghurt, caramelised with blistered
    bananas 357
yoghurt and passionfruit brûlée tarts 329

coffee
and brown sugar tray cake 101
and date upside-down cake 142
caramel bliss balls 133
caramel sauce (quick) 139
cheesecake with coffee syrup 92
chocolate tiramisu mousse 136
cookies, cocoa-dusted 89
cream puffs 137
cubes, iced 139
hazelnut and cocoa crisps 54
syrup 92
see also affogatos; mocha; tiramisu

cookies
and cream ice-cream sandwiches 355
almond doughnut 175
banana maple toffee 104
blackberry and banana oat 231
caramel-filled peanut (cheat's) 138
caramel popcorn, salted almond
    and malt 89
chewy cinnamon and date 219
chocolate, malt and pecan 21
chocolate s'more sandwiches 33

chocolate salted caramel 101
cocoa-dusted coffee 89
ginger molasses 184
granola and maple bourbon raisin 187
raw, chocolate-coated, with raspberry
    and coconut filling 77
salted chocolate brownie 27
salted peanut butter and choc-chip 42
sugar with jam and cream (cheat's) 203
white chocolate and rhubarb jam drops 252
crackles, cacao buckwheat 77
cranberry jam scrolls 258
cream cheese icing 172
creamy cashew icing 376
crème brûlée
    custard doughnuts 335
    yoghurt and white chocolate (cheat's) 357
crème fraîche
    glazed cinnamon scrolls 163
    and jam sweet buns 359
crepes, almond milk with whipped ricotta 219
crispy chocolate coconut bars 61
crostini, cinnamon sugar with ricotta 202
crostoli, ricotta and orange 358
crumble
    apple, berry, coconut and quinoa 210
    chocolate and pear (cheat's) 62
    pear, blackberry and hazelnut 290
    slice, blueberry 293
crunchy chocolate caramel layer cake 51
crunchy coconut, tahini and date fudge 216
crushed raspberry tart 280
cupcakes, cacao with ricotta maple
    frosting 68
custard
    doughnuts, crème brûlée 335
    tarts, chai portuguese 338
    tarts (cheat's) 207

dark chocolate
    caramel peanut crunch bars 148
    and fig teardrop truffles 24
    ganache (quick) 12
    layer cake, salted, with milk chocolate
        ganache 15
    pretzel cake 12
date
    and almond milk cake with creamy
        cashew icing 376
    and almond scones with whipped
        butter 166

caramel 148, 151
chocolate and peanut butter fudge 154
and cinnamon cookies, chewy 219
and coffee upside-down cake 142
crunchy coconut and tahini fudge 216
doughnuts with spiced sugar 181
and ginger tiramisu 148
meringue cake, sticky 125
sticky steamed pudding with spiced
    rum and maple glaze 86
and walnut cake with butterscotch
    toffee icing 122
and whiskey brioche pudding 276
doughnuts
    chocolate stout, with chipotle stout
        praline 45
    crème brûlée custard 335
    date with spiced sugar 181
    earl grey with brown butter glaze 178
    miso-glazed 196
    raw chocolate-glazed turkish delight 74
    ricotta and dulce de leche with
        smoked salt sugar 338
    salted caramel apple cider 128
dulce de leche
    lava cakes, molten 98
    and ricotta doughnuts with smoked
        salt sugar 338

earl grey doughnuts with brown
    butter glaze 178
eton mess, blackberry, lemon and
    yoghurt 280

f

fairy floss marshmallow ice-creams 314
fig
    and almond pies 267
    coconut and almond slice 370
    and dark chocolate teardrop truffles 24
    meringues 137
    yoghurt and honey parfaits 284
fillings – see icings and fillings
filo tarts, coconut and strawberry 203
flourless cacao cake 68
french toasts, one-bite salted caramel 135
friands, rhubarb and brown butter 252
frosting – see icings and fillings
frozen yoghurt and white chocolate bark 361
fruit and nut bread and butter puddings 204

fruit salad, lemongrass and kaffir lime 283
fudge
    chocolate and peanut butter date 154
    crunchy coconut, tahini and date 216
    hazelnut chocolate (cheat's) 60
    peanut butter 145
    peanut butter and caramel 135

ganache
    dark chocolate (quick) 12
    white chocolate 175
ginger
    and apple crumble muffins 222
    and caramel pecan pies (cheat's) 205
    and chocolate truffles 207
    and date tiramisu 148
    and lemon possets 360
    molasses cookies 184
    nut crunch bars 213
    nut tarts, lemon and blueberry 281
    and pineapple upside-down cake 264
    puddings, sticky 184
    and raspberry ice-cream cheesecakes 234
gingerbread cakes, caramel 95
glaze – see icings and fillings
glazed chocolate bundt cake 33
goji coconut bliss balls 71
granita
    coconut chai 204
    passionfruit and lime 367
granola
    and maple bourbon raisin cookies 187
    and mixed berry ice-cream bars 299
    yoghurt popsicles 373
grapefruit popsicles, pink 286

h

halva and pear crumble loaf 270
hazelnut
    chocolate fudge (cheat's) 60
    chocolate and pear upside-down cake 273
    coffee and cocoa crisps 54
    and cream layered slice 356
    orange and ricotta cake 335
    pear and blackberry crumbles 290
honey
    glaze, spiced 187
    orange syrup 210
    toffee sauce (quick) 132
hotcakes, ricotta with spiced sugar 200

ice-cream(s)
banana and honey sesame crunch
    ice-cream cake 373
banana and raspberry ice-cream 302
candied almond ice-cream 116
caramelised brioche with ice-cream
    and honeycomb 134
chocolate ice-cream pie 60
chocolate s'more ice-cream 36
coconut caramel with coconut
    ice-cream 376
coconut crumbed deep-fried
    ice-cream bars 347
cookies and cream ice-cream
    sandwiches 355
fairy floss marshmallow ice-creams 314
lamington ice-cream bars 45
limoncello and coconut ice-cream cake 314
mixed berry and granola ice-cream bars 299
mocha swirl ice-creams 113
passionfruit three-milk ice-cream cake 317
peanut butter brownie ice-cream bars 64
raspberry and ginger ice-cream
    cheesecakes 234
raspberry pavlova ice-cream (cheat's) 359
ricotta and buttermilk ice-cream 320
roasted peach and blueberry ice-cream
    sandwiches 249
salted caramel crunch ice-creams 116
strawberries and cream ice-cream bars 299
tiramisu soft-serve sandwiches
    (cheat's) 344
tiramisu swirl ice-cream waffle cones 341
vanilla soft-serve ice-cream with
    maple and bourbon syrup 344
white peach and bourbon vanilla
    ice-cream 234
see also popsicles
iced coffee cubes 139
icings and fillings
blackberry chia jam 71
blackberry and vanilla jam 231
blood orange jam 261
brown butter glaze 178
burnt butter filling 193
butterscotch toffee icing 122
chocolate caramel filling 51
chocolate coating 24
chocolate custard icing 15
chocolate ganache (quick) 12, 15
chocolate glaze 33, 48

chocolate icing 71
chocolate mousse topping 80
cranberry jam 258
cream cheese icing 172
creamy cashew icing 376
crème fraîche glaze 163
dark chocolate ganache (quick) 12
italian meringue 311
lemon glaze 243
lemon icing 347
maple glaze 193
marshmallow 39
marshmallow meringue topping 36
mascarpone cream 119
milk chocolate ganache (quick) 15
miso glaze 196
mocha mousse 119
raspberry jam 39
rhubarb jam (quick) 252
ricotta filling 338
ricotta icing 210
ricotta maple frosting 68
roasted raspberry jam 255
spiced honey glaze 187
spiced rum and maple glaze 86
strawberry chia jam 293
vanilla coconut cream 311
vanilla yoghurt cream 323
whipped mascarpone 122
whiskey frosting 27
white chocolate ganache 175
yoghurt drizzle 296
yoghurt topping 290
irish coffee affogatos 138
italian meringue 311

jam drops, white chocolate and rhubarb 252
jams – *see* icings and fillings
jellies, milk and honey 355

kisses, caramel and cardamom 104

l

lamington(s)
lamington ice-cream bars 45
raw lamingtons with blackberry jam 71
lavender and honey madeleines 160

lemon
and blueberry ginger nut tarts 281
cheesecake slice (cheat's) 283
chia cake 290
chia and ricotta muffins 243
curd impossible puddings 282
delicious, coconut and lime pudding 285
and ginger possets 360
glaze 243
icing 347
and raspberry three-milk cake 350
ricotta and almond cakes 320
and vanilla ricotta cheesecake 323
and yoghurt cake 347
and yoghurt panna cottas with
    passionfruit 370
lemongrass and kaffir lime fruit salad 283
limoncello and coconut ice-cream cake 314
lychee and coconut sorbet (quick) 354

m

madeleines, lavender and honey 160
magic chocolate molten puddings 64
maple
and bourbon syrup 344
and chocolate banana cake 12
and cinnamon roasted pears 206
glaze 193
and pear upside-down muffins 243
pecan tarts, upside-down 92
and spiced cream brioche trifles 205
toffee 104
toffee cookies, banana 104
marshmallow
chocolate and raspberry slice 39
filling 39
meringue topping 36
mascarpone
cream 119
and passionfruit shortbread
    sandwiches 360
meringue(s)
caramelised fig meringues 137
chocolate s'more meringue pie 36
coconut layer meringue cake 311
meringues poached in vanilla milk 308
salted caramel swirl meringues 128
see also pavlova
milk and honey jellies 355
milk chocolate ganache (quick) 15
miso-glazed doughnuts 196
mixed berry and granola ice-cream bars 299
mixed spice and raspberry slice 196

mocha
    meringue cake 119
    mousse 119
    swirl ice-creams 113
molten dulce de leche lava cakes 98
mousse, chocolate tiramisu 136
muffins
    apple and ginger crumble 222
    carrot cake with spiced honey glaze 187
    chocolate, banana and coconut 42
    fudgy brownie 24
    lemon, chia and ricotta 243
    one-bowl chocolate and coconut 65
    upside-down maple and pear 243
mulberries with smashed pavlova and
    roasted raspberry jam 255

n

nectarine
    and coconut brown butter tart 240
    and honey tray pie 237
    and semolina cake 237
no-bake chocolate and walnut brownies 65

o

oat cookies 77
oats, blackberry and banana cookie
    sandwiches 231
one-bite salted caramel french toasts 135
one-bowl chocolate and coconut muffins 65
orange
    and cinnamon syrup cake 222
    and ricotta crostoli 358
    ricotta and hazelnut cake 335
    ricotta soufflés 317
    slices, dried, chocolate-dipped 59
    see also blood orange

p

pancakes
    almond with spiced almond butter
        and maple syrup 172
    apricot and cinnamon 240
panna cotta(s)
    buttermilk panna cottas 308
    cocoa panna cottas 30
    lemon and yoghurt panna cottas
        with passionfruit 370
    yoghurt panna cotta tart 329
parfaits, fig, yoghurt and honey 284
passionfruit
    and coconut yoghurt brûlée tarts 329
    with lemon and yoghurt panna cottas 370

and lime granita 367
and mascarpone shortbread
    sandwiches 360
and pineapple pavlova 261
and summer peach trifles 282
syrup 246
syrup and yoghurt cake 246
tart with rum pineapple 246
three-milk ice-cream cake 317
pastries, vanilla yoghurt with lavender
    sugar 323
pastry
    rough puff 341
    shortcrust 329, 386
    sweet shortcrust 240, 246
    vanilla 323
    yoghurt 326, 329
pavlova
    chocolate-dusted with raspberries
        and pistachios 276
    raspberry ice-cream (cheat's) 359
    smashed, with mulberries and roasted
        raspberry jam 255
    summer pineapple and passionfruit 261
peach
    and blueberry ice-cream sandwiches 249
    and bourbon vanilla ice-cream 234
    honey and vanilla pie 267
    and passionfruit trifles 282
    and raspberry brioche bake 202
peanut
    caramels, salted 107
    cookies, caramel-filled (cheat's) 138
peanut butter
    brownie ice-cream bars 64
    brownies 30
    and caramel fudge 135
    and choc-chip skillet cookies 42
    and chocolate date fudge 154
    fudge 145
    raw caramel peanut crunch bars 148
    salted chocolate cups 59
pear
    blackberry and hazelnut crumbles 290
    and chocolate crumbles (cheat's) 62
    chocolate and hazelnut upside-down
        cake 273
    and chocolate sugared brioche pillows 200
    and halva crumble loaf 270
    maple and cinnamon, roasted 206
    and maple upside-down muffins 243
pecan
    caramel brownies 110

and chocolate cake 48
chocolate and malt cookies 21
ginger and caramel pies (cheat's) 205
maple tarts, upside-down 92
raw chia caramel pies 151
peppermint
    chocolate caramels 107
    slice, raw 80
pie(s)
    apple and caramel hand pies 285
    blackberry and elderflower pie 270
    chocolate ice-cream pie 60
    chocolate s'more meringue pie 36
    chocolate tiramisu pie 122
    fig and almond pies 267
    ginger and caramel pecan pies
        (cheat's) 205
    nectarine and honey tray pie 237
    peach, honey and vanilla pie 267
    raw chia caramel pecan pies 151
    rhubarb and almond hand pies 284
pikelets, buttermilk and ricotta 181
pina colada popsicles 286
pineapple
    caramelised rum 246
    coconut and lemongrass popsicles 287
    and coconut sorbet sandwiches 281
    and ginger upside-down cake 264
    and passionfruit pavlova 261
    pina colada popsicles 286
    syrup 264
pink grapefruit popsicles 286
pistachio
    and cardamom caramels 110
    rosewater and sour cherry squares 213
plum, lemon and juniper tart 228
plums, roasted with star anise and vanilla 201
popsicles
    pina colada 286
    pineapple, coconut and lemongrass 287
    pink grapefruit 286
    rockmelon and yoghurt 287
    yoghurt granola 373
possets, lemon and ginger 360
praline
    chipotle stout 45
    vanilla bean 341
pretzel and choc-toffee bark 133
pudding(s)
    brûlée black rice pudding with coconut
        gelato 190
    candied clementine and chocolate
        pudding 21

coconut chia puddings with passionfruit
and lime granita 367
coconut, lime and lemon delicious
pudding 285
date and whiskey brioche pudding 276
fruit and nut bread and butter
puddings 204
lemon curd impossible puddings 282
magic chocolate molten puddings 64
rose and strawberry chilled rice
puddings 358
steamed almond milk pudding with
almond and maple sauce 367
steamed sticky date pudding with
spiced rum and maple glaze 86
sticky ginger puddings 184
puff pastry, rough 341
puffed quinoa blueberry bars with
yoghurt 296
puffs, coffee cream 137

q

quick caramel sauce 134
quick coffee caramel sauce 139
quick dark chocolate ganache 12
quick honey toffee sauce 132
quick lychee and coconut sorbet 354
quick milk chocolate ganache 15
quick rhubarb jam 252
quinoa blueberry bars with
yoghurt, puffed 296

r

raspberry
apple, coconut and quinoa crumble 210
and banana ice-cream 302
and chocolate brownie trifles 63
and chocolate marshmallow slice 39
and coconut chocolate buttons 62
and cream angel food cake 311
and ginger ice-cream cheesecakes 234
jam 39, 255
and lemon three-milk cake 350
and mixed spice slice 196
and peach brioche bake 202
tart 280
and turkish delight rocky road 63
raw cacao, coconut and walnut cake 74
raw caramel peanut crunch bars 148
raw caramel slice 151
raw chia caramel pecan pies 151
raw chocolate, cherry and coconut bars 296

raw chocolate-glazed turkish delight
doughnuts 74
raw cookies, chocolate-coated, with
raspberry and coconut filling 77
raw lamingtons with blackberry jam 71
raw peppermint slice 80
rhubarb
and almond hand pies 284
and brown butter friands 252
jam (quick) 252
puree 249
soufflés 249
strawberry and ricotta tart 231
and white chocolate jam drops 252
and yoghurt loaf cake 364
rice pudding with coconut gelato, black 190
rice puddings, rose and strawberry,
chilled 358
rice, puffed
cacao buckwheat crackles 77
crispy chocolate coconut bars 61
raw caramel peanut crunch bars 148
ricotta
and buttermilk ice-cream 320
and buttermilk pikelets 181
and cinnamon cheesecakes, baked 178
cinnamon sugar crostini 202
and dulce de leche doughnuts with
smoked salt sugar 338
filling 338
hazelnut and orange cake 335
hotcakes with spiced sugar 200
icing 210
lemon and almond cakes 320
lemon and chia muffins 243
lemon and vanilla cheesecake 323
and lime filo cheesecake with lemon
balm, baked 326
maple frosting 68
and orange crostoli 358
orange and nutmeg cannoli 201
orange soufflés 317
rhubarb and strawberry tart 231
sweet baked, with honeycomb 356
whipped 219
roasted peach and blueberry ice-cream
sandwiches 249
roasted raspberry jam 255
rockmelon and yoghurt popsicles 287
rocky road, raspberry and turkish delight 63
rose and strawberry chilled rice
puddings 358
rough puff pastry 341

rum and maple glaze 86
rum and raisin truffles 39

s

s'more
caramel slice 98
chocolate meringue pie 36
cookie sandwiches 33
salted caramel
apple cider doughnuts 128
brownie squares 86
chocolate cookies 101
crunch ice-creams 116
french toasts, one-bite 135
swirl meringues 128
salted chocolate
brownie cookies 27
caramel tarts 132
layer cake with milk chocolate ganache 15
peanut butter cups 59
salted honey and apple tarte tatin 255
salted peanut butter and choc-chip skillet
cookies 42
salted peanut caramels 107
sauce
almond and maple 367
caramel 142
caramel (quick) 134
coconut caramel 145
coffee caramel (quick) 139
date caramel 148
honey toffee 132
see also syrup
scones, almond and date with whipped
butter 166
semolina
almond and blood orange syrup cakes 264
and nectarine cake 237
sheep's milk yoghurt with pistachio and
mint sugar 361
shortbread sandwiches: mascarpone
and passionfruit 360
shortcrust pastry 329, 386
sweet 240, 246
smashed pavlova with mulberries and
roasted raspberry jam 255
soft vanilla sponge cake 163
sorbet
lychee and coconut (quick) 354
sandwiches, pineapple and coconut 281
soufflés
orange ricotta 317
rhubarb 249

sour cherry, pistachio and rosewater
squares 213
spiced almond butter 172
spiced apple cake 273
spiced chai bundt cake 193
spiced cream and maple brioche trifles 205
spiced honey glaze 187
spiced layered apple cake 169
spiced rum and maple glaze 86
spiced sugar 181, 200
spiced vanilla biscuits 166
star anise and vanilla roasted plums 201
steamed almond milk pudding with
almond and maple sauce 367
steamed sticky date pudding with spiced
rum and maple glaze 86
sticky buns, burnt butter and salted maple 193
sticky date
meringue cake 125
pudding with spiced rum and maple
glaze 86
sticky ginger puddings 184
strawberry
chia jam and coconut slice 293
and coconut filo tarts 203
and cream ice-cream bars 299
ricotta and rhubarb tart 231
summer peach and passionfruit trifles 282
summer pineapple and passionfruit
pavlova 261
sweet shortcrust pastry 240, 246
syrup
amaretto 169
blood orange 264
coconut caramel 145
coffee 92
honey orange 210
maple and bourbon 344
orange cinnamon 222
passionfruit 246
pineapple 264
see also sauce
syrupy coffee and date upside-down cake 142

t

tart(s)
apple and honey tarte tatin, salted 255
blueberry and thyme tart 228
chai portuguese custard tarts 338
chocolate, banana and malt tarte tatin 258
coconut and nectarine brown butter
tart 240

coconut and strawberry filo tarts 203
coconut yoghurt and passionfruit
brûlée tarts 329
crushed raspberry tart 280
custard tarts (cheat's) 207
lemon and blueberry ginger nut tarts 281
passionfruit tart with rum pineapple 246
plum, lemon and juniper tart 228
salted chocolate caramel tarts 132
strawberry, ricotta and rhubarb tart 231
upside-down maple pecan tarts 92
yoghurt, mascarpone and cherry tarts 326
yoghurt panna cotta tart 329
tarte tatin
chocolate, banana and malt 258
salted honey and apple 255
tiramisu
caramel and biscotti 354
cheesecakes 125
ginger and date 148
mousse, chocolate 136
pie, chocolate 122
soft-serve sandwiches (cheat's) 344
sponge cake 119
swirl ice-cream waffle cones 341
toffee
butterscotch icing 122
maple 104
trifles
raspberry and chocolate brownie 63
spiced cream and maple brioche 205
summer peach and passionfruit 282
truffles
bourbon sugar and pretzel 190
chocolate and ginger 207
fig and dark chocolate 24
rum and raisin 39
turkish delight and raspberry rocky road 63

u

upside-down chocolate, hazelnut and
pear cake 273
upside-down maple and pear muffins 243
upside-down maple pecan tarts 92

v

vanilla
almond cake with tarragon and mint 160
bean praline 341
biscuits, spiced 166
and chocolate brûlée cheesecake 350
coconut cream 311
pastry 323

slice with vanilla bean praline 341
soft-serve ice-cream with maple and
bourbon syrup 344
sponge cake 163
yoghurt cream 323
yoghurt pastries with lavender sugar 323

w

wafer sandwiches, banoffee 136
walnut, cacao and coconut cake 74
whipped orange and nutmeg cannoli 201
whiskey-frosted brownie cake 27
whiskey frosting 27
white chocolate
and amaretti bundt cake 18
and frozen yoghurt bark 361
ganache 175
and rhubarb jam drops 252
and yoghurt crèmes brûlées (cheat's) 357
white peach and bourbon vanilla
ice-cream 234

y

yoghurt
caramelised coconut, with blistered
bananas (quick) 357
coconut, and passionfruit brûlée tarts 329
crème with blood oranges 332
drizzle 296
granola popsicles 373
and lemon cake 347
and lemon panna cottas with
passionfruit 370
mascarpone and cherry tarts 326
panna cotta tart 329
and passionfruit syrup cake 246
pastry 326, 329
and rhubarb cake 364
and rockmelon popsicles 287
sheep's milk, with pistachio and mint
sugar 361
topping 290
and white chocolate bark, frozen 361
and white chocolate crèmes brûlées
(cheat's) 357

thank you

In a quiet street in Sydney sits my light-filled studio. Inside is like a sanctuary for me, where I do my best work, but it's also where I have a team of hand-picked creatives, who help me keep the world of all things *donna hay* turning. Talented, dedicated and, let's be honest, a little mischievous, I adore working with you all. A big book such as this takes an extra level of commitment, so I'd like to send special thanks to a few of you.

To my creative director, Chi, your serene nature and superb vision are a powerful combination. Thank you for pulling this project together with such fresh inspiration, and for making it look so dreamy – I'm the luckiest!

Abby, my editor, you know my style so well. Your sharp eyes ensure every last proof that's sent to print is immaculate. Thank you for weaving your unique magic through all the (many, many!) words in this book.

My team of photographers, Will, Chris, Anson, Ben and Con, we've been working together for years now and I'm still in awe of the beauty, light and mood you're able to capture. You're all true masters in your craft.

Much of the styling throughout these pages is the stunning work of Steve and Justine. Be it in the studio or on crazy location adventures, it's not difficult to see you two are at the top of your game – thank you both.

To Jess and Georgie, my food editors, I'm grateful on a daily basis for your on-trend ideas and your fast and flawless ways in the *dh* kitchen. You, in fine company with Amber, Dolores, Hannah, Hayley and Amanda, are the reason these treats taste like pure perfection, down to the very last bite (and didn't we taste them all!).

Thank you Tony, in prepress, for your diligence and amazing skill – I know you always go above and beyond. To my magazine team, you guys know how I feel, I so appreciate your loyalty, resourcefulness and sense of fun.

Huge thanks, of course, must go to James, Catherine and the team at HarperCollins*Publishers*. Time after time you bring my ultimate book dreams to life – I'm very humbled by your ongoing support and faith in me. Thank you also to my amazing sponsors, Le Creuset, KitchenAid, Estée Lauder, Smeg and Cobram Estate. I'm always grateful to be working with such dynamic brands as yours, not to mention your exceptional products.

In my down-time outside the studio, my life is brightened and enriched by my friends and family. Thank you all for your love and laughter – you're so important to me. Karen, thank goodness you always have my back, as my sister and in business. And to my boys, Angus and Tom, it goes without saying you're my favourite people to bake for! Thank you for keeping me grounded and always inspiring me with those beautiful imaginations.

Donna Hay is Australia's favourite and most trusted home cook, and an international food-publishing phenomenon. Donna's 27 books have sold more than 6 million copies worldwide, been translated into 10 different languages, and her television cooking shows have brought her signature style to life for viewers in more than 14 countries. In Australia, her recent books have dominated the bestseller charts, with *Fresh and Light* (2012) selling 202,000, *the new classics* (2013) selling 160,000, *life in balance* (2015) selling 114,000 and *basics to brilliance* (2016) selling 106,000 copies to date.

Donna Hay is a household name. She is editor-in-chief of her own magazine (that's reached more than 730,000 readers) with a digital version that's been the number one of its kind in Australia. In addition, her food range is stocked in supermarkets nationally. She is also the working mum of two beautiful boys.

Books by Donna Hay include: *basics to brilliance kids*; *basics to brilliance*; *life in balance*; *the new easy*; *the new classics*; *Fresh and Light*; *simple dinners*; *a cook's guide*; *fast, fresh simple.*; *Seasons; no time to cook*; *off the shelf*; *instant entertaining* and the *simple essentials* collection.

donnahay.com

For more of my cookbooks, plus plenty of super simple recipes for weeknights and weekends, visit donnahay.com. You can explore my online store of gifts, hampers and beautiful homewares, or create a gift registry for your next special occasion. Follow me on social media for news, inspiration and all the latest on the magazine and my blog.

Connect with Donna on Facebook, Instagram and Pinterest

 facebook.com/donnahay

 @donna.hay

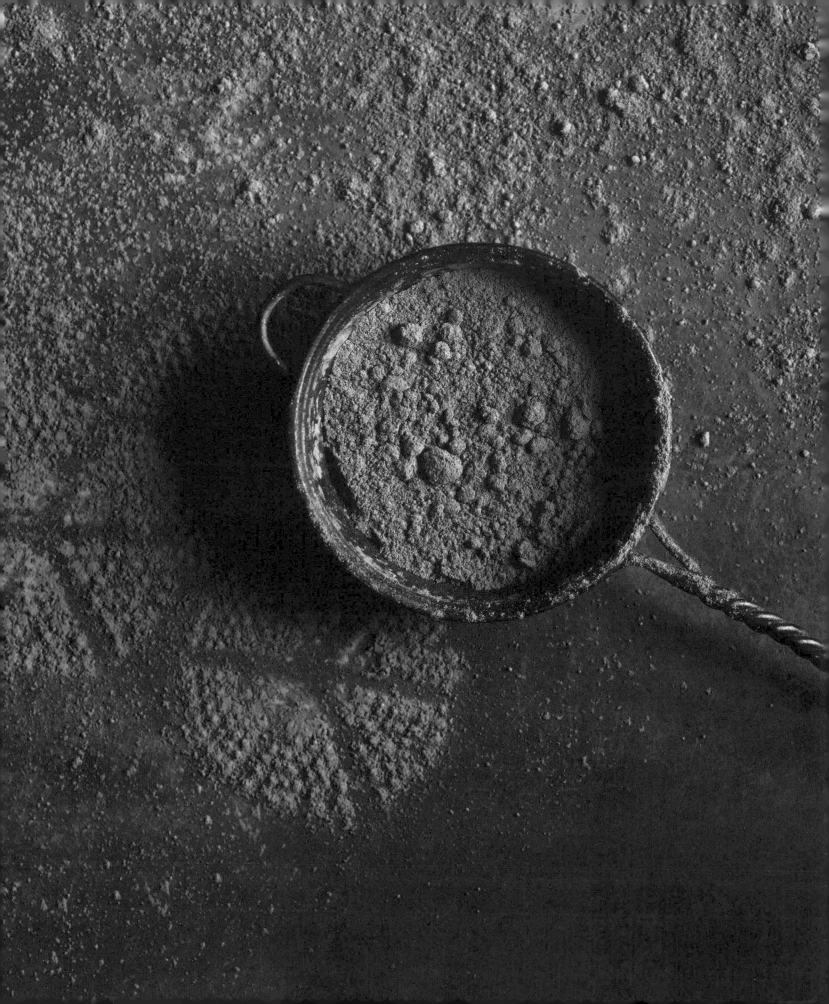